Solar Plexus Chakra 101: Power, Confidence, Will
Copyright © 2025 by Dr. Constance Santego.

Copy Editor & Interior Design: Constance Santego
Book Layout: ©2017 BookDesignTemplates.com

Ordering Information:
Quantity sales. Special discounts are available on quantity purchases by corporations, associations, and others. For details, contact the "Special Sales Department" at the address above.

Trade Paperback ISBN: 978-1-990062-98-8
Ebook ISBN 978-1-990062-99-5
Created and published In Canada. Printed and bound in the United States of America

First Edition
Published by Maximillian Enterprises
Kelowna, BC Canada
www.constancesantego.ca

Solar Plexus Chakra 101: Power, Confidence, Will

"Unlock the fire of your Solar Plexus — reclaim confidence, courage, and direction."

(Vol IV)

Dr. Constance Santego

Maximillian Enterprises
Kelowna, BC

Dedication

To everyone learning to trust their own light —
May you remember that true power is not found in control,
but in the quiet confidence of being fully yourself.
— Dr. Constance Santego

ALSO BY DR. CONSTANCE SANTEGO

NOVELS
Illegitimate Grace
Ashcroft Hollow

Okanagan Trilogy:
Beneath the Vineyards
Under the Okanagan Sun
Guardian of the Lake

The Nine Spiritual Gifts Series:
Journey of a Soul – (Vol 1 Michael)
Language of a Soul – (Vol 2 Gabriel)
Prophecy of a Soul – (Vol 3 Bath Kol)
Healing of a Soul – (Vol 4 Raphael)
Miracles of a Soul – (Vol 5 Hamied)
Knowledge of a Soul – (Vol 6 Raziel)
Wisdom of a Soul – (Vol 7 Uriel)
Faith of a Soul – (Vol 8 Pistis Sophia)

NONFICTION
The Intuitive Life, The Gift Of Prophecy, Third Edition
Fairy Tales, Dreams And Reality... Where Are You On Your Path? Second Edition
Your Persona... The Mask You Wear
Archangel Michael's Soul Retrieval Guide
Tesla And The Future Of Energy Medicine
Beyond Tesla: Advancing The Science Of Energy Healing
Tesla's Code: Mastering Energy, Frequency, And Creative Power
Beyond The Mind: Harnessing The Power Of Astral Projection For Creative Awakening
Bend, Don't Break: Finding Your Way Back To Abundance
Ring Therapy: A Guide To Healing And Balance
Ring Therapy Pocket Guide
Floraopathy™: The Art And Science Of Vibrational Healing With Essential Oils
Dear Older Me: A Memoir... Of Sorts
It's Just Like Poker: A Spiritual Guide To Playing The Cards Life Deals You
Signs And Meanings: What The Feet Reveal About Health, Stress, And The Body's Story
Auricions: Unlocking Subconscious Healing Through Quantum Medicine
Quick Fix Acupressure Method
Manifestation – The DREAM Method in 5 Steps
Confidence- Mastering the Dream Method

REIKI WISDOM, SERIES:
Angelic Lifestyle, a Vibrant Lifestyle
Angelic Lifestyle 42-Day Energy Cleanse
Reiki and the Power of The Joint Points: Unlocking Energy Pathways for Healing (Vol I)
Reiki and Karmic Healing: Releasing Patterns From Past Lives (Vol II)
Reiki and the Five Elements (Vol III)
Secrets of a Healer, Magic Of Reiki
The Reiki Master's Manual

CHAKRA SERIES:
Heart Chakra 101: The Bridge
Root Chakra 101: Building Safety, Survival, Foundation
Sacral Chakra 101: Creativity, Pleasure, Emotions
Solar Plexus Chakra 101: Power, Confidence, Will
Throat Chakra 101: Truth, Voice, Self-Expression
Third Eye Chakra 10: Intuition, Vision, Insight
Crown Chakra 10: Spiritual Connection, Transcendence.

SECRETS OF A HEALER, SERIES:
Magic Of Aromatherapy (Vol I)
Magic Of Reflexology (Vol II)
Magic Of The Gifts (Vol III)
Magic Of Muscle Testing (Vol IV)
Magic Of Iridology (Vol V)
Magic Of Massage (Vol VI)
Magic Of Hypnotherapy (Vol VII)
Magic Of Reiki (Vol VIII)
Magic Of Advanced Aromatherapy (Vol IX)
Magic Of Esthetics (Vol X)
The Reiki Master's Manual (Vol XI)

ADULT COLORING JOURNALS
SERIES-ZEN COLORING:
Quantum Energy and Mindful Living Journal (Vol 1)
Reiki Energy Journal (Vol 2)
Nine Spiritual Gifts Journal (Vol 3)
I Forgive Journal (Vol 4)

FOR CHILDREN
I am Big Tonight. I Don't Need the Light
The Magic Elf Book: 25 Days of Surprises

COOKBOOK
My Favorite Recipes, with a Hint of Giggle

BUISNESS
How To Use ChatGPT For Authors: From Idea To Published Book
Scaling Beyond 6 Figures: Strategies For Health & Wellness Professionals
The Academypreneur's Playbook: Turn Knowledge Into A
Revenue-Generating School

HUMOR/GIFT BOOK
How Do You Like Your Eggs? Crack Into Your Personality, Yolk and All

Contents

Solar Plexus Chakra 101: Power, Confidence, Will

"Unlock the fire of your Solar Plexus — reclaim confidence, courage, and direction."

(Vol IV)

Dr. Constance Santego

Preface

Introduction: Awakening the Fire Within

Our journey through the chakras began at the heart — the bridge between heaven and earth, the center of compassion and connection. From there, we descended to the Root Chakra, the ground of being that teaches safety, stability, and trust in life itself. Once anchored in the earth, we moved upward into the waters of the Sacral Chakra, where emotion, creativity, and pleasure awaken the rhythm of life.

Now, our path rises once more to the **Solar Plexus Chakra**, or **Manipura**, the radiant core of our personal power. If the root gives us the right to exist and the sacral grants permission to feel, then the solar plexus bestows the **power to act** — to transform inspiration into intention and intention into reality.

Manipura, meaning "lustrous gem," resides above the navel and below the heart. Its element is **fire**, the transformative force that fuels growth, digestion, and purpose. This fire is not merely physical but spiritual — the inner flame that propels us toward self-mastery, confidence, and willpower. When it burns steadily, we feel clear, courageous, and capable. When it dims, self-doubt, passivity, and indecision take hold. And when it blazes out of control, we may struggle with anger, control, or burnout.

The Solar Plexus Chakra governs the **digestive system**, the place where we metabolize not only food but experience. Here, we "digest life" — breaking down what we take in and transforming it into energy, understanding, and action. This is the realm of personal identity, where we discover who we are apart from others and how to assert that self in the world with integrity and grace.

Just as the heart teaches love, the root teaches strength, and the sacral teaches flow, the solar plexus teaches **empowerment through balance**. True power is not about dominance or control; it is the steady, radiant presence that arises when we are aligned with our higher purpose.

In this book, we will explore the wisdom, symbolism, and healing practices of the Solar Plexus Chakra — the center of fire within. Through breathwork, visualization, affirmations, and self-reflection, you will learn to awaken your inner sun: to transform fear into confidence, stagnation into movement, and uncertainty into decisive, inspired action.

As we continue this upward journey through the chakra system, remember — every flame begins with a spark. Your light has always been within you; it only awaits your permission to shine.

About the Chakra 101 Series

The **Chakra 101 Series** is a journey through the seven primary energy centers of the human body — a guided exploration of how spirit expresses itself through matter, and how healing unfolds layer by layer. Each book in this series blends ancient wisdom with modern energy practices, bridging spirituality, psychology, and embodiment to help readers rediscover balance and wholeness.

The series began with *Heart Chakra 101: The Bridge*, where love and compassion opened the way for inner transformation. From there, *Root Chakra 101: Building Safety, Survival, Foundation* grounded that love into the physical world, teaching stability, trust, and the sacredness of belonging. *Sacral Chakra*

101: Creativity, Pleasure, Emotions then carried the journey forward — from stability to movement, from survival to creation, from love as an ideal to love as an experience felt through the body.

Now, *Solar Plexus Chakra 101: Power, Confidence, Will* ignites the inner fire — the energy of purpose, determination, and self-mastery. It teaches how to transform fear into courage, uncertainty into action, and self-doubt into radiant confidence. Through this center, we learn what it means to stand in our power and direct our life with intention and grace.

Each book in this series builds upon the last, guiding you upward through the chakra system:

1. **Heart Chakra 101** – The Bridge of Love and Compassion
2. **Root Chakra 101** – Building Safety, Survival, Foundation
3. **Sacral Chakra 101** – Creativity, Pleasure, Emotions
4. **Solar Plexus Chakra 101** – Power, Confidence, and Will
5. **Throat Chakra 101** – Expression, Authenticity, and Truth
6. **Third Eye Chakra 101** – Intuition, Vision, and Clarity
7. **Crown Chakra 101** – Spirit, Consciousness, and Unity

While each volume stands on its own, together they form a complete map — a journey from earth to sky, from the physical to the divine. This path through the chakras mirrors the process of awakening itself: beginning with love, rooting into safety, awakening creative flow, discovering purpose, speaking truth, seeing clearly, and ultimately remembering our oneness with all that is.

Whether you are a student of energy medicine, a healer, or a seeker of self-understanding, the **Chakra 101 Series** is designed to guide you home — to your body, your energy, and your divine essence.

Chapter 1 – Igniting the Flame of Being

The Role of the Solar Plexus Chakra in the Chakra System

Every journey of energy unfolds step by step. After grounding ourselves in the Root Chakra and learning to flow through the Sacral, we now rise into the **Solar Plexus Chakra**, *Manipura* — the fire at the center of our being. Though this series began at the Heart, where love bridges heaven and earth, it is here, in the luminous core of the body, that love gains strength, direction, and purpose.

If the Root Chakra whispers, "You are safe; you belong," and the Sacral answers, "You may feel; you may create," then the Solar Plexus declares, "Now you may act; now you may become."
Here, desire is refined into determination, and emotion transforms into motion. It governs our **willpower, self-esteem, confidence, and sense of identity** — the sacred right to choose, to decide, and to shape one's own destiny.

Manipura's element is **fire**, ever-transformative and radiant. Its color is **brilliant yellow**, like sunlight warming the skin or flames dancing at dawn. Its symbol, the **ten-petaled lotus enclosing a downward-pointing triangle**, represents both the absorption of universal energy and

the alchemical transformation that occurs when spirit meets form. This is the inner sun — the place where energy is digested, transmuted, and directed outward into purposeful action.

In the chakra system, Manipura builds directly upon Svadhisthana. Without the emotional current of the Sacral Chakra, the fire of the Solar Plexus cannot burn with inspiration. Likewise, without the grounding of the Root, that fire can become unstable or self-destructive. But when the lower chakras are balanced, Manipura becomes a steady flame — warm, focused, and life-giving.

Think of Manipura as the fire within the hearth. The Root provides the bricks and foundation, the Sacral brings the water and life-force, and the Solar Plexus offers the heat that transforms raw material into sustenance. It is the energy of digestion — not only of food, but of life itself. Here we assimilate experience, extract wisdom, and generate the power to act in alignment with our values.

When Manipura is balanced, we stand tall in self-trust. We know who we are and what we stand for, yet remain open and compassionate. Our confidence radiates naturally, inspiring others without effort. But when this chakra is weak or blocked, self-doubt, fear, or indecision clouds our path. When overactive, the fire may flare into anger, dominance, or perfectionism — the need to control what cannot be controlled.

In the great ascent of the chakra system, the Solar Plexus represents **the will to evolve**. It is where personal energy becomes conscious direction — where passion from the Sacral finds purpose, and that purpose fuels the higher centers of love, truth, and awareness. Manipura is the bridge between feeling and doing, between desire and manifestation.

The Solar Plexus Chakra is an invitation to awaken your **inner power** — not the power that conquers, but the power that **creates**. It asks you to trust your intuition, to honor your boundaries, and to direct your energy with clarity and intention. When you align your will with your spirit, confidence is no longer something to achieve — it is something you *embody*.

Balanced, Manipura brings vitality, confidence, and radiant strength. Imbalanced, it can leave you drained, anxious, or overbearing. In its highest expression, it is the sun within you — shining with purpose, transforming fear into courage, and guiding you forward with unwavering light.

TRADITIONAL SANSKRIT NAMES

• **Manipura (मणिपूर)** – the most common Sanskrit name for the Solar Plexus Chakra, meaning **"city of jewels"** or **"lustrous gem."** The term derives from *mani* (gem, jewel) and *pura* (city, place), symbolizing the radiant inner treasure of confidence, vitality, and personal power that lies within the center of the being.

In the ancient yogic texts, *Manipura* represents the **seat of Agni**, the sacred fire that governs digestion, transformation, and willpower. It is described as a radiant lotus blazing like the rising sun — the inner furnace where energy is refined into strength and clarity. This fire transforms not only food into energy but also experiences into wisdom.

Associated with the element of **fire (Tejas)** and the **solar energy of Surya**, Manipura is said to illuminate both the physical and subtle bodies, providing the heat necessary for growth, purification, and transformation. It is the center of dynamism, vitality, and purpose — the inner sun that empowers the individual soul (*jivatman*) to act in harmony with the divine will.

COMMON ENGLISH NAMES

- **Solar Plexus Chakra** – The most widely used English name, referring to its location at the solar plexus, the network of nerves situated behind the stomach and below the diaphragm. The term highlights this chakra's role as the energetic "sun" of the body — a radiant center from which vitality, warmth, and willpower emanate.
- **Power Center** – Emphasizes Manipura's connection to personal strength, confidence, and self-mastery. It is the energetic source that fuels action and motivation, translating thoughts and desires into tangible results.
- **Center of Will** – Refers to its function as the chakra of determination and focused intent. This is where decisions are made, boundaries are set, and one's personal authority is claimed.
- **City of Jewels** – A poetic translation of *Manipura*, describing the chakra as a radiant inner treasure where clarity and brilliance reside. It reminds us that true power shines from within rather than being sought outside ourselves.

ELEMENTAL & SYMBOLIC ASSOCIATIONS

- **Fire Chakra** – Associated with the **element of fire (Agni)**, representing transformation, energy, and will. Fire governs digestion and metabolism, both physically and energetically, turning nourishment and experience into usable life force. It is the spark that fuels confidence, action, and purpose.
- **Sun Center** – Linked to the **solar energy of Surya**, the radiant sun that illuminates and empowers. Just as the sun sustains all life on Earth, this chakra sustains our personal vitality and inner drive. Its warmth radiates outward, giving strength and clarity to our intentions.

- **Yellow Chakra** – Identified by its brilliant yellow hue, symbolizing brightness, intellect, and the light of self-awareness. Yellow reflects optimism, clarity, and the illumination of truth through understanding.
- **Lotus of Ten Petals** – Represented by a ten-petaled lotus enclosing a downward-pointing triangle, symbolizing the transformative power of fire and the direction of energy inward for purification. Each petal corresponds to ten forms of prana, or vital energy currents, circulating through the body.

CULTURAL / ESOTERIC NAMES

- **City of Jewels** – A poetic name derived from the Sanskrit *Manipura*, representing the luminous treasure of energy and consciousness within. It symbolizes the hidden brilliance of personal power waiting to be uncovered and refined through self-awareness.
- **Seat of the Soul** – In various esoteric and mystical traditions, the solar plexus is viewed as the point where the individual soul (*jivatman*) expresses its unique will in the world. It bridges instinct and intellect, uniting personal desire with divine purpose.
- **Fire Center** – Recognized in many yogic and metaphysical systems as the **center of transformation**. It is the furnace of life-force where spiritual energy (*prana*) is converted into action, will, and vitality. This fire, known as *Agni*, purifies and empowers.
- **Sun Chakra** – In both Tantric and Western esoteric teachings, Manipura is often linked to the **solar principle**—illumination, vitality, and the masculine aspect of consciousness. It governs the inner "solar power" that radiates confidence, clarity, and warmth.
- **Power Chakra** – Within modern energy healing and psychology-based chakra interpretations, it is called the **Power Chakra** because it governs autonomy, personal

identity, and the will to act. It is the center of empowerment and the drive to fulfill one's life purpose.

- **Third Fire or Solar Gate** – In certain alchemical and Hermetic systems, the solar plexus is referred to as the third of the "fire gates," signifying the awakening of the transformative energy that leads from emotional awareness to spiritual mastery.

METAPHORICAL NAMES

- **The Inner Sun** – Symbolizing the radiant source of light and warmth within each person. Just as the sun sustains life on Earth, the Solar Plexus Chakra sustains the inner world with vitality, direction, and clarity. It is the sun of the subtle body — the place where energy rises to illuminate the mind and empower the spirit.
- **The Furnace of Transformation** – Representing the alchemical fire that refines raw emotion into willpower and purpose. Here, personal challenges become fuel for growth, and life's experiences are digested into wisdom. It is the hearth of the soul, where struggle becomes strength.
- **The Warrior's Core** – A metaphor for courage, discipline, and the ability to stand one's ground. This chakra embodies the noble strength of the inner warrior — one who acts with confidence, integrity, and honor, guided by clarity rather than ego.
- **The Golden Flame** – Reflecting the subtle fire of consciousness that burns steadily when aligned with truth. It is the light of discernment that cuts through fear and doubt, illuminating the path of self-realization.
- **The Seat of Purpose** – Describing the place where intention crystallizes into action. Here, dreams are given direction and will aligns with divine timing. It reminds us that purpose is not found — it is lived, one conscious choice at a time.

Manipura: The Fire of Personal Power

The Sanskrit name for the Solar Plexus Chakra is **Manipura**, a term rich with symbolic meaning. *Mani* translates to "jewel," and *pura* means "city" or "place." Together they form **"the city of jewels"** — the radiant center where the treasures of self-confidence, willpower, and inner strength reside.

If the Sacral Chakra teaches us to feel, Manipura teaches us to **act**. It is the inner forge where emotion becomes motion, and desire becomes direction. Here, the energy that once flowed like water is refined by fire — purified, focused, and given purpose.

From birth, our survival depends not only on grounding and emotional connection but also on our ability to assert, to decide, and to act upon the world. The instincts of Muladhara root us to life, the emotions of Svadhisthana help us feel alive, and Manipura gives us the power to **live with intention**. It is the flame that fuels individuality and transforms potential into achievement.

Manipura represents the **energetic intelligence of transformation**. It governs digestion — both physical and emotional — teaching us how to process experience, extract nourishment, and release what no longer serves us. Just as the digestive fire turns food into energy, this inner fire turns challenge into confidence and effort into accomplishment.

When Manipura is balanced, we radiate vitality and strength. Our decisions are clear, our actions purposeful, and our confidence natural — not forced or arrogant, but grounded in self-trust. We stand tall, guided by inner conviction rather than external validation.

When imbalanced, this fire may flicker or flare. Too little, and we feel powerless, indecisive, or trapped in self-doubt. Too much, and we may burn with impatience, anger, or the need to control. Both expressions signal a disconnection from the steady, luminous flame of true power — the kind that illuminates rather than scorches.

Manipura is the **sun of the subtle body**, the radiant jewel that fuels the heart above and draws strength from the waters below. Without this fire, our emotions stagnate, our confidence wanes, and our spiritual ascent falters. But when it burns bright and steady, it lights every level of our being — giving us the courage to act, to grow, and to shine.

Just as the sun transforms everything it touches, the Solar Plexus Chakra transforms everything it encounters. It turns fear into courage, inertia into action, and confusion into clarity. It reminds us that true power is not about control, but about illumination — the ability to see clearly and move forward with purpose.

It is here, in the golden fire of Manipura, that your journey into **power, confidence, and will** begins.

What Is Sanskrit and Why Does It Matter for Chakras?

The language most often associated with the chakras is **Sanskrit**, the ancient sacred language of India. Sanskrit is often called a **language of vibration** — each word carries not only meaning but also energetic resonance. Its sounds are designed to awaken specific frequencies within the body and mind, aligning us with the subtle dimensions of energy that shape our being.

For the Solar Plexus Chakra, the Sanskrit name is **Manipura**. *Mani* means "jewel," and *pura* means "city" or "place."

Together, they form **"the city of jewels,"** a luminous metaphor for the radiant center of inner power and transformation that glows within the human body. Just as the sun illuminates the world, Manipura represents the inner light that empowers and sustains us.

Unlike a simple label, each Sanskrit term is an **energetic code** — a vibration that carries the essence of the chakra it names. To speak *Manipura* is to invoke the qualities of radiance, courage, and vitality. The sound itself is fiery, resonating with willpower and determination.

Each chakra also has a **bīja mantra**, or seed sound, that activates its energy through vibration. For Manipura, that sound is **RAM** (pronounced "rum"). When spoken, sung, or chanted, *RAM* generates a powerful, warming vibration that can be felt in the solar plexus region — igniting the inner fire of strength and purpose. The sound stimulates digestion, confidence, and courage, helping to burn away inertia and fear.

Sanskrit is more than language; it is **vibration embodied**. The letters of the Sanskrit alphabet are said to correspond with subtle aspects of consciousness, and in traditional chakra imagery, each lotus petal bears a specific Sanskrit syllable. The **ten petals of Manipura** carry sounds that reflect the movement of pranic energy — the dynamic forces of vitality, ambition, and transformation. Together, they remind us that sound and consciousness are inseparable expressions of life itself.

Why does this matter today? Because **sound shapes energy**, and energy shapes reality. When we chant, speak, or meditate upon Sanskrit sounds, we align with ancient patterns of vibration that have harmonized body, mind, and spirit for millennia. To engage with the Sanskrit language of the chakras is to participate in an unbroken lineage of sound healing — one that transcends culture and connects us to the essence of being alive.

When you chant *"RAM,"* you are not just repeating a sound. You are declaring: **I am strong. I am confident. I act with purpose.**

Chanting this mantra awakens the solar fire — the **Agni** — that governs both physical digestion and the spiritual digestion of experience. It transforms stagnation into motion, confusion into clarity, and fear into focused courage. The vibration of "RAM" aligns the individual will with the higher will, reminding us that true strength is the harmony between action and awareness.

In the traditional mandala of Manipura, **ten Sanskrit syllables** are inscribed on the lotus petals, representing the ten forms of prana, or vital energy, that circulate through the human body. These sounds symbolize the dynamic forces of transformation, movement, and expression — all guided by the central fire of consciousness.

Why does this matter today? Because **language shapes energy**, and energy shapes reality. Sanskrit provides not only an ancient linguistic key but also a **vibrational map** of the human experience. When we chant or meditate on the sounds of Manipura, we are not invoking something external — we are awakening the radiant center that has always been within us.

When you chant "RAM," you are not merely speaking an ancient word; you are **becoming** it. You are affirming:
I transform. I trust myself. I am the light that acts.

The Solar Plexus Chakra and Maslow's Hierarchy of Needs

In the 20th century, psychologist **Abraham Maslow** introduced his *Hierarchy of Needs*, a model describing the progressive stages of human motivation and fulfillment. At its foundation lie physiological and safety needs — food, water, shelter, and stability. Once these are met, human energy naturally seeks belonging, esteem, and ultimately self-actualization.

This psychological framework mirrors the **chakra system** remarkably well. The ancient yogic tradition, much like Maslow's modern theory, recognized that consciousness unfolds in layers. Each stage of development — physical, emotional, and spiritual — builds upon the last. When one level is nourished, the next can awaken.

- **Root Chakra ↔ Physiological & Safety Needs**
  The Root Chakra provides grounding and security. Without stability, the entire energetic structure wavers. It corresponds to Maslow's first two levels — the basic human need for safety, survival, and trust in life.
- **Sacral Chakra ↔ Belonging, Intimacy & Emotional Flow**
  Once safety is established, energy rises into the Sacral Chakra, the realm of relationship, pleasure, and emotional connection. This aligns with Maslow's need for love and belonging — the ability to feel accepted, to connect, and to create.
- **Solar Plexus Chakra ↔ Esteem, Confidence & Personal Power**
  Here, the journey reaches the domain of *Manipura*, the "city of jewels." Once connection and belonging are secure, the next natural desire is for **self-respect, autonomy, and mastery**. This is Maslow's fourth level — *esteem*. Manipura governs our inner authority: the confidence to take action, make decisions, and direct our life with purpose.
  Just as Maslow recognized that esteem and self-efficacy build the bridge toward self-actualization, the yogic system teaches that the Solar Plexus transforms emotional energy into **empowered action**. It is where we begin to ask, *Who am I? What am I capable of?*

- **Heart Chakra ↔ Love & Compassion**
  When self-worth is secure, the heart opens fully. Love becomes unconditional — not a need to be filled, but an energy to be shared.
- **Throat Chakra ↔ Authentic Expression**
  With confidence and self-trust awakened, one's truth can be spoken clearly and without fear.
- **Third Eye Chakra ↔ Vision & Intuition**
  Inner clarity arises when the fires of ego are refined into awareness. Perception expands beyond the self.
- **Crown Chakra ↔ Self-Actualization & Transcendence**
  The highest stage of both Maslow's and the yogic systems reflects union — the realization of one's divine nature and purpose within the greater whole.

In this way, **Maslow's hierarchy and the chakra system** are not separate philosophies, but two expressions of the same human truth. Maslow described it as the movement from survival to self-actualization; yoga describes it as the ascent from root to crown.

The **Solar Plexus Chakra**, at the center of this ascent, marks a vital turning point — the shift from dependency to autonomy, from reaction to creation. It is the fire that transforms need into purpose and gives us the confidence to rise from instinct into awareness.

When we cultivate Manipura, we strengthen the bridge between emotion and action, body and mind, self and soul. Both psychology and spirituality agree: true empowerment begins not with control, but with inner alignment — the steady flame of knowing who you are and daring to shine.

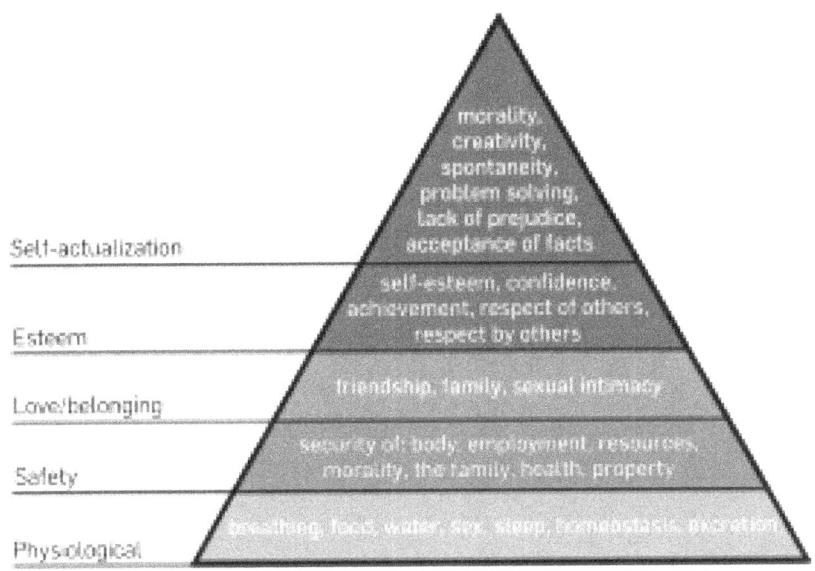

Mazlow's Hierarchy of Needs

Solar Plexus Chakra ↔ Esteem, Confidence & Personal Power

The **Solar Plexus Chakra (Manipura)** is the third energy center of the chakra system, just as *esteem* forms the fourth level of Maslow's Hierarchy of Needs. Once belonging and emotional connection have been established through the Sacral Chakra, the human spirit naturally seeks **autonomy, confidence, and self-mastery**. Without empowerment at this level, the journey toward love, expression, and higher awareness becomes unstable.

ESTEEM NEEDS: THE HUMAN DESIRE FOR WORTH AND ACHIEVEMENT

At its core, Manipura governs our sense of **identity, willpower, and inner authority**. It teaches that belonging is not enough — we must also know our own value and act upon it.

- **Self-Respect:** True esteem begins within. When Manipura is balanced, we hold ourselves with quiet confidence, neither inflated by ego nor diminished by doubt.
- **Autonomy:** This chakra governs independence — the ability to make choices, set boundaries, and trust one's judgment. It marks the shift from relying on others for validation to leading from inner conviction.
- **Achievement:** Manipura fuels ambition and the drive to accomplish goals. When directed consciously, it supports purposeful action rather than competition or control.
- **Integrity:** Healthy esteem is rooted in honesty. Acting in alignment with one's values strengthens both the will and the spirit.

CONFIDENCE: THE FIRE OF SELF-TRUST

Beyond the need for belonging, the Solar Plexus represents the *fire of self-belief*. It is where emotion transforms into motivation and inspiration becomes action.

- **Courage:** Manipura is the center of bravery — the strength to face fear, take risks, and step into the unknown.
- **Motivation:** This chakra is the engine of momentum. It gives direction to emotional energy, channeling it into productivity and purpose.

- **Focus & Discipline:** Like a steady flame, confidence must be maintained through mindful attention. Discipline transforms potential into mastery.
- **Self-Efficacy:** Believing in one's capacity to succeed ignites the energy to manifest ideas into reality.

PERSONAL POWER: THE ENERGY OF ACTION

Manipura's element is **fire**, symbolizing transformation. It governs both physical digestion and the spiritual digestion of experience. When balanced, it allows us to process life with clarity and resilience.

- **Boundaries:** Personal power includes the ability to say no without guilt and yes without fear. Boundaries protect our energy so confidence can grow.
- **Leadership:** A strong solar plexus radiates influence naturally, inspiring rather than dominating. True leadership uplifts others through presence and purpose.
- **Responsibility:** With power comes accountability. Manipura teaches that we are the creators of our own experiences — responsible for our choices and their impact.
- **Transformation:** This chakra refines raw emotion into willpower, turning insecurity into strength and resistance into progress.

WHY THIS MATTERS FOR ENERGY FLOW

Just as Maslow's hierarchy shows that unmet esteem needs lead to insecurity and stagnation, the chakra system teaches that blocked solar plexus energy restricts higher development. If Manipura is weak or unstable:

- The **Heart Chakra (Anahata)** may hesitate to open, for love requires the confidence to give without losing oneself.

- The **Throat Chakra (Vishuddha)** may struggle to express truth if self-worth is low.
- The **Third Eye Chakra (Ajna)** may find it difficult to trust intuition when the will is unsteady.

When Manipura is balanced, the entire system gains momentum. A radiant Solar Plexus Chakra provides the inner affirmation:
"I am worthy. I am capable. I am powerful."

With this assurance, energy rises freely toward love, clarity, and spiritual realization. The fire of Manipura becomes the steady sun that fuels all growth — illuminating the path between the self that acts and the soul that awakens.

Chapter 2 – Foundations of Manipura

Solar Plexus Chakra Basics: A Gentle Recap

If you are new to chakra study, the **Solar Plexus Chakra**, or **Manipura**, is the **third** of the seven main chakras. It is located in the **upper abdomen**, just above the navel and below the diaphragm, radiating through the stomach, liver, pancreas, and digestive system.

Where the Root Chakra grounds us in safety and the Sacral Chakra teaches us to flow with emotion and creativity, the Solar Plexus Chakra invites us to **act** — to step forward with purpose, confidence, and willpower. It is the **center of personal identity and empowerment**, the energetic fire that fuels self-trust and transformation.

The energy here is **radiant and dynamic**, like the sun itself. Manipura governs our **ability to take action**, to assert ourselves with clarity, and to manifest intentions into tangible results. Just as sunlight nourishes all life, the energy of the Solar Plexus nourishes our vitality, ambition, and sense of direction. Without strength at this level, we may feel disempowered, indecisive, or unable to sustain momentum toward our goals.

KEY QUALITIES OF MANIPURA

• **Element:** Fire — transformative, illuminating, energizing, purifying.
• **Color:** Brilliant yellow — the hue of sunlight, clarity, and

intellectual radiance.

• **Symbol:** A ten-petaled lotus enclosing a downward-pointing triangle, representing the transformative fire of Agni and the power to direct energy toward purpose.
• **Sound (Bīja Mantra):** *RAM* — the seed syllable that resonates with inner strength, focus, and the fire of will.
• **Location in the Body:** Upper abdomen, solar plexus, stomach, liver, pancreas, and diaphragm.
• **Organs and Systems:** Digestive system, metabolism, adrenal glands, and nervous system — all processes related to energy production and transformation.
• **Core Themes:** Confidence, self-esteem, willpower, autonomy, transformation, discipline, and purposeful action.

THE FIRE OF SELF-EMPOWERMENT

When **Manipura** is balanced, you feel capable, motivated, and self-assured. Your decisions are guided by clarity rather than fear, and your confidence radiates naturally. You act from integrity and know that your energy has purpose.

When it is **blocked or weak**, you may experience self-doubt, procrastination, low motivation, or a sense of powerlessness. Digestive issues, fatigue, or anxiety may arise as physical reflections of inner stagnation.

When it is **overactive**, the energy may be expressed as dominance, perfectionism, anger, or excessive control. The fire that once inspired can begin to burn too hot, consuming balance instead of sustaining it.

BALANCING THE INNER SUN

Manipura reminds us that **true power is not control — it is alignment.**
It is the quiet strength that comes from knowing who you are and acting in harmony with your truth. By tending to the Solar

Plexus Chakra, you ignite your inner flame — a light that transforms fear into courage and vision into action.

From this center of power, energy rises freely into the **Heart Chakra**, where will meets compassion, and confidence evolves into love in action.

The Solar Plexus Chakra is your invitation to stand tall in your own light — to trust your strength, honor your path, and live as the luminous being you were born to be.

Cross-Cultural Perspectives on the Solar Plexus

The concept of **personal power, will, and transformation** is not limited to yoga or Sanskrit philosophy. Across the world, cultures have long honored the sacred fire within — the energy that fuels vitality, courage, and purpose. Though the symbols and languages differ, the essence of **Manipura** is universal: without fire, there can be no illumination, no movement, and no life.

YOGIC TRADITION

In the yogic chakra system, **Manipura** is the third chakra — the energy center of fire (*Agni*), strength, and will. It is symbolized by the ten-petaled lotus, the downward-pointing red triangle, and the sound *RAM*. Ancient yogis described Manipura as the **seat of power and transformation**, where the fire of digestion refines not only food but also experience. It governs self-confidence, motivation, and spiritual energy, serving as the bridge between the lower chakras of survival and the higher chakras of love and wisdom.

Yogic texts such as the *Shat-Chakra-Nirupana* describe Manipura as "resplendent as the rising sun," where the dormant energies of the body awaken into action. Here, *Agni* — the sacred fire — burns away inertia and ignorance, awakening the light of awareness that propels the soul's evolution.

SHAMANIC TRADITIONS

In many **shamanic cultures**, the Solar Plexus corresponds to the **fire of the spirit** — the energy of will, courage, and transformation. Fire ceremonies are performed to release fear, burn away old patterns, and summon strength. The flame represents both purification and renewal, echoing Manipura's role as the power that transforms limitation into possibility.

Drumming, chanting, and movement rituals are often used to stoke this inner fire. Shamans recognize that illness, fatigue, or depression may reflect a dimming of this spiritual flame — a disconnection from one's purpose or life force. Through ceremony, the fire is rekindled, and the individual's inner sun is restored to balance.

INDIGENOUS PERSPECTIVES

Many **Indigenous traditions** across the world revere the element of fire as the living spirit of transformation and truth. Fire is used to seal commitments, to offer prayers, and to mark passages of initiation. It is seen as the messenger between the human and the divine — a sacred ally that teaches respect, discipline, and self-mastery.

In some First Nations teachings, fire represents **the will of the heart** — the courage to walk one's path with integrity. The tending of fire mirrors the tending of one's inner strength: if neglected, it fades; if overfed, it destroys; if balanced, it sustains life and light. This wisdom reflects Manipura's lesson of moderation and mindful empowerment.

SUN AND FIRE DEITIES

In countless mythologies, the **sun** and **fire deities** embody the essence of Manipura.

- In **Hinduism**, *Surya* is the solar god whose light sustains all beings, while *Agni*, the fire god, transforms offerings into divine connection.
- In **ancient Egyptian tradition**, *Ra* was the solar deity who traveled across the sky each day, symbolizing renewal and resilience.
- In **Greek mythology**, *Helios* and *Apollo* represent illumination, truth, and the radiant spark of creation. Across these traditions, the solar principle symbolizes the **radiance of consciousness** — the spark within each being that mirrors the sun in the sky.

FIRE-BASED SPIRITUALITY

Fire-based spiritual practices — from Vedic *homa* rituals to the Zoroastrian sacred flame, from Celtic *Beltane* fires to the candles of Christian devotion — all express reverence for the transformative power of light. To sit before flame is to commune with one's own spirit. Fire cleanses, empowers, and reminds us of our eternal capacity to rise renewed.

The Solar Plexus Chakra resonates with this same principle: when we honor our inner fire, we live with courage, clarity, and conviction. When we ignore it, our light dims; when we misuse it, we burn out. Balance comes from tending the flame with awareness — using power not to dominate, but to illuminate.

A SHARED UNDERSTANDING

Whether through yogic philosophy, shamanic ceremony, indigenous teaching, or solar worship, the message is clear: we are beings of fire and light. Our vitality depends on how we tend the flame within. **Manipura** reminds us that the true measure of power is not how brightly we outshine others, but how steadily we shine from within — transforming fear into faith, doubt into purpose, and energy into inspired action.

ORIGINS & HIDDEN HISTORY OF MANIPURA

The concept of **Manipura** arises from the ancient yogic traditions of India, where the chakra system was first articulated in the **Tantras**. Classical texts such as the *Shat-Chakra-Nirupana* (circa 16th century) describe Manipura as a **ten-petaled lotus**, radiant like the rising sun, located at the **navel or solar plexus region**. Within this lotus lies a **downward-pointing red triangle**, symbolizing fire, transformation, and the direction of energy toward purification. The element associated with this chakra is **Agni**, the sacred fire — both the physical flame of digestion and the spiritual fire of will and awareness.

This solar center was seen by yogic adepts as the seat of **personal power and vitality** — the forge where the energies of the lower chakras are refined into purpose and strength. The Sanskrit term *Manipura*, meaning "city of jewels," reflects the radiance and preciousness of this inner fire — a treasure hidden within, waiting to be ignited through self-mastery.

Yet the idea of a sacred center of fire, courage, and transformation is not unique to India. The essence of Manipura — illumination through inner strength — appears across civilizations and mystical systems throughout history:

Vedic India

In the earliest Vedic hymns, **Agni**, the fire god, is praised as the divine messenger and purifier. Fire was the means by which humans offered devotion to the gods, transforming matter into light. This act of transmutation mirrors Manipura's purpose — the conversion of raw experience into clarity and wisdom. The solar deity **Surya** was likewise revered as the radiant force of vitality and truth, the cosmic reflection of the inner sun that shines within all beings.

Egyptian Mysteries

In ancient Egypt, the **solar principle** was embodied by the god **Ra**, whose daily journey across the sky represented renewal, perseverance, and resurrection. Fire and sunlight symbolized divine order (*Ma'at*), courage, and creative power. Temples aligned with the sun's movement taught that illumination came from balance — not excess heat, but the measured flame of wisdom, much like Manipura's teaching of steady, conscious power.

Greek Philosophy

Greek philosophers such as **Heraclitus** regarded fire as the **fundamental element of transformation** — ever-living, ever-changing. The Delphic maxim *"Know thyself"* also echoes Manipura's call for self-awareness and mastery. The Greek god **Apollo**, the radiant sun deity, symbolized light, intellect, and clarity — qualities directly resonant with the solar plexus center.

Chinese Medicine

In **Traditional Chinese Medicine (TCM)**, the **Middle Dantian**, located near the solar plexus, is the center of **qi transformation** — where life energy is refined into strength, vitality, and emotional balance. Associated with the element of **fire** and the organ of the **stomach and spleen**, this region governs willpower and the harmonious exchange between nourishment and action — an energetic parallel to Manipura's role in digestion, metabolism, and self-empowerment.

Kabbalistic Mysticism

In **Kabbalah**, the sefirah **Tiferet**, meaning "beauty" or "harmony," corresponds to the radiant heart of the Tree of Life — balancing divine will and human action. It represents compassion infused with strength, mirroring Manipura's spiritual maturity: power guided by purpose and integrity rather than ego or control.

THE HIDDEN HISTORY OF MANIPURA

Over time, Manipura became more than the center of physical vitality; it evolved into the **seat of personal evolution**. Yogic sages taught that the fire of Manipura, when cultivated, awakens courage, clarity, and discernment — the very qualities needed to raise consciousness beyond instinct and emotion.

The "hidden history" of Manipura lies in how societies have treated **power and will**. Cultures that honored inner strength as sacred fostered leadership rooted in service, courage, and enlightenment. Those that distorted or feared power often birthed hierarchies of domination, control, and suppression — leading to collective wounds of disempowerment or abuse. These imbalances persist today as societal struggles over control, self-worth, and authentic leadership.

Understanding Manipura's origins is more than studying its symbols; it is a call to **reclaim the sacredness of power** itself. True power is not force — it is radiance. It is the inner light that illuminates without burning, transforms without consuming, and acts from integrity rather than fear.

Manipura reminds us that **will is divine when aligned with purpose**. To awaken this chakra is to remember that strength and service, courage and compassion, are not opposites — they are the twin flames of the same eternal fire.

THE SYMBOLISM OF THE SACRAL CHAKRA

Svadhisthana is associated with the element of **water**, the most fluid and adaptable of all the elements. Water represents movement, change, and emotional depth — the qualities that allow us to feel, connect, and create. Just as the body cannot live without fluids, the spirit cannot awaken without the flowing vitality of Svadhisthana.

Its color is **vibrant orange**, the hue of creativity and life's sweetness. Orange blends the energy of red with the joy of yellow, symbolizing passion transformed into pleasure, survival refined into expression. It is the color of ripe fruit, sunsets, and the inner fire that warms rather than burns. This orange vibration connects us to desire, stirs our imagination, and reminds us that life is meant to be felt and enjoyed.

THE YELLOW LOTUS

The lotus of **Manipura** is always depicted as **golden yellow**, radiant like the **sun at dawn**, glowing with the warmth of life, intellect, and purpose. It is the lotus of **fire and light**, symbolizing the awakening of inner power through self-awareness and will.

Its **ten petals** represent the **ten forms of pranic energy** that sustain human vitality — the subtle currents of breath, digestion, and motion that circulate through the body and mind. They also mirror ten emotional or mental tendencies that must be transformed through conscious mastery: **delusion, foolishness, desire, jealousy, shame, fear, ignorance, betrayal, thirst, and spiritual blindness**. When these are purified by the inner fire, they become jewels of strength, clarity, and confidence — the treasures of Manipura's "city of jewels."

At the heart of the lotus lies a **downward-pointing red triangle**, symbolizing the **element of fire (Agni)** and the transformative power of directed energy. The triangle points downward to signify energy moving inward — the digestion and integration of experience — and upward in its radiance, as the flame that nourishes all higher chakras.

Unlike the red lotus of **Muladhara**, which anchors us to the earth, or the orange lotus of **Svadhisthana**, which flows with emotion and creativity, the **yellow lotus of Manipura** teaches us to **shine** — to embody our unique light with confidence and integrity. It is the flower of action, transformation, and self-realization.

Where the root reminds us that we **exist**, and the sacral reminds us to **feel**, the solar plexus declares that we **can**. It is not the flower of stillness or surrender, but of conscious direction — the sacred bloom of human will guided by divine light.

THE COLOR YELLOW OF MANIPURA

When you close your eyes and visualize the **Solar Plexus Chakra**, the color most often seen is **brilliant yellow** — radiant, warm, and luminous like the midday sun. This is more than a symbolic image; it expresses a vibrational truth recognized across **Tantric, yogic, and healing traditions**. Yellow carries the resonance of **fire, light, and clarity** — the very essence of **Manipura**, the inner sun.

YELLOW: LIGHT, POWER, AND CLARITY

- **The Color of the Sun and Vitality:**
  Yellow is the hue of illumination — the light that reveals, nourishes, and awakens. It is the color of sunlight upon the skin, the golden fields of harvest, and the glow of inspiration. Just as the sun sustains all life, yellow reflects the sustaining energy of the Solar Plexus Chakra — the radiant force that fuels our motivation and sense of purpose.
- **The Fire of Transformation:**
  Associated with the element of **fire (Agni)**, yellow symbolizes transformation through heat and light. It reminds us that every challenge, like metal in a forge, can be refined by the steady flame of awareness. Yellow invites us to meet life's intensity not with fear, but with courage and confidence.
- **Clarity of Thought and Action:**
  Yellow is the color of intellect and discernment. It sharpens the mind and strengthens focus, illuminating the path forward. When the Solar Plexus Chakra is balanced, yellow energy radiates as clarity — the confidence to make decisions and the wisdom to act with purpose.
- **Confidence and Self-Worth:**
  Yellow awakens the inner sun of self-esteem. It empowers us to stand tall, to speak from strength, and to

shine without apology. In its highest expression, yellow reminds us that true confidence is quiet — it does not need to burn others to shine.

- **Radiance and Joy:**
  Like laughter and sunlight, yellow carries the vibration of joy. It opens the energy body to optimism and enthusiasm, dispelling heaviness and doubt. When we embody Manipura's golden light, we feel alive, inspired, and capable — our inner world illuminated by the steady flame of purpose.

Yellow is the color of awakening — of the soul remembering its own light.
It is the color that bridges the warmth of emotion and the brilliance of spirit, teaching us that to shine is not vanity, but vitality. To live in the radiance of Manipura is to stand fully in one's truth: **confident, clear, and illuminated from within.**

WHY YELLOW BELONGS TO THE SOLAR PLEXUS

Each chakra color resonates with a distinct frequency of light, forming part of the rainbow spectrum that mirrors the human energy system. **Yellow** vibrates just above orange, representing **energy in motion becoming direction** — life rising beyond emotion into **action, will, and clarity**.

- **The Third Color of the Rainbow:**
  Just as yellow follows orange, **Manipura follows Svadhisthana** in the chakra system — the natural next step after feeling is empowerment. Once the emotional waters are in balance, they are heated by the sun of the Solar Plexus, transforming sensitivity into strength and passion into purpose.
- **A Frequency of Illumination:**
  Yellow holds more vibrational energy than orange, resonating with mental clarity, alertness, and awareness. It bridges the warmth of emotion with the brilliance of

understanding. This balanced frequency supports both the **intellect** and the **will**, guiding energy toward conscious, decisive action.

- **Radiant and Expansive:**
  Yellow is the color of **expansion and radiance** — the light that naturally reaches outward. Just as the sun's rays illuminate the world, the Solar Plexus expands self-awareness into confidence, leadership, and inspired living. It reminds us that our light is meant to be shared, not hidden.

Yellow belongs to Manipura because it is the color of transformation — where warmth becomes power and energy becomes purpose.
It signifies the awakening of the inner sun, the steady flame that turns potential into strength and shines as the confidence to live boldly and authentically.

YELLOW IN DAILY LIFE

- **When you feel powerless or indecisive:**
  Wear **yellow clothing or jewelry** to boost confidence and motivation. Yellow activates the energy of action and helps you reconnect with your inner strength.
- **When your focus or will feels weak:**
  Visualize **breathing in golden-yellow light**, filling your solar plexus with clarity and determination. Let this light ignite your inner fire and sharpen your sense of purpose.
- **When self-doubt arises:**
  Place your hands gently over your upper abdomen and imagine a **radiant sun** glowing within. Feel its warmth expanding through your body, dissolving fear, and replacing it with courage and self-trust.
- **In rituals of empowerment and renewal:**
  Use **yellow candles, citrine or tiger's eye stones**, or golden fabrics to enhance focus, confidence, and

personal power. These tools help align your energy with Manipura's fiery vibration of transformation and will.

MEDITATION WITH YELLOW

1. **Close your eyes** and visualize a brilliant **yellow lotus** at your solar plexus, glowing like the morning sun.
2. **See the yellow light** radiating outward, warming your stomach, diaphragm, and entire core with strength and clarity.
3. With each breath, feel this golden fire expanding, filling your body with vitality and confidence as you repeat silently:

"I am strong. I am confident. I act with purpose."

WANT TO EXPERIENCE IT IN ACTION?...
Watch this video for the Sacral Chakra Meditation.

Watch it here: https://youtu.be/29IMppeKK70

THE DEEPER LESSON OF YELLOW

Yellow teaches us that **power, confidence, and purpose** are not separate from the sacred. To act with integrity, to speak with conviction, to shine without apology — these too are spiritual acts when aligned with truth. Just as fire must burn to give warmth and light, the soul must **ignite its will** to fulfill its divine potential.

The Solar Plexus' yellow light is both a **gift and a calling**. It is the gentle flame that whispers,
"You are strong. You are worthy. You are the light that transforms."

It reminds us that our inner fire was never meant to consume, but to **illuminate** — to guide us forward with courage, clarity, and love. When we honor the yellow light within, we remember that **to act with purpose is to live in alignment with spirit**, and that shining our light is not pride — it is our sacred responsibility.

The Ten-Petaled Lotus Of Manipura

At the heart of **Manipura's** symbolism lies a **golden-yellow lotus with ten petals** — brighter and more complex than the lotuses below it, yet not as ethereal as those above. It is the **lotus of fire and transformation**, where energy begins to move from the instinctual to the intentional, from survival and emotion to conscious direction. Each of its ten petals represents a vital aspect of **energy and awareness** that must be refined for power to become purposeful.

The Ten Syllables

Each petal of Manipura's lotus bears a Sanskrit **bīja (seed syllable)** — *ḍaṁ, ḍhaṁ, ṇaṁ, taṁ, thaṁ, daṁ, dhaṁ, naṁ, paṁ,* and *phaṁ.*
These are not mere phonetic sounds but **vibrational keys** that tune the chakra's frequency. Chanting them purifies the solar center, clears emotional residue, and activates the **ten prāṇas**, or vital airs, that circulate through the subtle body. These ten prāṇas govern movement, breath, metabolism, and transformation — all expressions of Manipura's fiery essence.

When these syllables are spoken or visualized, they resonate like sparks within the body's inner flame, strengthening focus, vitality, and will.

The Ten Qualities of Transformation

The ten petals are also associated with **ten tendencies** that must be purified and mastered for willpower to become wisdom. These tendencies are the shadows of ego that arise as one develops a sense of individuality. When balanced, they become the jewels of Manipura's "city of light."

- **Delusion** – dispelled through discernment and self-awareness.
- **Foolishness** – transformed into humility and openness to learning.
- **Desire** – refined into purpose and conscious creation.
- **Jealousy** – purified through self-confidence and gratitude.
- **Shame** – released by self-acceptance and forgiveness.
- **Fear** – burned away by courage and trust in divine will.
- **Ignorance** – illuminated by knowledge and inner reflection.
- **Treachery** – transmuted into integrity and loyalty.
- **Thirst (Greed)** – balanced through moderation and contentment.
- **Spiritual Blindness** – healed through surrender to the higher self.

Together, these ten energies represent the **alchemy of self-mastery**. When unrefined, they manifest as confusion, anger, and imbalance. When transformed, they ignite confidence, clarity, and unwavering will.

The Ten Directions of Power

The ten petals can also be viewed as **directions of energetic expansion** — radiating outward like the rays of the sun. They represent the multidimensional flow of human will: forward and backward (progress and reflection), left and right (analysis and intuition), above and below (heaven and earth), and the four diagonals of integration (mind, emotion, action, and spirit).

Manipura's energy expands in all directions, reminding us that personal power is not domination but illumination — the ability to shine light on every area of life with balance and grace.

The Ten Flames of Fire

In Tantric tradition, each petal of Manipura also corresponds to one of **ten flames of Agni**, the sacred fire that purifies all forms of energy. These flames govern not only digestion but also **mental and spiritual transformation**. They burn away ignorance and stagnation, allowing higher consciousness to rise like smoke toward the heavens.

When this fire is tended with awareness — not too weak, not too fierce — it becomes the **steady flame of inner mastery**, the mark of one who acts from truth rather than impulse.

The Sacred Geometry of Ten

The number **ten** holds special significance in sacred geometry, representing **completion and divine order** — the return to unity after the cycle of experience. It symbolizes **the perfected individual**, whose energy moves freely through all directions yet remains centered in light.

In the Solar Plexus Chakra, the ten-petaled lotus expresses this same harmony through balance between **will and wisdom**, **strength and compassion**. It teaches that true power is not achieved by force but by alignment with the higher purpose of the soul.

THE TRIANGLE OF FIRE: MANIPURA'S CORE GEOMETRY

At the center of Manipura's lotus lies a **downward-pointing red triangle**, the classical symbol of **Agni**, the sacred fire. Unlike the Root Chakra's square of stability or the Sacral Chakra's circle of flow, the triangle signifies **transformation through action**.

The Triangle

- The three sides represent the **trinity of will, knowledge, and action** — the three forces that manifest reality.
- The downward point reflects the **descent of divine energy into matter**, the alchemical process by which spirit is embodied.
- In meditation, this triangle becomes the hearth of the inner flame — the place where the individual's will is aligned with divine will.

The Fire

- Fire (*Agni*) purifies and illuminates. It digests not only food but experience, thought, and emotion.
- It is both destroyer and creator, consuming ignorance while kindling understanding.
- In the body, it governs metabolism, vitality, and transformation; in the soul, it awakens purpose and spiritual strength.

UNION OF LIGHT AND FIRE

Where the circle and crescent of Svadhisthana symbolized fluidity, the triangle of Manipura symbolizes **directed power**. Together, they reveal a greater truth: water flows and nourishes, but **fire transforms and ascends**.

Manipura's geometry teaches that life energy must first move (Sacral) before it can be refined and directed (Solar Plexus). It is through this sacred fire that the soul begins its ascent — rising from survival and emotion into awareness and purpose.

RETURNING TO RADIANCE

While the Root anchors us and the Sacral teaches us to flow, the Solar Plexus empowers us to **shine**. It reminds us that energy, when purified by the fire of awareness, becomes **light** — and that our task is not merely to survive or to feel, but to **act** with clarity and courage.

This is the secret wisdom of Manipura:
To be human is to **transform as well as to feel,**
to **shine as well as to flow,**
to **lead as well as to live**.

TRIANGLES IN TAROT SYMBOLISM
The Major Arcana

> **• The Magician (I):**
> The Magician raises one hand toward the heavens and points the other toward the earth — forming the invisible triangle of **as above, so below**. This embodies Manipura's principle of **directed will**: energy flowing consciously from divine inspiration into tangible creation.

> **• The Lovers (VI):**
> The composition of this card often forms a triangle — the two figures below and the angel above — representing the **union of opposites guided by higher will**. This echoes Manipura's fire of discernment: the power to choose alignment with love and truth over fear or temptation.

• The Chariot (VII):
The charioteer's posture, the balanced sphinxes, and the triangular canopy all suggest the strength of **focused direction**. The Chariot is Manipura in motion — confidence, control, and mastery through disciplined willpower.

• Temperance (XIV):
An angel pours liquid between two cups, forming the alchemical triangle of **transformation** — fire refining water into steam. This is the essence of Manipura: balance between passion and patience, power and peace.

• The Tower (XVI):
Lightning strikes the crown of a triangular tower — a warning of **power misused or unbalanced**. When ego burns too fiercely, fire consumes rather than enlightens. This card mirrors the shadow of Manipura: domination without integrity.

• The Sun (XIX):
The Sun radiates golden triangles of light, symbolizing **illumination, success, and vitality**. It is the full expression of a balanced Solar Plexus — radiant confidence born from authenticity.

The Minor Arcana

• The Suit of Wands:
Wands, aligned with the **element of fire**, are the natural companions of Manipura. Their pointed shapes often form triangles of energy and motion, representing creative drive, ambition, and transformation. The threefold symbolism — spark, flame, and light — mirrors the triangle's upward energy of growth and purpose.

• The Suit of Swords:
While Swords represent air and intellect, triangular compositions appear where **decision and direction** emerge. This reflects Manipura's mental aspect — the clarity and discernment needed to act with precision and power.

• The Suit of Pentacles:
The pentagram within a circle includes a subtle **inverted triangle at its base**, representing grounded fire — the act of manifesting spiritual will into material results. This is Manipura's energy anchored in the physical world.

SOLAR PLEXUS REFLECTIONS IN TRIANGULAR IMAGERY

• Transformation:
Triangles in Tarot symbolize the alchemical fire that **changes one state into another** — ignorance into wisdom, inertia into action, limitation into empowerment. This is Manipura's gift: transformation through awareness.

• Direction:
Unlike circles, which move endlessly, triangles **point** — they define a goal and move toward it. This directed energy reflects the Solar Plexus Chakra's nature as the **center of will and purpose**.

• Illumination:
The triangle's upward motion embodies **ascension through clarity and light**. It reminds us that true confidence is not about control, but about radiating truth and illuminating the path for others.

The triangle is the sacred geometry of **fire and evolution**.
In Tarot, as in Manipura, it reveals that growth comes not from
remaining still, but from the courageous act of transformation
— to rise, refine, and radiate the light within.

KEY CARDS TO MEDITATE ON FOR THE SOLAR PLEXUS CHAKRA

The Magician (I): Mastery of will and focused intention —
transforming thought into creation.
The Chariot (VII): Determination, discipline, and the
triumph of self-control through balance.
Strength (VIII): Inner power expressed through patience,
compassion, and courage.
Temperance (XIV): Alchemical harmony — blending
passion and purpose into enlightened action.
The Sun (XIX): Confidence, joy, and radiant authenticity
— shining as your truest self.
Three of Wands: Vision, confidence, and expansion
through clear direction.
Nine of Wands: Resilience and perseverance in the face of
challenge — the steady flame that endures.

Manipura is both the **fire and the forge** of the human journey.
It is the third chakra to awaken in early childhood, when
individuality and autonomy first emerge — the moment we
learn the word *"I can."* From that spark, the Solar Plexus
carries the lifelong imprint of self-worth, motivation, and
purpose.

It is the radiant center that fuels all transformation. Without
Manipura, the chakra system lacks momentum and vitality —
like a hearth without flame. With it, we gain the courage to act,
to lead, to create change, and to meet life's challenges with
clarity and confidence.

In this way, Manipura is not simply a phase of empowerment —
it is a **living teacher**. Every act of will, every choice to rise
above fear, every moment of inner strength is touched by its
light. As we ascend toward love, truth, and higher wisdom, the
Solar Plexus reminds us that enlightenment is not withdrawal
from power but its **refinement into purpose** — the sacred fire
that transforms both self and world.

Manipura in Yogic Practice

In the earliest **Tantric and yogic traditions**, the chakras were
understood not as physical organs but as **subtle vortices of
energy** — spiritual focal points for awakening, purification, and
the expansion of consciousness. Each chakra served as a portal
through which the practitioner could access deeper dimensions
of being, transforming the body into a vehicle of enlightenment.

For **Manipura**, the Solar Plexus Chakra, practice is centered on
fire, transformation, and willpower. The **bīja mantra**, or
"seed sound," of Manipura is **RAM** — a vibrational key that
ignites the element of **fire (Agni)** and harmonizes the body's
digestive, metabolic, and spiritual processes. By meditating on
the ten-petaled lotus and chanting "RAM," practitioners awaken
their **inner sun** — the radiant energy that fuels confidence,
discipline, and the drive to act in alignment with higher
purpose.

Yogis viewed Manipura as the **sacred forge of purification** —
where lower emotions and desires are refined into spiritual
strength. Through **pranayama (breath control), agni sara
(fire cleansing practices)**, and **visualization of golden light at
the navel**, they stoked the inner fire until it blazed steadily,
neither consuming nor fading.

The goal was not domination, but **mastery through awareness**.
Yogis understood that power and will could either enslave the

ego or liberate the soul, depending on how they were directed. When aligned with the heart and higher consciousness, the fire of Manipura becomes a tool of awakening — burning away illusion, fear, and weakness until only the light of truth remains.

Working with Manipura taught practitioners to embody **conscious action** — to act not from impulse or desire, but from clarity and conviction. In this way, the solar fire became a sacred ally in the **ascent of kundalini,** providing the strength and focus needed to rise toward love, wisdom, and divine realization.

THE INNER SYMBOL OF MANIPURA

At the center of **Manipura's lotus** rests a **downward-pointing red triangle**, radiant like the rising sun and surrounded by **ten golden petals**, each inscribed with sacred Sanskrit syllables. The triangle represents **fire (Agni)** — the transformative element that digests, refines, and empowers. Its downward point signifies energy moving inward, concentrating and purifying before ascending toward higher consciousness.

Encircling this fiery core are the **ten petals**, symbolizing the ten prānas — the subtle life currents that sustain vitality and movement throughout the body. Together, the petals and triangle illustrate the perfect balance of **containment and expansion, power and direction** — the harmony of a steady, controlled flame.

Within this sacred geometry lies the **bīja mantra RAM (रं)**, the seed sound of Manipura.
RAM is the **vibrational essence of transformation**, the sound that kindles the inner fire. When chanted, it resonates in the solar plexus, awakening courage, discipline, and radiant confidence. It burns away stagnation, fear, and doubt, leaving clarity and will in their place.

The symbol of Manipura reminds us that true power is born not from force, but from **illumined will** — the inner fire that purifies the self and lights the path toward wisdom.

WHAT RAM REPRESENTS

Vibrational Key:
RAM (रं) is the sacred sound that **"unlocks" the Solar Plexus Chakra**, activating the inner fire of willpower, confidence, and transformation. It awakens the luminous energy that fuels motivation, digestion (both physical and spiritual), and purposeful action.

Sound of Fire:
When chanted, **RAM** resonates deeply within the **solar plexus**, radiating warmth and light through the core of the body. It stimulates the digestive fire — **Agni** — and clears energetic stagnation, empowering the practitioner with vitality and focus.

Dissolver of Fear and Doubt:
Ancient teachings describe RAM as the mantra that **burns away fear, inertia, and self-doubt**, transforming weakness into strength and confusion into clarity. It purifies the ego's distortions, allowing true confidence — rooted in awareness, not control — to emerge.

Link to the Fire Element:
Each chakra corresponds to one of the five elements (*tattvas*). Manipura aligns with **fire (Agni Tattva)** — the element of digestion, transformation, and illumination. Through RAM, we harmonize with the sacred flame that turns experience into wisdom and action into achievement.

By meditating on **Manipura's ten-petaled lotus** and chanting **RAM**, yogis learned to harness the sacred energy of transformation — to transmute desire into determination, emotion into empowerment, and personal will into divine purpose.

The Solar Plexus Chakra was never seen as the seat of domination or ego, but as the **temple of illumination** — the fire that gives life direction, the strength that acts with integrity, and the radiant light that guides the soul toward awakening.

THE SEED SOUND OF MANIPURA: RAM

At the very center of the **Solar Plexus Chakra's symbol** lies not only sacred geometry, but also **sacred sound**. In Tantric and yogic philosophy, every chakra resonates with a specific **bīja mantra** — a "seed sound" containing the pure vibrational essence of that energy center.

For **Manipura**, the Solar Plexus Chakra, that sound is **RAM** (pronounced "Rahm," with an open "ah" sound).

Why Sound Matters

In the Sanskrit tradition, **sound is the essence of creation**. It is vibration made audible — frequency that gives form to energy. Just as the universe is said to have arisen from the primordial sound **OM**, each chakra represents a harmonic of that original vibration.

Chanting the bīja mantra of a chakra is like striking the precise **tone of resonance** that awakens and harmonizes its energy. For **Manipura**, that key is **RAM**, the sound of the **inner sun**, the sacred flame that transforms matter into light and will into purpose.

The Power of RAM

- **Resonance in the Solar Plexus:**
  When chanted, **RAM** vibrates through the **stomach, diaphragm, and solar plexus**, igniting the internal fire — both physical digestion and spiritual transformation.
- **Burning Away Fear and Inertia:**
  Manipura can become clouded by doubt, fear, or fatigue. **RAM** burns through these dense energies, rekindling clarity, motivation, and confidence.
- **Awakening Strength and Willpower:**
  The mantra energizes the **core of action**, empowering you to make decisions and act with integrity. It teaches that true will is not control, but conscious direction.
- **Honoring the Element of Fire:**
  RAM attunes the practitioner to **Agni Tattva**, the fire element. It symbolizes illumination, purification, and the spark of divine purpose that transforms all experience into growth.

Chanting RAM

Chanting **RAM** is a practice of empowerment — the **permission to act**, to lead, and to transform. It connects you to your inner flame — not the fire that destroys, but the one that **illuminates and refines**.

It is the vibrational key that opens the **"City of Jewels"** within, revealing the radiant power that arises when energy is aligned with awareness.

HOW TO CHANT RAM
Step 1 – Prepare the Body

• Sit upright, either cross-legged or with your feet flat on the floor.
• Place your hands gently on your **solar plexus**, just above the

navel.
• Take 3–5 slow, deep breaths, feeling your abdomen expand and contract like a steady flame — warm, calm, and alive.

Step 2 – Focus on the Solar Plexus

• Visualize a **brilliant yellow lotus** glowing in the center of your abdomen.
• See its petals illuminated like the rays of the sun, pulsing gently with each breath.
• Imagine this golden light spreading through your torso — warming, strengthening, and clearing your energy.

Step 3 – Chant the Sound

• Inhale deeply. As you exhale, chant slowly and clearly: **RAAAAAHHHHMmmmm…**
• Let the "Rah" rise from deep in your core, like heat from a glowing ember.
• Allow the "mmm" to vibrate in your upper abdomen and chest, radiating power and confidence throughout your body.

Step 4 – Repeat Rhythmically

• Chant **RAM** 7, 12, or 108 times.
• With each repetition, visualize the **ten golden petals** of Manipura's lotus opening one by one, releasing fear, doubt, and hesitation.
• Feel the energy within you grow stronger, brighter, and more focused — a steady flame of will and purpose.

Step 5 – Silent Resonance

• After chanting, rest your awareness at the solar plexus.
• Sense the subtle warmth and vibration of **RAM** glowing like sunlight within.
• Sit in this radiant stillness, breathing gently as you affirm:

"I am strong. I am confident. I act with purpose."

WAYS TO USE RAM IN PRACTICE

- Morning Empowerment:
  Chant RAM three times upon waking to ignite your
  inner fire and set the tone for clarity, focus, and strength
  throughout your day.
- Confidence Reset:
  When you feel uncertain, anxious, or drained, chant
  RAM until your breath deepens and your energy feels
  centered and strong. Let the vibration rekindle courage
  and motivation.
- Healing Sessions:
  Practitioners can chant RAM silently or softly while
  working near the stomach, diaphragm, or solar plexus to
  encourage balance, digestion, and renewed vitality.
- Movement Integration:
  Pair chanting with core-activating yoga poses such as
  Boat Pose (Navasana), Warrior I (Virabhadrasana I), or
  Plank. You can also flow with intentional breathwork or
  sun salutations to embody Manipura's dynamic energy.
- Group Practice:
  Chanting RAM together builds a powerful shared field
  of radiant energy — magnifying confidence, unity, and
  purposeful action within the group.

SOLAR-CENTERED AFFIRMATION WITH RAM

**"As I chant RAM, my inner fire awakens. I am strong. I am
confident. I act with purpose and clarity."**

THE ANIMAL SYMBOL OF MANIPURA: THE RAM

At the base of each chakra lotus rests a **sacred animal**,
symbolizing the instinctual or elemental energy that fuels that
center.

For the **Solar Plexus Chakra**, the guardian and carrier of its power is the **Ram**, or **Aries**, representing the fiery energy of **Agni** — the force of courage, action, and transformation.

Why The Ram?

- **Fire Element:**
  As a creature of both earth and fire, the Ram embodies Manipura's element — **Agni**, the sacred flame. Its bold and forward-moving nature mirrors the unstoppable drive of willpower when guided by purpose.
- **Determination and Leadership:**
  The Ram climbs mountains with focus and persistence, symbolizing **courage, endurance, and strength**. It reflects Manipura's lesson: power is not about domination, but about the unwavering commitment to rise and overcome.
- **Action and Initiative:**
  Just as the Ram charges forward fearlessly, this chakra fuels our **ability to take initiative**, to act decisively, and to manifest our goals. It is the energy of movement, assertion, and progress — the fire that propels life forward.
- **Transformation through Challenge:**
  The Ram's horns, spiraling upward, signify **spiritual ascent through trial and mastery**. They remind us that obstacles are not barriers but opportunities to refine our inner fire into light.
- **Solar Power:**
  Linked to the **zodiac sign Aries**, ruled by **Mars**, the Ram embodies solar vitality and pioneering spirit — the willingness to begin, to strive, and to lead with confidence.

The Ram teaches that true strength arises not from aggression, but from balance — a will that is **steady, conscious, and luminous**. It is the sacred guardian of Manipura's fire, reminding us that power, when aligned with wisdom, becomes light — the light that guides, transforms, and empowers all creation.

THE SHADOW OF THE RAM

The Ram embodies strength and will — yet, like all power, its energy holds both light and shadow. When Manipura is imbalanced, the fire that should illuminate can instead burn or consume.

- **Aggression and Control:**
  When willpower becomes domination, the Ram charges without awareness. This shadow expresses as anger, competitiveness, or the need to control outcomes and others.
- **Ego and Pride:**
  The brilliance of Manipura can inflate into arrogance when the ego mistakes confidence for superiority. The shadow Ram forgets that true strength serves rather than conquers.
- **Burnout and Overdrive:**
  Unchecked fire leads to exhaustion. Constant striving without rest can deplete energy, leaving the inner flame flickering weakly — ambition without nourishment.
- **Fear of Weakness:**
  Sometimes the opposite occurs: fear of failure or rejection dims the fire entirely. Suppressed willpower results in passivity, indecision, or loss of self-trust.

THE WISDOM OF THE RAM

Balanced, the Ram becomes a symbol of **courageous awareness** — strength guided by heart and purpose.

- **Focused Power:**
  Like the Ram that climbs with steady resolve, we can

learn to direct our energy deliberately, channeling will into disciplined, purposeful action.

- **Courage through Challenge:**
Every obstacle is an invitation to rise higher. The Ram teaches perseverance — to meet resistance not with force, but with clarity, confidence, and endurance.
- **Strength in Humility:**
True mastery blends strength with compassion. The Ram bows its head before it charges — a gesture that reminds us that humility precedes true empowerment.
- **Sacred Fire:**
The Ram's fire, when balanced, purifies rather than destroys. It becomes the steady warmth that fuels transformation and lights the path of integrity and service.

The **Ram** teaches that power is sacred when aligned with wisdom. Its horns spiral like the journey of the soul — upward, inward, evolving.

When we honor Manipura's fire with awareness, we discover that strength is not about force, but about **illumined will** — the courage to lead, to act, and to shine without burning.

THE RAM IN TANTRIC SYMBOLISM

In Tantric depictions of the **ten-petaled lotus of Manipura**, the **Ram** is drawn beneath the lotus as its **vehicle (vāhana)**. The Ram is the sacred carrier of **Agni**, the Vedic god of fire — the divine spark that burns within all beings.

Agni rides the Ram across the heavens, illuminating the world with light and warmth. This imagery reminds us that **willpower and fire are not meant to destroy but to transform**. Just as fire cooks food and refines gold, the inner flame of Manipura purifies the self — turning raw experience into strength and ignorance into wisdom.

The Ram, therefore, symbolizes **disciplined power** — energy harnessed through awareness, courage, and devotion. It teaches that personal will is most sacred when it serves higher consciousness, becoming not ego's flame, but the light of the soul.

MEDITATING ON THE RAM

- **Visualization:**
  Imagine a **Ram standing atop a golden mountain**, radiant beneath the sun. Its breath glows with light, its stance unwavering. This is your solar energy — strong, steady, and alive with purpose.
- **Affirmation:**
  "I honor my inner fire. I act with clarity, courage, and integrity."
- **Integration:**
  Work with **fire imagery** — the rising sun, a candle's steady flame, the warmth of breath — to connect with your own willpower and determination. Feel how the fire within transforms resistance into action and fear into light.

The Deities of the Solar Plexus Chakra

In **Tantric tradition**, each chakra is presided over by divine figures who represent its essential forces. These deities are not external gods to be worshipped, but **archetypal energies within**, embodying the sacred qualities that can be awakened through meditation and spiritual practice.

For **Manipura**, the Solar Plexus Chakra, the presiding deities express the power of **fire, transformation, self-discipline, and illumination**. They guide us to refine raw energy into willpower and instinct into conscious action.

AGNI – THE GOD OF FIRE AND TRANSFORMATION

- **Agni**, the Vedic god of fire, is the presiding male deity of Manipura. In the ancient hymns, Agni is the divine messenger — the sacred flame that carries human offerings to the heavens and brings divine wisdom to earth.
- Within the Solar Plexus Chakra, Agni represents the **inner digestive fire (Jatharagni)** — not only the power that metabolizes food, but also the subtle flame that digests thoughts, emotions, and experiences into understanding.
- Agni is the **transformer of energy**. Just as physical fire turns matter into light and warmth, spiritual fire turns ignorance into wisdom, fear into courage, and inertia into will.
- Meditating on Agni within Manipura awakens the strength to act with clarity and integrity. His fire teaches discernment — to burn away what no longer serves, and to shine with the steady radiance of self-awareness.

LAKINI – THE SHAKTI OF MANIPURA

- The feminine guardian of the Solar Plexus Chakra is **Lakini**, a radiant goddess of strength, self-mastery, and discipline. She is often depicted with **three faces and four arms**, clothed in yellow or red garments, seated upon a blazing lotus of fire.
- In one hand, Lakini holds **a thunderbolt (vajra)** — the weapon of truth and focused power. In another, she holds a **spear or arrow**, representing direction and precision. Her other hands bestow blessings of nourishment and liberation.
- Lakini embodies the **divine will** (*Iccha Shakti*), the power of alignment between desire and purpose. She teaches that true power is born from inner order, not

chaos — from the harmony of strength and compassion, determination and humility.

- Meditating on Lakini awakens **self-respect, vitality, and radiant confidence**. She reminds us that discipline is not restriction, but devotion — the sacred structure that allows fire to burn steadily rather than wildly.

TOGETHER: AGNI AND LAKINI

Together, **Agni and Lakini** reflect the dual essence of Manipura:

• **Agni** provides the sacred fire — the purifying force that transforms energy into illumination.

• **Lakini** provides the conscious direction — the divine will that channels that energy toward purpose and right action.

Their union symbolizes the harmony between **power and awareness, fire and form, masculine radiance and feminine discipline**.

When these archetypes awaken within us, we remember that willpower is not domination but alignment — the fire of divine intention burning through human action. Manipura becomes not just the center of strength, but the **temple of transformation**, where every act of courage, integrity, and service becomes an offering to the inner flame.

SOLAR DEITIES IN OTHER TRADITIONS

Though Tantra specifically names **Agni** and **Lakini** as the guardians of Manipura, many cultures throughout history have personified the **solar plexus energy** — the fire of transformation, courage, and illumination — through their own sacred figures.

- **In Hindu tradition, Surya**, the Sun God, embodies the radiant essence of Manipura. He rides a golden chariot across the sky, bringing light, vitality, and discernment. His brilliance mirrors the chakra's inner fire that fuels strength, purpose, and consciousness.

- **In Greek mythology, Apollo,** god of the sun, music, and prophecy, represents clarity, reason, and the illuminating power of truth. Like Manipura, Apollo's energy transforms chaos into harmony and ignorance into wisdom through light and discipline.
- **In Egyptian cosmology, Ra,** the sun deity, sails daily across the heavens in his solar barque, symbolizing rebirth and endurance. His fiery eye wards off darkness, reflecting the Solar Plexus Chakra's role in courage and self-protection.
- **In Indigenous and shamanic traditions,** the **Sun Spirit** is honored as the giver of life and energy — the fire that sustains all growth. Ceremonies invoking the sun often focus on renewal, vitality, and the courage to walk one's true path.
- **In Western mysticism, Archangel Michael** embodies the light of divine will. His sword of truth cuts through illusion and fear, much like Manipura's fire that burns away doubt and restores inner strength and conviction.
- **In Japanese Shinto belief, Amaterasu,** the sun goddess, represents radiant presence and the power of inner light to dispel darkness. Her emergence from the cave of withdrawal symbolizes awakening one's true power after periods of doubt or suppression.

Across these traditions, the **Solar Plexus energy** is consistently revered as the **fire of divine will and transformation** — the sacred flame that lights the path between fear and faith, ignorance and wisdom, action and purpose.

Where the **Sacral Chakra** flows like water, **Manipura burns like the sun** — illuminating, energizing, and empowering all that it touches. The universal message is clear: when we honor

the light within, we become a vessel for divine power —
radiant, courageous, and alive with purpose.

THE ELEMENT OF MANIPURA: FIRE (AGNI / TEJAS)

Each chakra aligns with one of the **five great elements** of
nature (*Pancha Mahabhutas*). For the **Solar Plexus Chakra**,
that element is **Fire — Agni or Tejas in Sanskrit**.
This is more than symbolic: it is the living expression of
Manipura's essence — **energy, transformation, and the
radiant power of will**.

FIRE AS THE POWER OF TRANSFORMATION

Fire is life's great alchemist. It transforms the raw into the
refined — wood into warmth, food into vitality, experience into
wisdom.
In Manipura, fire represents **the inner light that digests life
itself**, transmuting what we take in — physically, emotionally,
and spiritually — into energy, understanding, and purpose.

Qualities of Fire

- **Transformation and Willpower:**
  Fire consumes and refines. It represents the power to act,
  to decide, and to change. When Manipura is balanced,
  our will is strong but not domineering, purposeful yet
  steady — a sacred flame that fuels growth.
- **Illumination and Awareness:**
  Fire brings light to darkness, revealing truth and
  direction. The Solar Plexus is the inner sun that shines
  through confusion, awakening clarity, discernment, and
  self-confidence.
- **Digestion and Metabolism:**
  Fire governs digestion — not just of food, but of
  thoughts and emotions. When Manipura burns evenly,

we assimilate life with ease. When it weakens, we feel sluggish, doubtful, or powerless.
- **Purification and Renewal:**
Fire purifies what it touches. It burns away impurities, leaving behind only what is essential. A balanced Manipura transforms anger, fear, and ego into courage, purpose, and radiant strength.

BALANCE AND IMBALANCE

When the fire of Manipura burns **too low**, we feel cold, passive, indecisive, or drained of motivation.
When it burns **too fiercely**, we become irritable, controlling, or consumed by ambition.
When **balanced**, it glows like a steady flame — warm, powerful, and self-contained — giving light without burning, and strength without domination.

Like the sun that sustains all life, **the fire of Manipura** teaches us to use energy wisely — not to destroy, but to illuminate and transform.
Through this sacred fire, we awaken our **inner light**, radiating confidence, courage, and purpose in harmony with the world around us.

WHY FIRE BELONGS TO THE SOLAR PLEXUS

The chakras ascend through the elements — **earth (root), water (sacral), fire (solar plexus), air (heart), and ether (throat)** — each one becoming lighter, more expansive, and more conscious.
After the fluid motion of water, **fire** is the next evolution — the spark of transformation, illumination, and will.

Fire belongs to **Manipura** because this chakra governs our **inner sun** — the seat of personal power, digestion, and self-confidence.

Just as fire refines raw material into light and warmth, Manipura refines experience into wisdom, emotion into purpose, and desire into decisive action.

Manipura asks us to:

• **Transform rather than react.**
• **Shine rather than shrink.**
• **Act with purpose rather than burn with impulse.**

Fire is the element of **empowered embodiment** — the commitment to live with integrity, courage, and radiant awareness.
It reminds us that true strength is not domination, but direction: energy guided by consciousness.

MEDITATING ON FIRE

Bringing the element of fire into Solar Plexus Chakra practice awakens confidence, clarity, and motivation.

1. **Fire Visualization:**
   Sit comfortably and imagine a golden-yellow sun glowing in your solar plexus, just above the navel. With each breath, feel its warmth spreading through your chest and spine, dissolving fear and doubt.
2. **Breath of Fire (Kapalabhati):**
   Take short, rhythmic exhales through the nose, pumping the belly gently.
   This awakens inner fire, clears stagnation, and builds vitality.
3. **Candle Meditation:**
   Gaze at a candle flame. As you inhale, draw in its light; as you exhale, imagine your own inner flame glowing brighter.
   Whisper: **"I am strong. I am confident. I act with purpose."**

When we meditate with the fire element, we align with the sacred truth of Manipura:
You are the light of your own life.
Let your inner flame guide you — not to consume, but to illuminate.

FIRE IN DAILY LIFE

• **When motivation feels dim:**
Light a candle and focus on its flame. With each breath, imagine your inner light growing steadier and stronger, awakening courage and direction.

• **When fear clouds your confidence:**
Step into the sunlight. Feel its warmth on your skin and visualize golden light filling your abdomen, dissolving hesitation and igniting purpose.

• **When anger burns too hot:**
Place your hand over your solar plexus and breathe slowly. Imagine a steady, gentle fire — controlled, calm, and radiant — transforming tension into clear strength.

• **When energy feels low:**
Practice deep belly breathing or a few rounds of Breath of Fire (Kapalabhati). Feel the inner flame of Manipura rekindling vitality and focus.

• **When self-doubt arises:**
Repeat softly, *"I am strong. I trust my power. I act with purpose."* Let the fire of belief illuminate every shadow of uncertainty.

THE LESSON OF FIRE

Fire teaches that true power is not about control — it is about **illumination**.
It burns away confusion and fear, lighting the path of clarity, courage, and self-mastery.
Just as a steady flame warms without destroying, balanced fire empowers without consuming.

Manipura reminds us that confidence and action are sacred expressions of the soul's fire.
When aligned with purpose, your inner flame becomes a beacon — radiant, transformative, and unshakable.

A Solar Plexus Chakra aligned with fire becomes the sun itself: **brilliant, life-giving, and free to shine.**

BRINGING THE SYMBOLS TOGETHER

Taken together, these symbols form a complete picture of the **Solar Plexus Chakra's** role — the radiant center of personal power and transformation:

- **The ten lotus petals** represent the refinement of energy through discipline, willpower, and right action — the purification of ego into conscious strength.
- **The downward-pointing triangle** embodies the element of fire — transformation, digestion, and the direction of energy from spirit into form.
- **The ram (Aries)** symbolizes courage, determination, and momentum — the primal force that propels us toward purpose and mastery.
- **The color yellow** radiates confidence, clarity, and illumination — the light of inner awareness that burns away doubt and fear.

- **The seed sound RAM** vibrates through the core, activating the will and harmonizing the fire of transformation within.

To meditate on these symbols is to awaken your **inner sun** — the balanced fire that empowers without consuming, purifies without destroying, and illuminates without blinding.
Each image reminds you that **strength, confidence, and transformation** are sacred acts of alignment — the radiant expression of your divine fire.

When the symbols of Manipura unite, they whisper one truth: **You are the light. You are the fire. You are the power that transforms life itself.**

THE SOLAR PLEXUS AS THE SACRED FLAME

Long before chakras were illustrated as spinning wheels of light, ancient sages described **Manipura** as an **inner fire — the sacred flame of transformation** burning at the body's core. This fire was not imagined as destructive, but as purifying — a divine heat that digests life itself, turning experience into wisdom, and will into radiant action.

The Flame Within

Where the Sacral was seen as a hidden pool, the Solar Plexus was envisioned as a **central hearth** — the luminous fire that warms the body, powers digestion, and fuels the soul's evolution.
Yogis taught that when awareness rests in the region above the navel, one can sense this subtle flame — steady, golden, and alive — illuminating the path between instinct and insight.

Here burns the **Agni**, the fire of transformation. It is the source of vitality, clarity, and discernment — the power that refines raw desire into purpose, emotion into strength, and energy into light.

Why the Solar Plexus?

The Solar Plexus is the seat of **conscious will**, the alchemical fire that turns the fuel of experience into illumination. To enter its flame is to recognize your power not as dominance, but as presence — the light of awareness directing the currents of your life.

- **In Tantra:** Manipura is the dwelling place of **Tejas**, the subtle fire element, where energy is refined through awareness and discipline.
- **In Yoga:** It is the **"city of jewels,"** the radiant core of self-mastery, where ego transforms into enlightened action.
- **In Alchemy:** The fire represents the crucible of transformation, where the base self is transmuted into gold — the soul awakened through inner heat.
- **In Indigenous Mysticism:** The **sacred fire** is the heart of the community, a living spirit of purification, guidance, and renewal — mirroring the fire within each person's being.

A SHARED WISDOM

Across traditions, the Solar Plexus has always been linked to **fire, the sun, and the golden light of consciousness**.
Where the Root grounds and the Sacral flows, Manipura ignites — it is the **moment of transformation**, when energy becomes empowerment and awareness becomes action.

The lesson of the Solar Plexus is clear:
Tend your fire. Feed it with truth, guide it with purpose, and let it illuminate your path.

When the flame of Manipura burns steady and bright, you stand as your own sun — radiant, centered, and fully alive.

THE SOLAR PLEXUS AS A MAP

The Solar Plexus Chakra's lotus — with its ten petals, downward-pointing triangle, and blazing yellow sun — can be seen as a **map of inner fire**.
The petals are the flames of transformation, the triangle is the crucible of will, and the sun is the radiant heart of consciousness. Together they guide awareness inward into the sacred fire of **Manipura**, where purpose, strength, and clarity dwell — holding the memory of courage and the seed of power.

A Practice: Entering the Flame

1. **Close your eyes.** Place your hands on your upper abdomen, just above the navel.
2. **Visualize** a golden sun glowing within you, its light pulsating like a steady, living fire.
3. **Step inward** in your mind's eye, walking toward the heart of this radiant flame.
4. **At the center,** see the fire burn clean and bright — warm, not harsh — transforming doubt into confidence, fear into focus, and hesitation into inspired action.
5. **Stand before this inner sun** with reverence. Know that it is your sacred hearth — the source of will, courage, and luminous awareness.

The Deeper Lesson

The flame of the Solar Plexus reminds us that spirituality is not about escaping life, but **illuminating it from within**.
The world may challenge you, fears may rise, uncertainty may cloud your path — but within you burns a light that never wavers.

To return to this fire is to return to strength.
To live from this fire is to act with clarity, confidence, and radiant purpose.

When you trust your inner flame, you do not seek power — **you become it.**

THE WESTERN ADAPTATION

When the chakra system reached the West in the late 19th and early 20th centuries, its original Tantric and yogic depth was translated into language that fit the emerging Western understanding of the mind and self. Early Theosophists like **C.W. Leadbeater** and **Alice Bailey** reinterpreted the chakras not solely as subtle energy centers of meditation, but as reflections of **psychological and spiritual evolution**.

In this adaptation, the **Solar Plexus Chakra (Manipura)** came to represent **personal power, confidence, and the development of individual identity**. Rather than being viewed only as the fire of transformation or digestion in the subtle body, it was understood as the **seat of the ego, self-esteem, and will** — the center through which human beings learn to act with intention and mastery in the world.

Psychology found a natural resonance with this interpretation. **Freud's exploration of ego development and instinctual control**, and **Jung's concept of individuation** — the process of integrating the self — both mirror the evolution of Manipura's fire: transforming raw emotion and desire into directed energy and conscious purpose. The Solar Plexus became, in Western thought, the **forge of selfhood** — the inner alchemist that tempers passion with discipline and turns impulse into empowered choice.

By the mid-20th century, as the **New Age movement** expanded, Manipura was commonly described as the **center of**

empowerment, self-confidence, and motivation. Healers, yogis, and energy practitioners began teaching it as the chakra of will, self-worth, and personal transformation — a place where fear is burned away and courage ignited.

Workshops, meditations, and therapies began focusing on themes of **assertiveness, boundaries, leadership, and self-belief** — translating ancient fire practices into psychological language.

Today, in Western Reiki, yoga, and holistic wellness, the Solar Plexus Chakra is widely recognized as the **seat of empowerment** — the bridge between instinct and compassion, between survival and love. Practitioners often focus on balancing Manipura to overcome self-doubt, reclaim confidence, or restore the inner flame of purpose.

While this Western lens sometimes simplifies Manipura's deeper esoteric meaning — reducing the fire of transformation to mere motivation — it still honors the core truth: **without inner fire, there is no action; without confidence, there is no creation.**

The journey of the Solar Plexus in the West reminds us that **power is not dominance but presence**, and that the sacred fire within each person is not meant to consume, but to **illuminate the path of conscious living**.

As we continue in this book, we will weave together both the ancient yogic teachings of Manipura and the psychological insights of the modern world, creating a bridge between **spiritual fire and personal empowerment**, so that this chakra may once again be understood as the radiant heart of transformation — the **inner sun that gives life to all growth.**

ARCHETYPES OF THE SOLAR PLEXUS CHAKRA

Every chakra expresses itself through distinct patterns of thought, emotion, and behavior. These patterns often take the form of archetypes — universal roles or inner identities that reveal both the **light and shadow** of each energy center.
For the **Solar Plexus Chakra (Manipura)**, two archetypes stand out: **The Warrior** and **The Leader.**

The Warrior

The Warrior embodies Manipura's essence — the fire of willpower, courage, and self-discipline. This archetype represents our ability to take action, assert boundaries, and stand firmly in integrity.
The Warrior teaches that true strength is not about domination but about clarity, focus, and the willingness to act from purpose rather than fear.

In Balance:
The balanced Warrior is brave, focused, and resilient. They face challenges with confidence and determination while honoring ethics and compassion. Their fire burns steadily — not to destroy, but to illuminate. A balanced Warrior stands strong without aggression, motivated by purpose rather than ego.

In Shadow:
When unbalanced, the Warrior may become domineering, defensive, or power-hungry. Fear of vulnerability can manifest as control or anger. In its shadow form, the Warrior uses force instead of wisdom, seeking victory rather than truth.
The lesson: power without awareness burns out. True courage includes knowing when to act — and when to yield.

The Warrior reminds us that **personal power must be guided by conscience**. When we channel our inner fire through discipline and compassion, we become unstoppable forces of light.

The Leader

If the Warrior masters action, the Leader embodies **vision and empowerment** — the ability to inspire others while remaining rooted in authenticity. This archetype reflects Manipura's higher function: transforming personal will into collective strength.

In Balance:
The Leader radiates confidence and integrity. They uplift others, empowering them to see their own potential. Their sense of purpose comes from service rather than control. The balanced Leader acts decisively, guided by clarity and compassion.

In Shadow:
When distorted, the Leader becomes the Tyrant or the Martyr. The Tyrant seeks to dominate, believing control equals security. The Martyr sacrifices too much, believing self-worth comes from servitude. Both lose connection to the golden middle path — where will and wisdom meet.

The Leader teaches us that **true leadership is not about commanding others but mastering oneself.** When inner fire is balanced, we lead not through authority, but through example.

TOGETHER: THE WARRIOR AND THE LEADER

Together, these archetypes reveal the dual power of Manipura:

- The **Warrior** brings the courage to act.
- The **Leader** brings the wisdom to guide.

One embodies the heat of transformation; the other, the light of purpose.
When balanced, they ignite the golden fire of the soul — the power to stand firm, act with integrity, and inspire others through example.

LIVING ARCHETYPALLY

Both the Warrior and the Leader live within us. Sometimes one voice is louder — the driven, action-oriented fire of the Warrior, or the visionary, guiding light of the Leader. Recognizing which one leads (and when) helps us transform raw ambition into conscious power.

Living archetypally with Manipura means balancing **the Warrior's courage with the Leader's wisdom** — action with reflection, assertion with empathy. Together, they remind us that empowerment is not about control, but about **alignment with truth and purpose.**

SOLAR PLEXUS ARCHETYPE REFLECTION EXERCISE

Take a few quiet moments for this exercise. Sit upright, feeling your spine long and your breath steady. Place one hand over your solar plexus, just above your navel. With each breath, imagine a golden flame burning brighter, filling you with warmth and confidence. Reflect on the questions below and record your thoughts in a journal.

Exploring the Warrior

1. When have I acted with courage or determination, even when afraid?
2. How do I respond to a challenge — with clarity, or with control?
3. What strengths does my inner Warrior bring to my life?

4. When might my Warrior slip into shadow — aggression, defensiveness, or burnout?
5. What practice helps my Warrior channel fire into focused strength instead of reaction?

Exploring the Leader

1. When do I feel most empowered to inspire others or take initiative?
2. How do I balance my drive for success with humility and compassion?
3. In what ways do I express leadership — in my family, work, or community?
4. Where might my Leader archetype become unbalanced — trying to control outcomes or over-giving to please others?
5. What would it feel like to lead from inner calm and authenticity rather than pressure or pride?

Integration

- Which archetype feels stronger in me right now — the Warrior or the Leader?
- Where do I sense imbalance or shadow in my expression of power?
- What small step can I take this week to bring my Solar Plexus energy into harmony?

Reflection Mantra:

"I honor the Warrior within me for giving me strength. I honor the Leader within me for guiding that strength with wisdom. Together, they ignite my inner fire — steady, radiant, and true."

Chapter 3 – The Energetic Blueprint of the Solar Plexus

The Solar Plexus Chakra and the Aura

The Solar Plexus Chakra does more than generate confidence or drive ambition — it fuels the **energetic engine of vitality and purpose** within the aura. If the Root provides grounding and the Sacral gives flow, then the Solar Plexus ignites **direction and radiance** — the organizing force that turns movement into intention and energy into creation.

When **Manipura** is strong and balanced, the aura glows with a **brilliant golden-yellow light** that radiates outward from the upper abdomen. This luminosity resembles sunlight — warm, powerful, and invigorating. The entire field feels **energized, focused, and alive**, pulsing with clarity and strength. Others may sense this as confidence, presence, or inner authority — the quiet magnetism of someone who knows who they are and acts with purpose.

Emotionally, a balanced Solar Plexus Chakra manifests as motivation, discipline, and a healthy sense of self-worth. You feel capable, decisive, and directed — able to face challenges without collapsing into fear or overexertion. Your energy radiates naturally, influencing your surroundings with warmth and focus.

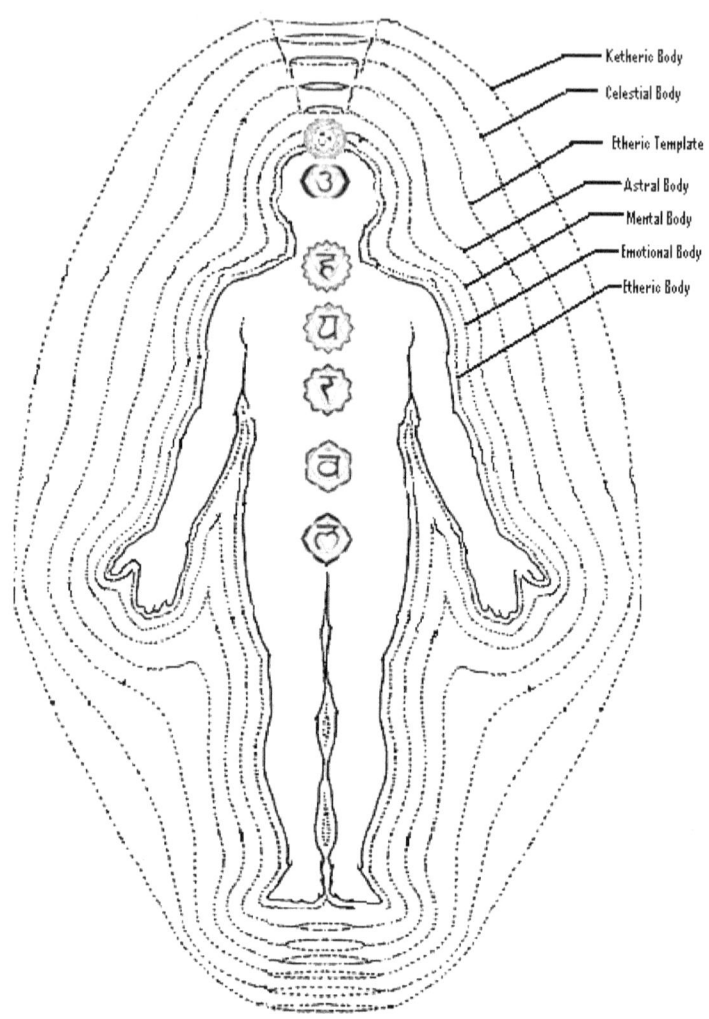

Ketheric Body

Celestial Body

Etheric Template

Astral Body

Mental Body

Emotional Body

Etheric Body

When **Manipura** is weak or blocked, however, the aura may appear dim, faded, or fragmented around the stomach and diaphragm. This often corresponds with low energy, fatigue, indecision, or self-doubt. The person may feel invisible or unable to assert their will. On the other extreme, when the Solar Plexus is **overactive**, the aura may flare too brightly or sharply, creating energetic tension, irritability, or the urge to control. Both imbalances reflect fire that has lost its balance — either extinguished or burning too hot.

The Solar Plexus governs **the distribution of energy throughout the aura**, much like the sun governs the solar system. It is the center where **raw vitality is refined into usable power**. This is why solar practices — such as standing in sunlight, practicing breathwork (especially Kapalabhati or "Breath of Fire"), visualizing a glowing sun in the belly, or chanting the bija mantra **RAM** — restore balance. These practices awaken Manipura's sacred flame, sending a message through the aura:

"I am strong. I am confident. I act with purpose."

In response, the energy field brightens, becoming vibrant, centered, and coherent — like the steady glow of a lantern in the dark.

From a practitioner's perspective, the Solar Plexus Chakra is often the **energetic blueprint of empowerment**. It reveals how an individual manages their personal energy — whether they burn with steady purpose or flicker with uncertainty. Even if the lower chakras are stable and the higher centers awakened, without the fire of Manipura, the aura lacks vitality and direction. Like a lamp without flame, it cannot illuminate or inspire.

In this way, **Manipura serves as the energetic blueprint of radiance for the aura** — the inner sun that fuels action, confidence, and transformation. It is the center where will becomes light and light becomes life.

The Aura of Fire: How Manipura Radiates Through the Energy Field

When the **Solar Plexus Chakra (Manipura)** is balanced, its golden radiance extends far beyond the body.
This is the light people sense before you speak — the quiet power of presence that fills a room without demanding attention.
It is confidence without arrogance, leadership without control, warmth without expectation.
In the aura, this appears as a soft yet luminous golden glow radiating from the upper abdomen, spreading outward like sunlight through mist.

THE QUALITY OF LIGHT

Manipura's energy expresses through the element of fire — bright, vibrant, and transformative.
When the fire burns cleanly, the aura shimmers in hues of gold, amber, and yellow, often with streaks of white or radiant silver.
This light communicates vitality, integrity, and clarity of intention.
Others may describe feeling "uplifted" or "safe" in your presence, as though your energy provides both warmth and illumination.

When the Solar Plexus is underactive, the aura appears dim or faded in the midsection, reflecting low vitality, timidity, or indecision.
When overactive, the glow may seem harsh or overly intense — the energy pushes outward, creating dominance rather than radiance.
True balance lies in a steady flame — light that warms but does not burn.

THE FIELD OF CONFIDENCE

The Solar Plexus governs personal identity and willpower, and its radiance in the aura represents **self-containment** — the ability to hold one's energy without leaking or absorbing others' emotions.
This containment is not rigidity; it is sovereignty.

When Manipura is balanced, you move through the world with energetic integrity.
You can enter crowded or emotionally charged spaces without losing your sense of self.
You empathize without merging, lead without overpowering, and assert boundaries with grace.

The aura becomes a golden shield — not as defense, but as natural coherence.
It says to the world: *"I am centered in my own light."*

INFLUENCE AND MAGNETISM

A balanced Solar Plexus magnetizes opportunities, people, and experiences aligned with your higher purpose.
This is not manipulation — it is resonance.
When your inner fire burns steadily, it naturally attracts others who share your frequency of authenticity, courage, and drive.

In this way, Manipura serves as the **magnet of manifestation** — converting intention into reality through focused energy.
Your words carry weight, your presence inspires action, and your clarity creates trust.

This radiant influence is why leaders, teachers, and healers often have a strong Solar Plexus field — their confidence empowers others to believe in their own.

ENERGY EXCHANGE AND BOUNDARIES

The Solar Plexus is also where energetic cords of power are most frequently formed — those invisible lines through which people exchange influence, expectation, or control.
When Manipura is healthy, these exchanges remain balanced: giving without depletion, receiving without guilt.
If the chakra is weak, energy may be drained through over-giving or people-pleasing; if excessive, energy may unconsciously dominate others.

Maintaining balance means practicing awareness — noticing when your light dims from overextension or flares from defensiveness, and gently returning to center.
Breathing into the Solar Plexus while visualizing a steady golden flame restores harmony instantly.

THE RADIANCE OF RIGHT POWER

At its highest vibration, the Solar Plexus becomes the **light of right power** — power used in service of truth, not ego.
In this state, the aura expands effortlessly, reflecting both confidence and compassion.
The fire purifies, illuminates, and inspires rather than consumes.

To walk in this light is to embody leadership through being, not doing —
to shine because it is your nature, not because you seek to prove your worth.

This is the essence of a balanced Manipura: a sun that neither hides nor burns too brightly,
but radiates warmth, courage, and illumination — a living flame of inner sovereignty.

Flow of Energy from the Solar Plexus Upward

The Solar Plexus Chakra is not merely a center of will and confidence — it is the **great transformer** within the human energy system, the place where raw life force becomes conscious direction. In yogic tradition, this current of energy is called **prana**, and in Tantra, it is guided upward by **Kundalini** as she ascends through the body's central channel, the **sushumna nadi**.

At **Manipura**, the fluid emotional energy of the Sacral Chakra refines into something new: **personal power, clarity, purpose, and radiant self-awareness**. Here, the life force takes on form and focus — the formless flow of feeling becomes the steady flame of intention.

Once this transformation occurs, the energy continues to rise, moving through successive layers of awakening:

- **From Manipura (Solar Plexus) → to Anahata (Heart):** Personal will is tempered by compassion. Power expands beyond self-interest and becomes service, empathy, and love.
- **From Anahata → to Vishuddha (Throat):** Love finds its expression through truth. The courage of the Solar Plexus gives voice to authenticity.
- **From Vishuddha → to Ajna (Third Eye):** Expression refines into insight. Action gives birth to perception and inner wisdom.
- **From Ajna → to Sahasrara (Crown):** Vision dissolves into unity, and the fire of individuality merges with divine consciousness.

This upward current mirrors a universal truth: **energy seeks refinement**. Emotion rises into power; power matures into compassion; compassion blossoms into wisdom; and wisdom dissolves into divine light.

When **Manipura** is balanced, this upward flow is steady and luminous. The will acts in harmony with intuition, and confidence arises from inner alignment rather than ego. The aura radiates coherence — clear, strong, and focused. But when the Solar Plexus is **blocked or unbalanced**, the current wavers. Power becomes control, or the fire dims into apathy and indecision. Without balance here, higher centers like the Heart and Throat cannot fully open, for love and truth both depend on a foundation of authentic selfhood.

Practitioners often describe Manipura as the **sun of the energy body** — the center that ignites every other chakra. If its flame burns too low, the upper centers grow dim; if it flares uncontrollably, it scorches the delicate currents above. But when it glows steadily, it radiates warmth and vitality throughout the entire system, empowering all levels of being.

The Solar Plexus does not hoard energy — it **refines and releases** it, transforming the heat of desire into the light of purpose. Just as the sun converts fire into life for the earth, Manipura converts will into wisdom, guiding the life force upward with focus, discipline, and illumination.

THE SOLAR PLEXUS AS THE SEAT OF POWER AND PURPOSE

If the heart is the seat of love, and the sacral is the seat of emotion, then the solar plexus chakra is the **seat of power and purpose**.

Manipura governs the fire of transformation — the energy that fuels action, confidence, and the pursuit of self-mastery. This is not the raw instinct of survival nor the flowing emotion of desire; it is **directed will**, the conscious use of energy to shape one's life with clarity and intention.

From an evolutionary perspective, **Manipura** reflects the stage of human development when emotional and relational needs have been met and the individual begins to assert autonomy and purpose.
Our ancestors, once secure in community and sustenance, turned toward leadership, innovation, and mastery. They learned to cultivate fire — to cook food, forge tools, and illuminate the dark. Likewise, the Solar Plexus is our **inner fire**, transforming the raw materials of experience into confidence, motivation, and action.
It is the bridge between feeling and doing, between emotional flow and conscious creation.

When the Solar Plexus Chakra is **balanced**, energy radiates steadily from the core. You feel confident without arrogance, decisive without domination, motivated yet calm. Your actions arise from alignment, not from impulse or fear. Challenges are met with clarity, and boundaries are maintained with integrity. Manipura in harmony allows you to act — not react — embodying the quiet strength of self-trust.

When **Manipura** is out of balance, the fire of will either weakens or burns uncontrollably.

- **When underactive**, it manifests as low energy, self-doubt, procrastination, or a sense of powerlessness — the flame flickering in insecurity.
- **When overactive**, it appears as dominance, anger, perfectionism, or control — fire turned to wildfire.
  In both cases, energy is misdirected: either smothered by fear or consumed by ego.

Manipura also influences the **digestive and metabolic systems**, the body's mechanisms for turning nourishment into usable energy. In the same way, it governs the psyche's ability to "digest" life — to transform experiences into wisdom and challenges into growth. When this center is aligned, we assimilate lessons with ease and act from discernment rather than reaction.

Modern life often challenges Manipura's balance. External pressures, competition, and self-comparison can distort the natural rhythm of empowerment. The result is burnout, self-criticism, or the illusion that worth must be earned. Healing the Solar Plexus restores the **truth of personal power** — that it arises not from control, but from alignment with one's inner fire.

When balanced, **Manipura** awakens the radiant light of self-confidence and purpose.
You act with integrity.
You lead with clarity.
You transform fear into fuel.

The Solar Plexus teaches that empowerment is not domination, but illumination — the fire that lights the way for yourself and others.
To honor Manipura is to remember that your will is sacred, your confidence divine, and your purpose the flame that keeps your soul alive.

In this way, flow is both universal and deeply personal. It can be as simple as dancing to a rhythm, painting with color, or sitting by water — yet as profound as awakening the truth that your emotions, your creativity, and your relationships are sacred currents of life itself.

Svadhisthana holds this truth: flow is not a distraction, nor a luxury — it is a gift. The gift of being alive, sensual, and in harmony with the waters of creation.

A UNIVERSAL UNDERSTANDING OF FIRE

Though the chakra system originates in the yogic and Tantric traditions of India, the experience of **fire** — both literal and symbolic — is universal. Across cultures and ages, humanity has gathered around flame for warmth, illumination, and transformation. Fire is life's purifier and awakener: the power that cooks our food, forges our tools, and ignites the inner light of consciousness.

To live with fire is to live with **purpose, passion, and illumination** — the sense of *"I act. I choose. I transform."* Whether through ritual, innovation, leadership, or courage, cultures across the world have honored fire as the force that turns potential into power. It is the sacred reminder that energy, when directed with wisdom, becomes light.

CROSS-CULTURAL EXPRESSIONS OF FIRE

Indigenous Traditions:
In many Indigenous and First Nations teachings, fire is the living heart of the circle — the bridge between human and spirit. Fire ceremonies are used for cleansing, renewal, and courage. Flames consume what no longer serves, transforming it into light and smoke that carries prayers to the Creator.

Eastern Systems:
In yogic philosophy, Manipura's element is **Agni**, the inner fire that governs digestion, vitality, and will. In Ayurveda, balanced Agni sustains life; too little leads to weakness, and too much to burnout. Fire is both the physical heat of metabolism and the spiritual light of awareness — the same flame that burns in the belly and in the soul.

Greek Philosophy:
For the ancient Greeks, fire was the element of divine intellect and transformation. Heraclitus declared that *"all things are*

exchanged for fire, and fire for all things" — expressing the eternal cycle of change that defines existence. The fire of Prometheus, gifted to humanity, symbolizes the awakening of knowledge and creative potential.

Alchemy:
In Western alchemical traditions, fire is the agent of refinement — the crucible through which base metals (and the human ego) are transmuted into gold. This inner alchemy mirrors Manipura's role: to burn away fear and transform raw energy into clarity, confidence, and illumination — the true "city of jewels."

Western Mysticism and Tarot:
The element of fire is embodied in the **Suit of Wands**, representing inspiration, drive, and creative will. Wands mirror the Solar Plexus energy of determination and vision — the spark that begins all manifestation. Spiritually, the flame also symbolizes divine presence: the burning bush, the sacred candle, the Pentecostal light.

THE UNIVERSAL LESSON OF FIRE

In every culture, fire is a **teacher of transformation**. It asks not for possession but for respect — for mindfulness in how we tend our flame. When we repress fire, we lose vitality and purpose; when we let it rage uncontrolled, we destroy what we wish to create.
Balance lies in the **sacred tending** — feeding the flame enough to warm, guide, and illuminate, without letting it consume.

Across traditions, this same wisdom endures:

- Fire purifies.
- Fire reveals.
- Fire transforms.

Whether we call it Agni, divine spark, life force, or creative will, the essence is the same:
When our inner fire burns clear and steady, we awaken the light of Manipura — the power to act, to illuminate, and to transform our world from within.

How Practitioners Work with the Solar Plexus Chakra

For healers and energy practitioners, the **Solar Plexus Chakra — Manipura — ** is known as the **center of power and transformation**. Located in the upper abdomen, just above the navel, it governs personal will, confidence, motivation, and the ability to act with purpose.
When Manipura is balanced, a person radiates strength, clarity, and vitality — they move through life with focus and conviction.
When blocked, energy feels heavy or scattered, self-doubt clouds decision-making, and personal power becomes either suppressed or overexerted.

ASSESSMENT

Practitioners begin by tuning into a client's relationship with power, self-worth, and direction in life. They may explore questions such as:

- How confident do you feel making decisions or asserting boundaries?
- Do you often feel drained, unmotivated, or indecisive?
- Are you overly controlling or fearful of taking action?
- How do you respond to criticism or failure — with resilience, or with collapse?

Energetically, healers sense **Manipura** as a vibrant yellow field radiating from the solar plexus.

- A balanced center feels **warm, bright, and focused**, like a steady flame.
- An underactive Manipura may appear **dull, cool, or withdrawn**, suggesting low energy or self-esteem.
- An overactive one may feel **sharp or volatile**, signaling anger, tension, or control issues.

ENERGY HEALING TECHNIQUES

• Reiki & Hands-On Healing:
Energy is channeled into the upper abdomen and diaphragm to rekindle the inner flame. Practitioners often visualize a golden light radiating outward, strengthening the client's will and clarity.

• Sound Healing:
The bija mantra **RAM** resonates with the Solar Plexus, activating the fire element and harmonizing digestion, both physical and emotional. Drums, gongs, or deep brass bowls often accompany sessions, echoing the steady pulse of empowerment.

• Crystal Healing:
Yellow and golden stones — such as **citrine, tiger's eye, amber, pyrite, and yellow calcite** — are placed over the solar plexus to enhance confidence, focus, and vitality.

• Aromatherapy:
Energizing oils like **lemon, ginger, black pepper, frankincense, and rosemary** awaken Manipura's fiery essence, promoting motivation and mental clarity.

BODYWORK PRACTICES

Because Manipura governs digestion, movement, and energy conversion, physical work is essential in restoring balance:

- **Core-strengthening yoga poses** (Boat, Plank, Warrior III) build stability and ignite inner strength.
- **Breathwork** — especially *Kapalabhati* (Breath of Fire) — activates the diaphragm and clears stagnant energy.
- **Abdominal massage or reflexology** supports digestion and the release of emotional tension stored in the gut.
- **Qi Gong or martial arts** help channel energy into disciplined, focused motion — fire directed through mastery.

SPIRITUAL AND ANCESTRAL HEALING

Practitioners working at the Solar Plexus often focus on clearing the energetic imprints of fear, shame, or disempowerment passed through lineage or past experiences.
Common practices include:

- **Guided visualizations** to reclaim personal power or retrieve lost confidence.
- **Cord and vow release** to dissolve unhealthy energetic attachments to control, approval, or fear of failure.
- **Fire ceremonies or candle rituals** to symbolically burn away limitations and invite clarity, courage, and will.

INTEGRATION

Healing Manipura is the art of **transforming energy into action**. Practitioners encourage clients to embody empowerment through consistent practice:

- Set one clear goal each day and take aligned action.

- Practice **mindful posture** — stand tall, breathe deeply, and let your body remember its strength.
- Speak affirmations aloud: *"I am strong. I am capable. I act with purpose."*
- Engage in **sunlight meditation** or time outdoors to recharge the body's solar energy.
- Reflect on successes — large or small — to reinforce a positive sense of self.

For healers, the Solar Plexus Chakra represents the **alchemy of will** — the point where energy is refined into purpose, and confidence becomes light.

It reminds us that true power is not force — it is clarity.

When Manipura burns steady and golden, we lead not from dominance, but from radiant presence.

Chapter 4 – Signs of Imbalance

Shadow Aspects of the Solar Plexus Chakra

Every chakra carries both light and shadow. The **Solar Plexus Chakra — Manipura** — governs power, confidence, will, and transformation. It is the flame of purpose that propels us into action and helps us shape our destiny. Yet when this fire is distorted or misused, it burns unevenly — flaring too hot or dimming to embers.

Instead of fueling clarity, motivation, and confidence, an imbalanced Solar Plexus manifests as **control issues, low self-esteem, anger, or exhaustion**.

The shadows of Manipura are not punishments but **signals from the inner fire**, showing where our relationship with power has become misaligned — where we have either given it away or wielded it without awareness. They invite us to tend our flame with respect, transforming dominance, fear, or insecurity into radiant strength.

LOW SELF-WORTH AND POWERLESSNESS

When Manipura is underactive, the inner fire wanes. You may feel small, invisible, or incapable of directing your life. Indecision, procrastination, and fear of judgment replace confidence. Life feels like something happening *to* you, not *through* you.

Physically, this may show up as fatigue, poor digestion, or shallow breathing — signs that your internal energy is not being transformed into vitality. The fire of purpose has grown weak, leaving you disconnected from motivation and self-trust.

OVERCONTROL AND DOMINATION

When Manipura burns too hot, it manifests as overcontrol — needing to direct people or outcomes, micromanaging life, or refusing vulnerability. The desire to maintain order becomes a shield against uncertainty. This imbalance often masks fear: the fear of powerlessness, failure, or betrayal.

Overactive Solar Plexus energy can feel sharp, tense, or fiery — leading to anger, irritability, or burnout. The fire that once illuminated now consumes, leaving little room for collaboration or peace.

ANGER AND FRUSTRATION

The Solar Plexus governs the emotion of anger — the heat of personal will. When this energy is blocked or misdirected, anger festers beneath the surface, leading to chronic frustration, resentment, or internalized rage.

Unexpressed anger may manifest as digestive discomfort, tightness in the diaphragm, or a constant knot in the stomach. Healing does not mean suppressing anger but **transmuting it** — allowing it to become fuel for courage, clarity, and rightful action.

INSECURITY AND EXTERNAL VALIDATION

At its core, the shadow of Manipura reveals the wound of **disempowerment** — the belief that one's worth depends on others' approval or success in the outer world.

This can lead to perfectionism, overachievement, or people-pleasing — trying to prove value through doing rather than being. The Solar Plexus dims when self-worth is outsourced, and reignites when we reclaim our right to define ourselves.

LACK OF DIRECTION OR MOTIVATION

When Manipura is sluggish, even small goals can feel
overwhelming. The mind may be full of ideas, but the will to
act is absent. Doubt replaces drive. This often occurs after
disappointment, criticism, or a loss of faith in one's abilities.
In such times, gentle action rekindles the flame: one clear
intention, one honest decision, one courageous step at a time.

BURNOUT AND OVEREXERTION

Just as underactivity leads to stagnation, overactivity leads to
depletion.
The constant need to *do more* or *prove more* eventually
exhausts the system. The fire burns through its own fuel.
Physically, this can appear as digestive issues, adrenal fatigue,
or chronic stress. Emotionally, it feels like pushing through life
instead of flowing with it.
True empowerment is not endless effort — it is sustainable
energy guided by purpose.

THE HIDDEN WOUND

At the heart of every Solar Plexus imbalance lies a simple truth:
a wound to personal power.
Somewhere along the path, you may have learned that your
light was too bright, your voice too strong, or your will too
dangerous. The result is internal conflict — the fear of your
own strength or the guilt of using it.
Healing Manipura is not about dominance or submission. It is
about **authentic power** — the confidence to act in alignment
with truth.

You heal not by forcing control, but by rekindling trust in your
own inner flame.
Each small act of courage — saying no, setting a boundary,
speaking your truth, or taking initiative — feeds the fire again.

Like the rising sun after night, **your inner power returns gradually, yet inevitably.**
The light was never gone — only waiting for your permission to shine.

Excess or Overactive Solar Plexus Energy

When the Solar Plexus Chakra becomes overstimulated, its steady inner flame turns into a wildfire.
Instead of illuminating, it burns — consuming rather than empowering.
An overactive **Manipura** can manifest as domination, perfectionism, aggression, or relentless striving. The person may appear confident and driven, but beneath the surface, their energy burns too fast, leaving them exhausted, tense, and disconnected from inner peace.

This excess often develops when the drive for power, achievement, or control is fueled by fear rather than purpose. It may also arise in those raised in environments that valued success, productivity, or authority above emotional awareness — teaching the nervous system that to be powerful is to never rest.
The result is **fire without focus — action without reflection.**

CONTROL AND DOMINATION

When Manipura overfires, the desire for control overshadows trust. You may feel compelled to direct people, outcomes, or even the emotions of others.
Rather than leading through confidence, the energy seeks to dominate — out of fear that surrender equals weakness.
Relationships can feel strained as cooperation gives way to competition, and love is confused with control.

ANGER AND IRRITABILITY

Excess fire in Manipura often shows up as impatience, anger, or frustration. The smallest obstacles may ignite large reactions, and the inner dialogue becomes harsh or judgmental.
Though anger can be sacred fuel for transformation, when untamed it scorches instead of refines. The lesson is to learn **how to channel heat into light** — to speak with strength, not burn with reaction.

PERFECTIONISM AND OVERACHIEVEMENT

Overactive Solar Plexus energy drives the constant need to *do more, be more, prove more.*
The individual may appear highly productive, but beneath the surface lies chronic tension and fear of inadequacy. Rest feels unsafe; stillness feels like failure.
The fire burns endlessly, never satisfied, because it's fueled by self-judgment instead of inspiration.

ARROGANCE AND EGO INFLATION

When Manipura becomes excessive, the light of confidence can distort into ego.
One may feel overly self-important, dismissive of others, or obsessed with recognition and status. The fire of will, untempered by humility or heart, separates rather than connects.
This imbalance often conceals deep insecurity — the fear that without superiority, one will disappear.

BURNOUT AND EXHAUSTION

An overcharged Solar Plexus eventually depletes the very energy it seeks to expand.
The nervous system stays in overdrive, digestion weakens, and chronic stress becomes the norm. The body may signal imbalance through adrenal fatigue, ulcers, tension in the

abdomen, or shallow breathing.

Manipura's lesson is clear: **even fire must rest** — flames need oxygen and space to burn cleanly.

AGGRESSION AND IMPULSIVITY

Excess fire can erupt as impulsive decisions or reactive speech. Words or actions are taken before reflection, often followed by regret. The person may swing between high motivation and sudden collapse — the energetic equivalent of overheating an engine.

The cure lies in *discipline over force*, learning that true power moves deliberately, not explosively.

THE HIDDEN LESSON

Overactive Solar Plexus energy teaches that **power without presence becomes destruction.**

Just as fire can warm or consume, Manipura's energy must be guided by awareness and compassion.

Healing begins not by extinguishing the flame, but by learning to **tend it wisely** — transforming intensity into illumination. Meditation, deep breathing, and grounding practices invite the fire to burn steadily and bright.

When the will is aligned with truth and the ego bows to purpose, the Solar Plexus becomes what it was always meant to be: **the radiant sun of personal power — strong, focused, and life-giving.**

The Experience of an Imbalanced Solar Plexus

When the **Solar Plexus Chakra (Manipura)** is out of balance, life feels like a fire that flickers without fuel — sometimes dim, sometimes blazing, never quite steady.
Because this chakra governs personal power, confidence, motivation, and digestion (of both food and life experience), its imbalance reaches into nearly every aspect of being: how we act, how we decide, how we assert boundaries, and how we believe in our own worth.

An imbalanced Solar Plexus often reveals itself through the struggle between control and surrender — between trying too hard and giving up entirely. You may feel restless but uninspired, determined yet doubtful. The fire that once fueled direction and purpose begins to waver, either burning out or flaring up uncontrollably.

EMOTIONAL SIGNS

Emotionally, an unbalanced Manipura often feels like tension between confidence and insecurity. You may swing between self-assurance and self-criticism — one moment feeling unstoppable, the next doubting every choice.
Frustration, irritability, and impatience can surface easily, especially when things don't go according to plan.
Alternatively, a dim Solar Plexus may leave you feeling powerless, invisible, or unsure of your place in the world. The emotional flame struggles to hold steady, making trust in your own decisions difficult.

MENTAL AND BEHAVIORAL SIGNS

On the mental level, imbalance often manifests as **overthinking, perfectionism, or paralysis by analysis.**

When overactive, the mind races with plans, lists, and worries — an endless need to organize or control.
When underactive, procrastination or avoidance replaces action. You may find yourself seeking approval from others, doubting your intuition, or hesitating to take responsibility for fear of failure. Manipura's imbalance clouds clarity, replacing focused will with scattered effort.

MOTIVATIONAL SYMPTOMS

The Solar Plexus governs the ability to act — to turn ideas into motion.
When blocked, motivation fades; the smallest task feels monumental. The inner dialogue may echo: *"What's the point?"* or *"I can't do this."*
When overactive, you may push yourself past exhaustion, unable to rest or delegate. The balance between drive and surrender disappears, and the fire burns too hot or too low to sustain real progress.

RELATIONAL DYNAMICS

Because Manipura governs personal boundaries, imbalance often appears through **power struggles or passivity**.
When excessive, the energy seeks dominance — controlling, correcting, or criticizing others to maintain superiority.
When deficient, boundaries collapse — you absorb others' opinions, suppress your truth, and mistake compliance for peace.
In both extremes, relationships lose their balance of respect and autonomy. True connection becomes clouded by either force or fear.

PHYSICAL MANIFESTATIONS

Physically, the Solar Plexus corresponds to the stomach, liver, pancreas, and digestive system — the body's center of transformation.

Imbalance may show as poor digestion, acid reflux, ulcers, nausea, or adrenal fatigue. You might notice tightness in the diaphragm or shallow breathing.

These symptoms reflect difficulty "digesting" life — holding tension instead of processing experience, controlling rather than trusting.

THE INNER EXPERIENCE

At its core, an imbalanced Solar Plexus feels like being **disconnected from your own inner power.**

You may question your direction, hesitate to speak up, or feel lost between wanting to lead and fearing to be seen.

The world may seem overwhelming, or worse — under your constant need to control.

The lesson of Manipura is that true power is not about dominance or submission, but **alignment** — the quiet confidence that arises when will, purpose, and action move as one.

When the Solar Plexus returns to balance, the fire burns steady and clear.

Action feels natural, not forced. Confidence flows from within rather than from approval.

You act not to prove worth, but to express it.

Balance at Manipura is not about power over others — it is about **power within.**

The gentle strength to act with clarity, purpose, and radiant self-trust.

Chapter 5 – Causes of Disturbance

Childhood Control and Powerlessness

If the Root Chakra is where we learn that life is safe, and the Sacral is where we learn that life can be felt, then the **Solar Plexus Chakra** is where we learn that *we have influence* — that we can make choices, act on our will, and shape our own experience.
During early to middle childhood, Manipura begins to form as we explore independence: learning to say *yes* or *no*, asserting our opinions, and discovering the pride of self-accomplishment.

When this natural growth of autonomy is supported, a healthy Solar Plexus develops. We learn that personal power is safe, that effort brings results, and that confidence grows from experience.
But when control, criticism, or chaos dominate our early environment, the developing sense of power becomes distorted. The inner flame that should burn steadily begins to flicker between rebellion and submission.

AUTHORITARIAN ENVIRONMENTS AND LOSS OF AUTONOMY

Children raised in overly controlling or punitive homes often learn that obedience is safer than authenticity. Their natural impulses — curiosity, independence, defiance — are met not with guidance but with suppression.
This teaches the child that power belongs only to others.

As adults, this can manifest as chronic self-doubt, indecision, or difficulty asserting needs. The Solar Plexus remains dim, unable to trust its own authority.

Alternatively, some may swing to the opposite extreme — overcompensating by becoming rigidly self-reliant or controlling toward others. Both responses stem from the same wound: *a fractured relationship with power.*

CRITICISM AND CONDITIONAL APPROVAL

When love and praise are given only for achievement or perfection, self-worth becomes performance-based.
The message received is subtle but lasting: *I am valued only when I succeed.*
This pattern keeps the Solar Plexus overactive — constantly striving, proving, and pushing — or underactive, paralyzed by fear of failure.
In both cases, the natural confidence of Manipura is replaced by anxiety and comparison. The joy of action becomes burdened by the weight of expectation.

INSTABILITY AND LACK OF STRUCTURE

Children thrive within consistent boundaries. Without them, the inner fire burns without direction.
When parents are unpredictable, emotionally volatile, or neglectful, the developing Solar Plexus struggles to find a sense of order. The child learns that effort does not guarantee results, and control feels impossible.
This can lead to lifelong patterns of confusion, procrastination, or overcompensation through perfectionism and control.

HUMILIATION AND SHAMING OF WILL

One of the most damaging experiences for the Solar Plexus is humiliation — being mocked, dismissed, or punished for speaking one's truth.

These moments teach the child that visibility is dangerous and that their willpower must be hidden to stay safe.

As adults, this wound may appear as fear of confrontation, avoidance of leadership, or deep resentment toward authority figures. The flame of Manipura burns beneath the surface, longing to be expressed but fearful of rejection.

ROLE REVERSAL AND OVER-RESPONSIBILITY

Some children are forced to grow up too soon — taking on responsibilities far beyond their years. They become the caretakers, peacekeepers, or achievers in unstable homes. While this builds resilience, it also wires the Solar Plexus for **hypervigilance and over-control**. The child learns that rest equals danger, that everything depends on their effort.

In adulthood, this often manifests as burnout, anxiety, or difficulty delegating — an inner belief that "if I don't do it, everything will fall apart."

NEGLECT OF ENCOURAGEMENT AND INDEPENDENCE

A healthy Manipura thrives on encouragement — the gentle assurance that trying matters more than perfect success. When this support is missing, the will withers.

Without affirmation, the child doubts their competence, and the internal dialogue becomes self-defeating. Creativity, motivation, and leadership instincts fade. The Solar Plexus learns hesitation instead of confidence.

THE LASTING IMPACT

Childhood experiences that distort power and autonomy teach the body that self-expression is unsafe or futile.

As adults, we may either overexert — grasping for control and authority — or collapse into passivity, fearing our own strength.

Both stem from the same root wound: *a loss of trust in our ability to shape life with purpose.*

Healing the Solar Plexus begins with **reclaiming the right to choose**.
Through boundary-setting, mindful action, and gentle self-discipline, we remind the inner child that it is safe to stand tall again.

Each act of self-trust — speaking up, completing a task, honoring intuition — rekindles Manipura's golden flame.
As we remember that confidence is not domination but self-respect, the Solar Plexus begins to shine again — steady, warm, and radiant with authentic power.

Poverty, Scarcity, and Power Deprivation

The **Solar Plexus Chakra (Manipura)** governs not only confidence and willpower but also our capacity to believe in our own worth — to feel capable, deserving, and empowered to act in the world.
When life is dominated by fear, criticism, or lack of opportunity, the result is not just material scarcity but **power deprivation** — a starvation of the inner fire.
Where the Root asks, *"Am I safe?"* and the Sacral asks, *"Am I allowed to feel?"* the Solar Plexus asks, *"Am I enough?"*
When that question goes unanswered, a deep sense of inner poverty takes hold — not of the body, but of the spirit.

EMOTIONAL DEPRIVATION OF POWER

Emotional power deprivation begins in environments where independence, self-expression, or achievement were met with indifference or disapproval.
The child learns that standing out is dangerous, that effort goes unnoticed, or that confidence is arrogance.

Instead of developing pride in their abilities, they internalize smallness — a belief that taking up space will invite rejection. In adulthood, this often manifests as chronic self-doubt, fear of decision-making, or the need for external validation to feel capable. The person may appear competent yet feel hollow — *a quiet fatigue from constantly proving worth that never feels enough.*

SCARCITY OF SELF-WORTH

Just as financial scarcity breeds fear of losing security, **self-worth scarcity** creates fear of inadequacy.
Those with an undernourished Solar Plexus struggle to celebrate success or feel pride in accomplishment. Even achievements are downplayed — "It was nothing," or "Anyone could have done it."
This internalized modesty is not humility but a learned discomfort with power.
It often arises from cultural or familial teachings that equate confidence with ego or ambition with selfishness. Over time, these beliefs extinguish the inner flame of Manipura, replacing purpose with hesitation and joy with self-critique.

SURVIVAL THROUGH OVERCONTROL

When the inner fire dims, control often becomes a substitute for strength.
The person may micromanage details, cling to routines, or push themselves relentlessly to avoid feeling powerless.
Externally, they appear driven; internally, they are burning out.
Control creates the illusion of safety, but it also locks the Solar Plexus in tension — preventing the free flow of authentic confidence and trust.
The result is effort without ease, action without fulfillment, and exhaustion without satisfaction.

INTERGENERATIONAL SCARCITY OF POWER

Just as financial or emotional scarcity can be inherited, so can beliefs about worth and capability.
Families who endured hardship or oppression may unconsciously teach caution over courage: *"Don't get your hopes up,"* or *"People like us don't succeed."*
This legacy of limitation becomes a silent inheritance — generations shrinking themselves to stay safe.
Healing this lineage begins when someone chooses to light the fire again: to believe that empowerment is not arrogance, and that personal success uplifts the whole family line.

LONG-TERM EFFECTS

Living with a deprived Solar Plexus can lead to:
• Chronic self-doubt and fear of failure
• Difficulty setting or maintaining boundaries
• Overachievement without inner fulfillment
• Dependence on external approval
• Fear of visibility or leadership
• A deep sense of "never enough," no matter the success achieved

HEALING THE ENERGY OF WORTH AND EMPOWERMENT

Healing Manipura begins by reclaiming the right to **stand tall and shine.**
It asks us to remember that power is not domination — it is the steady warmth of self-trust.
Through small acts of courage and confidence — completing a task, speaking your truth, setting a healthy boundary — the inner flame reignites.

Where the Root heals through stability and the Sacral through flow, the **Solar Plexus heals through empowerment.**

Each time you act from your authentic will instead of fear, Manipura strengthens.

The mantra becomes:
"I am enough. I am capable. I am worthy of success."

As empowerment replaces deprivation, Manipura transforms from a dwindling spark into a radiant sun — a steady source of purpose, confidence, and inner sovereignty.

Ancestral Patterns of Fear, Control, or Disempowerment

The **Solar Plexus Chakra (Manipura)** does not hold only our personal confidence and will — it carries the energetic memory of our lineage's relationship to power, control, and courage.
Just as we inherit physical DNA, we also inherit subtle imprints in the energetic body — memories of how our ancestors faced fear, leadership, loss, and survival.
When generations before us experienced war, domination, forced migration, or suppression of voice, those memories often remain encoded within the fire of Manipura.

Even in peaceful lives, descendants may carry the echo of those ancestral wounds: fear of visibility, guilt around success, or an unspoken hesitation to step into full strength — as though power itself might bring danger.

INHERITED FEAR OF POWER

Manipura governs the right to act — to shape destiny through choice and will.
When ancestors lived under oppression, servitude, or constant threat, they learned that visibility and power were unsafe.
Over generations, this becomes an energetic inheritance:

descendants feel small, cautious, or apologetic for their own strength.

You might notice an inner tension — the desire to lead coupled with fear of standing out.
This is not just insecurity; it is ancestral conditioning whispering, *"Stay safe by staying small."*

Healing begins by remembering that your courage honors those who could not express theirs. Each step you take in confidence restores the lineage's lost sovereignty.

DISPLACEMENT AND LOSS OF DIRECTION

When families are uprooted through war, colonization, or migration, the Root may lose its grounding — but the Solar Plexus loses its compass.
Direction and purpose become diffused; generations may wander without a clear sense of mission or belonging.
This manifests as difficulty committing to goals, chronic uncertainty, or a feeling of "carrying others' burdens" without knowing why.

Ancestral disempowerment often appears as restlessness — a constant need to prove, achieve, or fix, rooted in the subconscious drive to restore what was once taken.
Healing this pattern involves redefining what success means on your terms, not through inherited survival scripts.

INHERITED CONTROL AND HYPERVIGILANCE

Families shaped by fear or instability often pass down an unconscious rule: *"If you can control everything, you'll stay safe."*
This imprint fuels perfectionism, over-responsibility, and the inability to relax — the flame of Manipura burning too hot.
Descendants may carry deep anxiety around failure, believing

rest equals danger.
The nervous system stays alert, even in safety, replaying ancestral vigilance.

Healing comes through trust — learning to act from inner power rather than outer control. When the fire burns steadily instead of fiercely, Manipura transforms anxiety into strength.

SILENCED VOICE AND SUPPRESSED WILL

In patriarchal or authoritarian lineages, the expression of will — particularly for women or marginalized voices — was often denied or punished.
Over time, this suppression weaves into the Solar Plexus as hesitation, guilt, or shame around speaking truth and asserting needs.
Descendants may unconsciously dim their light to maintain harmony or avoid conflict, perpetuating generations of silenced willpower.

Reclaiming Manipura means breaking the ancestral vow of silence: allowing yourself to speak, act, and shine without apology.
In doing so, you heal the unspoken stories of those who had to endure in silence.

THE LEGACY OF FEAR AND COURAGE

The energy of fear that once ensured survival can, generations later, become resistance to growth.
Families that survived by endurance may unconsciously transmit caution rather than confidence.
But when awareness transforms fear into wisdom, the same energy becomes fuel for empowerment.
Each act of courage — each choice to lead, create, or believe in your own capability — rewrites the ancestral script from submission to sovereignty.

HEALING THROUGH EMPOWERED ACTION

To heal ancestral patterns within the Solar Plexus Chakra:
• Acknowledge the histories of fear, oppression, or silence within your lineage.
• Honor your ancestors' endurance, but release the belief that you must live in their caution.
• Engage in actions that affirm courage — speaking truth, taking initiative, or standing firm in integrity.
• Use fire rituals or candle meditations to symbolically transform inherited fear into light and strength.
• Affirm: **"I honor the courage of my ancestors, and I reclaim the power they could not express."**

THE DEEPER LESSON

Where the Root carries inherited memories of physical survival, and the Sacral holds emotional memory, the **Solar Plexus carries the legacy of power** — how our lineage learned to act, lead, and believe in itself.
When generations lived under suppression, Manipura learned caution; when they fought to rise, it learned resilience.

By transforming fear into purpose and shame into confidence, you do more than empower yourself — you become the flame that rekindles your family's dormant fire.
The Solar Plexus no longer carries the story of endurance alone, but the awakening of courage — the ancestral sun rising again within you.

Inherited Beliefs About Success and Failure

The **Solar Plexus Chakra (Manipura)** is the energy center of willpower, self-worth, and achievement — the inner sun that fuels purpose and direction.
Yet for many, this light is dimmed not by personal failure but by **inherited beliefs** about what success and power mean. These

beliefs often originate in the struggles, sacrifices, or values of those who came before us.

Where the Root passes down survival instincts and the Sacral transmits emotional memory, the Solar Plexus inherits the stories of ambition, control, and worth — the ancestral scripts that tell us how bright we're allowed to shine.

Inherited Guilt Around Success

In families that endured poverty, oppression, or hardship, success can carry unconscious guilt.
The message — never spoken but deeply felt — might be: *"If I have more than they did, I am betraying them."*
Descendants may unconsciously sabotage opportunities, downplay achievements, or give away resources as soon as they're gained.

This pattern often shows up as chronic under-earning, fear of recognition, or discomfort with praise.
The Solar Plexus learns to dim its glow to protect others from discomfort — not realizing that genuine success uplifts the entire lineage.

Healing begins with permission: to thrive is not betrayal.
Every step into abundance honors the resilience that made it possible.

Fear of Failure and Perfectionism

When ancestors survived through vigilance, endurance, or strict discipline, their descendants may internalize a deep fear of failure.
The unspoken rule becomes: *"Mistakes are dangerous."*
Perfectionism then replaces curiosity. Ambition becomes burden. The natural joy of progress is overshadowed by the terror of imperfection.

In Manipura, this belief constricts the inner fire — too afraid to burn freely.
The nervous system interprets risk as threat, locking the will in hesitation or overdrive.
Healing requires re-teaching the body that failure is not fatal — it is feedback.
Success becomes sustainable when effort is guided by purpose, not fear.

INHERITED BELIEFS ABOUT HIERARCHY AND POWER

Across many lineages, ideas about power are polarized — either revered or distrusted.
Families who suffered under tyranny may fear authority altogether, while those who wielded control may equate leadership with dominance.
Both extremes distort Manipura's natural balance between confidence and humility.

If your lineage carries distrust of authority, you may hesitate to lead, feeling safer in the background.
If it carries patterns of domination, you may unconsciously replicate control instead of empowerment.
Healing this polarity means remembering that true power serves — it uplifts rather than conquers.
Manipura, in its essence, is not a throne but a sun — a light that radiates, not rules.

Inherited Work Ethic and the Fear of Rest

Many families carry ancestral vows of toil: *"Hard work is virtue."*
For those who survived through relentless labor, rest equated to risk.
Generations later, their descendants may feel anxious when idle, guilty when resting, or unable to celebrate accomplishments.

This inherited tension burns in the Solar Plexus as overdrive — productivity as proof of worth.

The body may run on adrenaline while the spirit quietly hungers for peace.

Healing this belief involves reclaiming balance: knowing that ease is not weakness and rest does not diminish power.

Manipura glows brightest when its fire burns steadily, not constantly.

Inherited Limitation and Self-Sabotage

When generations believed, *"People like us don't get ahead,"* that belief becomes an energetic barrier — a ceiling over the Solar Plexus flame.

You may notice a pattern of near-success followed by collapse, or opportunities arriving but slipping away.

These moments are not fate; they are ancestral echoes asking for resolution.

Each time you affirm, *"I am allowed to succeed,"* you rewrite centuries of silent limitation.

Healing Manipura at this level means embodying a new truth: that your worth is not conditional, your dreams are not disloyal, and your power does not harm — it heals.

Healing the Lineage of Power

To clear inherited patterns of success and failure within the Solar Plexus:

• Reflect on your family's stories around money, work, and recognition.

• Identify sayings or beliefs that shaped their view of achievement.

• Offer gratitude for their resilience — then consciously choose your own truth.

• Use fire rituals to release limiting beliefs (writing and burning them as symbolic transmutation).

• Affirm: **"I honor the effort of those who came before me. Their endurance gives me strength, and I am free to create success with joy and integrity."**

The Deeper Lesson

Where the ancestors toiled in survival, you are invited to thrive in purpose.
Where they labored under fear, you are asked to lead with light.
Each success you embody becomes a healing prayer for the lineage — proof that their sacrifices blossomed into empowerment.

As inherited beliefs dissolve, Manipura's fire steadies into golden confidence.
No longer dimmed by guilt or driven by fear, the inner sun radiates freely — a living testament that power, when reclaimed with love, becomes legacy transformed.

Environmental and Energetic Toxins: Violence, Stress, Societal Instability

The **Solar Plexus Chakra (Manipura)** is the energetic center of power, confidence, and self-governance — the fire that fuels our sense of purpose and agency in the world.
While the Root anchors physical survival and the Sacral processes emotion, the Solar Plexus determines how we respond: whether we act from fear or from inner authority.
In a world marked by violence, chronic stress, and instability, Manipura often becomes both shield and casualty — trying to stay strong in a sea of external pressure.

Where the Sacral absorbs emotion like water, the Solar Plexus absorbs tension like heat.
It flares in response to aggression, injustice, and chaos —

burning too hot with anger or too low with defeat.
Over time, the world's turbulence can distort this vital fire,
leaving the individual exhausted, anxious, or disconnected from
personal will.

THE REACTIVE NATURE OF MANIPURA

Manipura's element is **fire**, and like any flame, it is sensitive to
its environment.
It thrives in clarity, purpose, and integrity — yet flickers when
surrounded by deceit, hostility, or fear.
In toxic or volatile surroundings, the Solar Plexus often
compensates by either hardening into defense (overactive) or
collapsing into apathy (underactive).
The energy field tightens, and the body reflects it — tension in
the stomach, shallow breathing, or digestive unease.

Each time we witness cruelty, experience conflict, or absorb the
collective anxiety of the world, Manipura registers it as a threat
to personal power.
The subconscious reads this as *"It isn't safe to shine, to speak,
to lead."*
The flame dims to stay safe — but with it, our vitality and
confidence fade as well.

EXPOSURE TO VIOLENCE AND AGGRESSION

Exposure to violence — whether direct, witnessed, or through
media — sends shockwaves through the Solar Plexus.
This center governs the instinctive "fight or flight" response,
and continual exposure keeps it on high alert.
Even witnessing aggression can train the nervous system to
equate visibility with danger.

The result is often chronic muscle tension in the abdomen,
digestive issues, irritability, or hypersensitivity to criticism.
For some, this overstimulation leads to aggression and control

issues; for others, it causes withdrawal and powerlessness.
Manipura burns unevenly — too intense one moment,
extinguished the next.

Healing begins by separating personal truth from collective
chaos — learning that we can stand strong without internalizing
the world's turbulence.

CHRONIC STRESS AND OVERDRIVE

Modern life constantly stokes Manipura's fire.
High performance demands, nonstop communication, and
societal pressure to "succeed" keep the solar energy burning on
overdrive.
At first, this creates productivity and drive — but without rest,
the fire consumes its own fuel.

The body's stress hormones rise, digestion weakens, sleep
suffers, and emotional balance erodes.
Manipura's brilliance turns harsh, leaving irritability, fatigue, or
cynicism in its place.
Instead of confidence, we feel pressure; instead of
empowerment, exhaustion.

True strength is not intensity — it is endurance balanced with
calm.
When we learn to modulate our energy rather than force it, the
Solar Plexus becomes a steady light instead of a wildfire.

SOCIETAL INSTABILITY AND COLLECTIVE FEAR

Manipura governs how we hold power — both individually and
collectively.
In times of social upheaval, corruption, or economic insecurity,
this chakra often reflects the collective anxiety of lost control.
Even those with stable lives may feel restlessness, frustration, or
despair, echoing the collective disempowerment of humanity.

The more unstable the external world becomes, the more individuals tighten internally — trying to maintain order through willpower alone.
This tension breeds burnout and hopelessness, cutting off the natural current of optimism and trust.

Healing Manipura within collective chaos means remembering the distinction between **control** and **clarity.**
You cannot control the world's storms — but you can keep your inner fire lit through discernment, boundaries, and faith in your own strength.

ENERGETIC CONTAMINATION

Beyond physical stressors, the Solar Plexus is sensitive to environments charged with conflict, competition, or manipulation.
Because this chakra governs personal sovereignty, it easily reacts to power struggles — in families, workplaces, or communities.
Unspoken resentment, jealousy, or domineering energy can drain Manipura's field, leaving sensations of heaviness, fatigue, or self-doubt.

Energetic hygiene for this chakra involves **cleansing through clarity and choice**: removing yourself from toxic dynamics, speaking truth without aggression, and consciously reclaiming authority over your attention and energy.

HEALING THROUGH FIRE PURIFICATION

The antidote to Manipura's energetic pollution is purification through light and breath — practices that rekindle clarity and calm.
• Limit exposure to violent, fear-based media or high-conflict environments.
• Breathe deeply into your solar plexus, imagining a golden

flame burning away tension and fear.
• Practice discernment: engage only in conversations and commitments that align with your integrity.
• Reconnect with sunlight — walk, meditate, or simply absorb its warmth to reset your fire.
• Use energy-clearing tools such as sound, movement, or intention-setting to release collective fear.

THE DEEPER LESSON

Manipura teaches that power without peace burns out, and peace without power fades away.
In chaotic times, the goal is not to harden against the world but to strengthen the inner sun — calm, radiant, and self-sustaining.

To feel the world without being consumed by it is true mastery of the Solar Plexus.
To lead without reacting, to act without aggression, to shine without fear — this is the alchemy of Manipura.

When we tend the fire with awareness, we transform stress into strength and chaos into clarity — becoming beacons of steady light in a world still learning how to find its power.

Power Abuse, Control, and the Violation of Will

The **Solar Plexus Chakra (Manipura)** is the seat of personal power — the fire of individuality, confidence, and purpose.
It governs the right to act, to choose, and to direct one's own life.
When that right is violated — through manipulation, control, humiliation, or domination — the core of Manipura is shaken.
Its natural flame of autonomy dims into fear, self-doubt, or submission.

Just as the Sacral Chakra governs the sacred flow of emotion, the Solar Plexus governs the sacred flame of will.
When this flame is extinguished through coercion or emotional oppression, the individual may lose trust in their ability to decide, lead, or stand up for themselves.
It is a wound not only of confidence, but of **sovereignty** — the very essence of one's inner authority.

ENERGETIC IMPACT OF POWER VIOLATION

When personal boundaries are crossed — physically, emotionally, or psychologically — the Solar Plexus contracts to protect the self.
The body holds this memory as tightness or pressure in the stomach, diaphragm, or solar region.
People may experience sensations of nausea, digestive tension, or the feeling of "a knot in the gut" when recalling experiences of being controlled, criticized, or made small.

Energetically, the aura around Manipura becomes constricted or cloudy, reflecting internalized fear of power — both one's own and others'.
You may find yourself avoiding confrontation, doubting decisions, or giving away authority to keep peace.
For others, the opposite occurs: the wound expresses through overcompensation — becoming overly dominant or rigid to prevent ever being powerless again.

Both reactions — submission or overcontrol — stem from the same wound: **a loss of trust in one's own agency.**

THE LEGACY OF HUMILIATION AND SHAME

Shame is one of the heaviest burdens on the Solar Plexus.
It enters through words meant to belittle: *"Who do you think you are?"* or *"You'll never amount to anything."*
Such conditioning fractures the inner flame, replacing self-belief with chronic self-criticism.

Cultural systems of hierarchy and domination reinforce this imbalance, teaching that obedience equals virtue and power equals corruption.
Over time, individuals learn to hide their light, fearing that confidence will be punished or that leadership means arrogance.

But Manipura's true power is **dignity**, not dominance — the quiet strength that stands firm without aggression, and shines without apology.

EMOTIONAL AND PSYCHOLOGICAL VIOLATION

Not all Solar Plexus wounds are overt. Emotional manipulation, gaslighting, or controlling relationships can gradually erode willpower.
When choices are constantly questioned, or when someone's emotions are weaponized to force compliance, the psyche learns to equate disagreement with danger.

This subtle form of violation teaches the body to freeze, the voice to shrink, and the will to go silent.
It manifests as chronic indecision, fear of rejection, or dependence on external approval.
The fire of Manipura becomes trapped beneath layers of compliance and guilt.

Healing begins by re-establishing **inner permission** — the right to say no, to act, and to trust one's instincts again.

PHYSICAL MANIFESTATIONS

Because the Solar Plexus governs the digestive system and metabolism, trauma or chronic disempowerment often manifests physically.
Symptoms may include ulcers, IBS, acid reflux, adrenal fatigue, or chronic exhaustion.
The body quite literally "can't stomach" unresolved fear, resentment, or anger.

When energy is suppressed in this region, digestion — both physical and emotional — becomes compromised.
The system cannot assimilate nourishment or experiences fully until the inner fire is allowed to burn clearly once more.

PATHWAYS TO HEALING THE SOLAR PLEXUS

Healing Manipura after experiences of control or disempowerment is the act of reclaiming **inner authority** — the ability to choose and act from truth.
This is not about dominance but about remembering the sacred right to self-direction.
The process unfolds gradually as confidence, courage, and discernment return to the body.

Key Approaches Include:

• **Ground First:** Anchor into the Root before rebuilding power. Safety is the foundation for authentic strength.
• **Reconnect to the Body:** Practice mindful breathing into the diaphragm. Feel the rise and fall of your belly as a reminder of agency and life-force.
• **Voice Activation:** Speak affirmations aloud, practice toning or chanting "RAM," the seed sound of Manipura, to awaken strength and presence.
• **Boundaries as Healing:** Practice saying no without justification. Boundaries rebuild trust in your will.

• **Transform Anger into Purpose:** Anger is Manipura's signal that power was crossed. Channel it into assertive action or creative direction rather than suppression.
• **Supportive Guidance:** Work with therapists, energy healers, or mentors who honor autonomy rather than impose authority.
• **Affirmations of Empowerment:**
   "My will is sacred."
   "I trust my choices."
   "I act with clarity, courage, and compassion."

THE DEEPER LESSON

Violations of Manipura — whether through oppression, manipulation, or shame — remind us how fragile and precious personal power truly is.
But the Solar Plexus also holds the gift of transmutation: the ability to turn pain into purpose, and humiliation into humility anchored in strength.

Each time you reclaim your right to choose, to speak, and to act in alignment with your truth, the inner sun of Manipura brightens.
It burns away the residue of fear and reignites dignity, courage, and confidence.

To reclaim will after suppression is not an act of rebellion — it is an act of sacred remembrance.
It is to say:

I am not powerless.
I am not defined by others' control.
My power is not to dominate, but to shine.

Chapter 6 – Signs of Balance

Empowered Presence: Confidence, Purpose, and Vitality

When the **Solar Plexus Chakra (Manipura)** is balanced, there is a radiant sense of inner strength and clarity.
You feel centered in your own power — neither dominating nor shrinking — but glowing with a steady confidence that comes from knowing who you are.
The mind is calm, the will is focused, and actions flow naturally from purpose.

Just as the sun lights the world without effort, a balanced Manipura illuminates your life from within.
You act with integrity, speak with conviction, and trust yourself to move forward even when outcomes are uncertain.
Life feels purposeful, energized, and guided by an inner compass that does not waver in the face of doubt or comparison.

CONFIDENCE AND SELF-WORTH

A harmonious Solar Plexus radiates quiet assurance — not arrogance, but self-respect.
You recognize your inherent worth without needing validation.
Decisions feel grounded because they arise from authenticity rather than fear of judgment.
You can say yes when it aligns and no when it doesn't, maintaining peace instead of guilt.

Confidence becomes compassion in action — strength used not to control but to uplift.
The balanced Manipura reflects maturity: you no longer seek approval to exist; you embody self-trust as your natural state.

PURPOSE AND RIGHT ACTION

Manipura governs direction and discipline — the ability to turn vision into reality.
When this chakra is balanced, purpose feels clear and motivation flows effortlessly.
You take decisive action without forcing outcomes, guided by intuition and reason in harmony.
Work, creativity, and service align with personal values, creating a deep sense of fulfillment.

Challenges become opportunities for mastery rather than threats to identity.
You trust your ability to navigate life — not because it is easy, but because your fire burns steady.

VITALITY AND ENERGY BALANCE

The Solar Plexus is also the body's energetic furnace, transforming life force into usable power.
When balanced, energy levels remain consistent — vibrant yet sustainable.
Digestion, metabolism, and willpower all function harmoniously, mirroring the clarity of inner fire.

You awaken with enthusiasm for life, yet rest without guilt.
This balanced rhythm allows productivity without burnout, passion without compulsion, and ambition without anxiety.

EMOTIONAL STABILITY AND BOUNDARIES

A balanced Manipura brings emotional sovereignty.
You no longer absorb others' moods nor feel responsible for
their reactions.
Empathy remains, but with boundaries that protect inner peace.
Anger becomes assertiveness, fear becomes discernment, and
sensitivity becomes wisdom.

This emotional steadiness creates confidence in relationships
and leadership alike.
You meet conflict with calm authority rather than reactivity,
transforming friction into understanding.

INTEGRITY AND AUTHENTIC POWER

True power at the Solar Plexus is not control but alignment.
It is the ability to act according to truth even when it is
uncomfortable.
Integrity replaces ego, and humility refines strength.
The balanced Manipura honors the principle: *Power that serves
life expands; power that dominates diminishes.*

You no longer chase external power because your internal
authority is intact.
In this state, influence arises naturally — people feel your
presence as warmth, not force.

THE FEELING OF EMPOWERED FLOW

Confidence, purpose, and vitality weave together to create the
luminous feeling of balance at Manipura.
There is clarity without rigidity, strength without aggression,
and freedom without chaos.
You are self-directed yet connected, disciplined yet spontaneous
— living in harmony with the rhythm of your own inner fire.

In this state, life feels like a steady flame — bright, peaceful, and self-sustaining.
You trust your instincts, express your truth, and meet challenges with grace.
To live with a balanced Solar Plexus Chakra is to embody the quiet brilliance of the sun within — radiant, unwavering, and alive with purpose.

Physical Vitality: Digestive System, Core Muscles, and the Fire Element

The **Solar Plexus Chakra (Manipura)** governs the realm of transformation — both physical and energetic.
Where the Sacral Chakra is the river of life, Manipura is the inner fire that fuels motion, clarity, and power.
It is the seat of metabolism, digestion, and vitality — the alchemical furnace that turns food, emotion, and experience into energy and purpose.
When this fire burns steadily, the body feels strong, the mind clear, and the spirit courageous.

DIGESTIVE SYSTEM: THE FURNACE OF TRANSFORMATION

The digestive organs — stomach, pancreas, liver, gallbladder, and small intestine — are the physical home of Manipura.
They embody the chakra's essential function: **transformation.**
Just as the body digests food into nourishment, the Solar Plexus digests experience into wisdom and confidence.

When this system is balanced, digestion is smooth, metabolism steady, and the core feels warm and vital.
You assimilate not only nutrients but life itself — taking in what serves you and releasing what does not.

When imbalanced, you may experience indigestion, ulcers, sluggish metabolism, or fatigue — physical reflections of emotional or energetic overload.
The body, like the mind, struggles to "process" too much at once.

Balanced Solar Plexus energy keeps the digestive fire burning bright but controlled — transforming without consuming.

CORE MUSCLES: THE SEAT OF STRENGTH AND STABILITY

The muscles of the abdomen and lower back form the physical structure supporting Manipura.
This is the body's center of gravity — where balance, posture, and strength converge.

When this area is strong and flexible, you move through life with stability and assurance.
The body mirrors the spirit: upright, centered, and confident.

When energy here is weak, you may feel physically or emotionally collapsed — unable to "stand your ground."
When overactive, tension may accumulate in the solar region, reflecting excess control, anxiety, or defensiveness.

Strengthening and softening the core in equal measure restores harmony to Manipura — the balance between effort and ease, power and presence.

LIVER AND PANCREAS: THE ALCHEMISTS OF ENERGY

The **liver** and **pancreas** play key energetic roles in the Solar Plexus system.
The liver governs detoxification — both physically and emotionally — releasing anger, resentment, and stagnant

energy.
The pancreas regulates blood sugar, symbolizing balance
between energy intake and output, giving and receiving.

When Manipura is balanced, these organs work in rhythm,
sustaining steady energy and mood.
When the fire burns too fiercely, frustration or inflammation
may arise; when too low, fatigue and indecision follow.
The key is moderation — a steady, golden flame that nourishes
rather than consumes.

THE ELEMENT OF FIRE

Fire is the essence of Manipura — transformative, luminous,
and empowering.
It is the principle of **conversion:** turning potential into action,
thought into will, and energy into creation.
When balanced, fire purifies without burning, giving light
without destruction.

A healthy Solar Plexus teaches us the sacred art of right use of
energy — to act with precision, to speak with clarity, and to live
with purpose.
Just as the sun rises each day without strain, Manipura
expresses strength that is radiant yet calm.

THE FEELING OF PHYSICAL POWER

A balanced Solar Plexus Chakra brings a sense of embodied
vitality.
You feel centered in your power, energized without
restlessness, decisive without aggression.
The breath deepens, posture aligns, and warmth radiates
through the body like sunlight in motion.

Movement feels empowered, grounded, and intentional — each
action guided by inner strength rather than external pressure.

Energy flows upward, illuminating the heart and mind, creating harmony between body, will, and purpose.

To live with a balanced Manipura is to carry the sun within — a fire that transforms, uplifts, and sustains all that you are.

Spiritual Qualities: Willpower, Integrity, and Divine Purpose

When **Manipura** is balanced, spirituality takes on the form of empowered action — the divine expressed through purpose, clarity, and conscious choice.
The Solar Plexus reveals that true spiritual power is not about dominance or control, but about aligning personal will with divine will.
It teaches that enlightenment is not found only in meditation or stillness, but in every courageous act of integrity, every moment you stand in truth, and every choice made from the light of awareness.

WILLPOWER AS SACRED ALIGNMENT

The Solar Plexus transforms the raw desire of the lower chakras into disciplined will — the sacred capacity to act with intention and faith.
When this fire is balanced, willpower becomes devotion in motion.
Each task, no matter how small, becomes an offering — a chance to bring spirit into form.

You begin to understand that strength is not about forcing outcomes but about holding steady in clarity until life unfolds through you.
Your will becomes the hand of divine intelligence, moving with both power and humility.

INTEGRITY AS THE PATH OF ILLUMINATION

At the level of the Solar Plexus, integrity becomes a spiritual practice.
It is the commitment to live in truth — to speak honestly, act consciously, and align behavior with belief.
Integrity purifies the inner fire, transforming ego-driven ambition into enlightened purpose.

When Manipura is in harmony, you feel guided by an inner sun that never deceives.
You no longer need to seek validation, because your conscience itself becomes your compass.
Integrity is light made visible through your choices.

PURPOSE AS SPIRITUAL SERVICE

Manipura is the meeting point between personal desire and divine direction.
When balanced, you recognize that your talents and ambitions are not random — they are tools through which the universe expresses its creative intelligence.
Purpose, then, becomes a spiritual path: living your truth in a way that benefits the greater whole.

This understanding turns work into service and goals into prayers.
Action becomes meditation, and success becomes fulfillment through alignment rather than accumulation.
You move with confidence not because you know the outcome, but because you trust the light within to guide each step.

THE FIRE OF TRANSFORMATION

Spiritually, the Solar Plexus embodies the alchemy of transformation — the ability to transmute fear into faith, inertia into motion, and doubt into determination.

This is the sacred fire that purifies illusions and strengthens the soul.
You learn that trials are not punishments but initiations —
flames through which your essence becomes clear and refined.

When you stand in this fire willingly, resistance melts into resilience, and every challenge becomes a chance to evolve.
This is the deeper teaching of Manipura: power and humility must coexist.
Only when both burn together does the light of wisdom emerge.

CONNECTION TO DIVINE WILL

The highest spiritual expression of Manipura is surrender — not of weakness, but of alignment.
It is the moment when personal will merges with universal intelligence and the ego bows to the soul.
Here, you no longer strive to control life; you allow life to move through you.
In this union, action becomes effortless, decisions become clear, and energy flows freely through the body and spirit.

This is the spiritual radiance of the Solar Plexus:
to act with conviction, to speak with clarity, and to live with courage — not as separate from the Divine, but as its living flame.

The Experience of a Balanced Solar Plexus Chakra

When the **Solar Plexus Chakra (Manipura)** is in harmony, life feels purposeful, radiant, and empowered.
You move through the world with confidence and clarity — neither dominating nor submitting, but acting from inner strength and alignment.

Energy flows upward with steadiness; choices arise from trust rather than fear.
You feel illuminated from within — the quiet assurance that your life has meaning and direction.

PHYSICAL EXPERIENCE

The core feels warm, strong, and centered.
The digestive fire burns steadily — neither sluggish nor overactive — reflecting harmony in metabolism and vitality.
Posture aligns naturally, and movement carries both strength and grace.
You feel energized but calm, grounded in your power yet free of tension.
The body becomes a vessel of balanced fire — radiant, healthy, and alive.

EMOTIONAL EXPERIENCE

Emotionally, a balanced Manipura brings stability and self-assurance.
You respond to challenges with calm determination instead of reaction.
Confidence replaces self-doubt, and self-respect replaces the need for approval.
You can stand your ground without aggression, and yield when wisdom calls for it.
Your inner fire burns cleanly — transforming anger into motivation, fear into courage, and uncertainty into purpose.

MENTAL EXPERIENCE

The mind of a balanced Solar Plexus is sharp, focused, and clear.
You make decisions with confidence, guided by intuition and reason working in harmony.
Mental clutter fades, replaced by discernment and insight.

You can organize, plan, and follow through with discipline, yet remain flexible when life shifts.
Thought becomes action, and action aligns with truth.

SPIRITUAL EXPERIENCE

Spiritually, Manipura awakens the understanding that true power is service — the expression of divine will through human action.
You feel guided by an inner sun that illuminates your path without the need for control.
Life itself becomes an act of sacred leadership: living with integrity, inspiring others through example, and trusting your inner light as the reflection of divine strength within.
The ego no longer seeks to dominate; it becomes a vessel for spiritual purpose.

OVERALL EXPERIENCE

To live with a balanced Solar Plexus Chakra is to live with radiant empowerment.
You feel strong without force, confident without pride, and purposeful without pressure.
Your energy is consistent and magnetic, your emotions steady and luminous.
You no longer strive to prove your worth — you embody it.

In this state, the light of Manipura burns brightly and clearly — the golden flame of will, wisdom, and divine purpose shining from the core of your being.

The Body Trinity: Earth, Water, and Fire — The Sacred Foundation of Light

Before the higher centers of the heart, throat, and crown can awaken fully, the soul must first find stability within the body. The **three lower chakras** — Root (Muladhara), Sacral (Svadhisthana), and Solar Plexus (Manipura) — form the energetic foundation upon which consciousness rises. They are the sacred pillars of embodiment: **Earth that grounds, Water that flows, and Fire that transforms.**

Together, they anchor spirit into matter and prepare the vessel for higher illumination.

1. ROOT — THE EARTH OF EXISTENCE (MULADHARA)

The Root Chakra governs survival, stability, and the primal sense of belonging to the world. It anchors consciousness in the body, granting safety and trust in life's foundation. Its wisdom whispers: *"You are meant to be here."*

When balanced, Muladhara brings grounded presence — a calm certainty that life supports you. The nervous system relaxes, instincts align, and a quiet strength settles into the bones. Only from this rooted stillness can energy safely rise.

Keywords: Grounding · Safety · Presence · Trust
Element: Earth
Mantra: *LAM*
Affirmation: "I am safe, supported, and rooted in the rhythm of life."

2. SACRAL — THE WATERS OF CREATION (SVADHISTHANA)

Once safety is established, energy begins to flow.
The Sacral Chakra governs emotion, pleasure, and creative expression — the currents of feeling that give life color and movement.
Through Svadhisthana, we learn that to feel is to live, and to create is to participate in the sacred dance of existence.

When balanced, emotions flow freely, intimacy feels safe, and creativity blossoms naturally.
Water teaches adaptability — to move with change, to release resistance, to trust the tides of life.

Keywords: Flow · Emotion · Creativity · Intimacy
Element: Water
Mantra: *VAM*
Affirmation: "I flow with grace and honor my emotions as sacred currents of life."

3. SOLAR PLEXUS — THE FIRE OF TRANSFORMATION (MANIPURA)

The Solar Plexus ignites personal power, clarity, and will.
Here, the fluid energy of emotion becomes focused action — the ability to choose, commit, and manifest.
Manipura is the hearth of transformation where self-awareness becomes purpose.

When balanced, you act with confidence and integrity, guided by the steady flame of inner truth.
The ego no longer seeks control; it becomes the instrument of the soul's intention.

Keywords: Power · Purpose · Confidence · Transformation
Element: Fire

Mantra: *RAM*
Affirmation: "I act with clarity and shine from the light of my inner fire."

THE TRINITY OF EMBODIMENT

Together, these chakras create the **energetic geometry of life**
—

Earth anchors, Water flows, and Fire transforms.

- **The Root** grounds the soul into matter.
- **The Sacral** animates that matter with emotion and creativity.
- **The Solar Plexus** empowers that creativity into purpose and form.

When one falters, the entire current is affected.
Without Earth, Fire burns out of control; without Water, Earth becomes barren; without Fire, nothing evolves.
When all three are in harmony, they form the triangle of embodied consciousness — stable, expressive, and radiant.

THE EMBODIED PATH TO SPIRIT

The three body chakras are not lower in value; they are *foundational.*
They teach that enlightenment is not escape from form but **full presence within it.**
When Earth, Water, and Fire unite, the human vessel becomes a temple capable of holding divine light.

Only through grounding can flow be sustained.
Only through flow can power be purified.
And only through power can love and wisdom rise to their full illumination.

Chapter 7 – Hidden Secrets & Esoteric Wisdom

Tantra and the Solar Plexus Chakra

In Tantric philosophy, **Manipura** — the Solar Plexus Chakra — is the **chamber of transformation**, the alchemical fire where energy becomes power, desire becomes will, and matter becomes light.
If the Root anchors us to Earth and the Sacral teaches flow through Water, then the Solar Plexus is the sacred Fire that refines both — the furnace where spirit gains direction, purpose, and radiance.

Here, **Kundalini Shakti** begins to burn with conscious intent. The movement that began as emotional flow in Svadhisthana now becomes focused flame — the awakening of personal sovereignty and divine purpose.
Manipura is where the **individual self realizes its role as co-creator with the divine**, transforming raw energy into spiritual gold.

Kundalini's Ascent Through Fire

When Kundalini reaches Manipura, she enters the realm of Agni — the sacred fire.
This is the moment when awareness begins to illuminate itself, where instinct and emotion merge into disciplined power.

Tantric texts describe this center as the **"City of Jewels"** —
radiant, brilliant, and full of potential — for within this fire lies
the seed of spiritual mastery.

Through the Root, Kundalini gains grounding.
Through the Sacral, she learns movement and feeling.
But it is in the Solar Plexus that she **discovers direction and
purpose.**
The once fluid energy of emotion now rises as focused will —
the determination to act, serve, and shine with integrity.

This marks the second great transformation on the Tantric path:
from **emotion to empowerment**, from **flow to focus**, from
pleasure to purpose.

The Fire of Conscious Transformation

In the alchemy of Tantra, **fire** represents awareness in motion
— the ability to see, digest, and transmute.
Just as physical fire digests food, the fire of Manipura digests
experience.
It turns pain into wisdom, challenge into growth, and passion
into sacred purpose.

Kundalini's flame here purifies both body and mind.
Old emotions, patterns, and attachments are offered to the inner
Agni as fuel for awakening.
Each act of courage, honesty, or self-discipline becomes a spark
of spiritual illumination.

This process is not about control but about **clarity** — seeing
through illusion and acting from truth.
The mantra of Manipura is not domination, but devotion:
"May my will be aligned with divine will."

The Body as the Furnace of Light

Tantra honors the Solar Plexus as the **seat of personal divinity within the body** — the glowing core from which confidence, vitality, and integrity arise.
Located near the navel, Manipura is the body's sun, radiating energy through every cell.
When this sun burns steadily, life feels luminous and purposeful.
When it falters, the light of clarity dims into confusion or self-doubt.

Here, the **body itself becomes a sacred furnace**.
The fire of digestion mirrors the fire of transformation: one metabolizes food, the other metabolizes emotion and experience.
When both are balanced, the being shines with vitality — known in Tantra as **Tejas**, the radiance of pure spiritual fire.

Shakti and Shiva in Dynamic Union

In Manipura, Shakti's fiery ascent is witnessed by Shiva's still consciousness.
Their dance becomes one of illumination — awareness igniting form.
Where in Svadhisthana Shakti flowed with emotion, here she rises as willpower — sharp, brilliant, disciplined.
Shiva, the silent witness, gives that will direction and discernment.

Together, they create the sacred polarity of **power and wisdom, fire and form**.
Tantra teaches that this union generates true mastery: power without ego, energy without chaos, light without blindness.
When these forces unite, the self is no longer driven by impulse — it becomes the conscious flame of divine purpose.

Tantric Practices for Manipura

Traditional Tantric disciplines to awaken and harmonize the Solar Plexus Chakra focus on cultivating radiant awareness, courage, and alignment of will:

- **Bija Mantra — RAM:**
  Chant *RAM* to kindle the inner fire.
  Feel the vibration ignite within the navel center, expanding as warmth and golden light throughout the body.
- **Trataka (Candle Gazing):**
  Meditate on the flame of a candle, symbolizing your inner sun.
  Let your gaze soften until you feel the fire within you and the fire before you merge.
- **Agni Pranayama (Breath of Fire):**
  Use rhythmic breathing to awaken Manipura's heat, releasing lethargy, fear, and self-doubt.
  Each exhale becomes an offering to your inner altar.
- **Solar Meditation:**
  Visualize a radiant sun spinning at your navel.
  With every breath, feel it expand — warming your confidence, purifying your emotions, and fueling your purpose.
- **Rituals of Empowerment:**
  Honor the color yellow or gold.
  Light candles or burn incense to connect with the element of fire.
  Speak affirmations of strength, integrity, and divine alignment.

The Deeper Tantric Lesson

Tantra teaches that Manipura is not merely a center of personal power — it is the **gateway to divine empowerment.**
Here, individuality becomes a vessel of the universal will.

The energy that once served survival and pleasure now becomes
service and illumination.

When the fire of Manipura burns clear, it purifies ego and
transforms self-centered desire into sacred purpose.
You begin to act not from impulse, but from inspiration — no
longer driven by control, but guided by clarity.
The light that burns within becomes the same light that guides
the world.

This is the secret of the Solar Plexus in Tantra:
the realization that true power is not domination, but **radiance**
—
the steady flame that warms, transforms, and enlightens all it
touches.

THE SECRET WISDOM OF THE SOLAR PLEXUS

The hidden Tantric teaching of **Manipura** is that **power
becomes sacred when it is conscious**.
It is not domination but illumination — an acknowledgment
that will, courage, and transformation are divine expressions of
the soul in motion.

Where the Root taught grounding and survival, and the Sacral
taught surrender and flow, the Solar Plexus teaches **mastery
through awareness**.
It is the fire of discernment that transforms instinct into purpose
and emotion into radiant strength.

Where the Root declared, *"I exist,"* and the Sacral whispered,
"I feel, I create, I connect," the Solar Plexus proclaims, *"I act. I
choose. I shine."*
Here, **Kundalini's flame** reveals that the path to enlightenment
is not withdrawal from the world but the conscious
transmutation of its energy into light.

The same force that once drove survival or desire now becomes the fire of awakening — the will that serves truth, the passion that fuels purpose, the brilliance that guides creation.

In the language of Tantra, the Solar Plexus is not merely the center of personal power —
it is the **sun of the subtle body**, the inner hearth where Shakti refines herself into radiance.
This is the sacred fire through which consciousness ascends toward the infinite —
not by burning away life, but by **illuminating it from within**.

KUNDALINI: AWAKENING THROUGH THE FIRES OF THE SOLAR PLEXUS CHAKRA

The Serpent Ignites

At the Root, **Kundalini** rests in stillness — silent and coiled, the latent potential of divine power.
Through the Sacral, she learns to flow and feel.
But as she ascends into **Manipura**, her movement transforms — no longer water, but fire.
Here, the fluid current of Shakti becomes flame, rising with purpose, focus, and radiance.

This is the moment when **energy learns direction**.
The creative waters of Svadhisthana evaporate into light, and the serpent becomes luminous — shimmering gold within the solar fire.
The body begins to awaken not just as sensation, but as **will made conscious**.
Pleasure evolves into purpose; emotion transforms into clarity.
This is the sacred ignition of **personal power aligned with divine will**.

Where the Sacral whispered, *"I feel,"* Manipura declares, *"I act. I choose. I transform."*

The Dance of Fire

As Kundalini rises into the Solar Plexus, her rhythm quickens.
Her undulating waters become spirals of flame — energy
seeking refinement rather than indulgence.
This is the **alchemy of Shakti**, where instinct is burned into
insight, and desire becomes luminous devotion.

The ancient Tantras describe this moment as the **"awakening of
Agni,"** the sacred fire that digests all experience.
In Manipura, Agni consumes impurities, transforming darkness
into fuel for awareness.
Each fear becomes courage, each doubt becomes clarity, each
limitation becomes a spark of transformation.
The fire no longer destroys — it **illumines**.

Signs of Awakening

When Kundalini activates the Solar Plexus Chakra, her presence
is unmistakable.
The awakening may unfold gradually or arrive as a sudden
surge of inner heat and illumination.
Common signs include:

• A spreading warmth or tingling radiating from the navel
• Heightened vitality, confidence, and motivation
• Clearer perception of purpose and direction in life
• Sudden bursts of insight, courage, or determination
• A desire to release old fears, guilt, or self-doubt
• Waves of energy rising upward through the torso or spine
• Dreams or visions involving light, sun, or sacred fire

This is **Shakti refining the inner flame** — burning away
inertia and illuminating the path of conscious action.
The process can be intense, yet deeply liberating.
Through awareness, you learn not to fear the heat of

transformation, but to stand within it — steady, luminous, and awake.

Balancing the Fire

Fire gives life, but it can also consume.
A balanced Manipura burns steadily — a sun that warms, not a wildfire that scorches.
When Kundalini's fire becomes excessive, it manifests as anger, ego, or overexertion.
When too weak, it dims into doubt, lethargy, or victimhood.

The Tantric path teaches **containment through consciousness**: to hold the fire with reverence, not repression.

- **Ground through the Root**: Stability keeps fire purposeful rather than reactive.
- **Flow through the Sacral**: Emotional intelligence cools the intensity of power.
- **Open through the Heart**: Love refines ambition into service.

Through this trinity — Earth, Water, and Fire — the serpent's ascent remains balanced, radiant, and wise.

The Sacred Flame Within

Tantra teaches:
"To know the fire is to know transformation; to master it is to know illumination."

As Kundalini rises through Manipura, she becomes **Tejas** — spiritual brilliance, the fire of awakened awareness.
This is the light that guides both personal evolution and divine service.
The energy that once sought control now radiates as

compassion.
The will that once demanded becomes the will that serves.

When you surrender to the sacred fire of Manipura, life itself becomes a process of alchemy — where every challenge feeds the flame, every action becomes prayer, and every breath fans the embers of awakening.

TANTRIC SECRETS OF THE TRANSFORMATIVE FIRE

The Element of Fire and the Light Within It

The **Solar Plexus Chakra (Manipura)** is the realm of fire — luminous, dynamic, and purifying. It is the sacred furnace where the raw energies of life are refined into will, purpose, and radiance.
If the Sacral taught surrender through water, Manipura teaches **transformation through flame**.

Fire is the alchemist of the elements — it does not destroy for destruction's sake, but transforms what it touches. In Tantra, this inner fire represents *Agni*, the sacred light of awareness that digests not only food but also experience, emotion, and thought.

When Kundalini rises into the Solar Plexus, the emotional waters of Svadhisthana are set ablaze with purpose. The soft glow of feeling becomes a steady flame of clarity. Energy no longer drifts — it **directs**. Emotion becomes will, desire becomes creation, and the self begins to shine from within.

Power as Presence

In Tantra, **power is not control — it is consciousness in action**.
The true mastery of Manipura is not domination, but alignment — the ability to act from clarity rather than compulsion, to move with purpose rather than pride.

When fire burns unconsciously, it consumes. When tended with awareness, it illuminates.
The Tantric adept learns to keep the inner flame steady —
glowing in the belly like a sun, neither suppressed nor wild, but radiant and alive.

In this state, every action becomes sacred.
Each choice made with integrity is a form of prayer.
Each moment of courage is a spark of awakening.

Power becomes presence, and presence becomes light.

Purpose as Devotion

Manipura reveals that **true purpose is born from devotion, not ambition.**
When the ego yields to consciousness, action becomes selfless and radiant.
Tantra teaches that every act — when performed with awareness and sincerity — is an offering to the divine fire within.

To live from this place is to understand that purpose is not something to achieve but something to *embody.*
The fire of Manipura burns away self-doubt, fear, and hesitation, leaving behind the clear gold of inspired will.
Through this sacred alchemy, **work becomes worship**, and service becomes the natural expression of spiritual maturity.

The Inner Marriage of Shiva and Shakti

Within the Solar Plexus, the eternal union of **Shiva and Shakti** takes the form of **clarity meeting action.**
Shiva, pure awareness, is the light that sees.
Shakti, divine energy, is the fire that moves.
Together, they create the **radiance of transformation** —
consciousness set in motion with wisdom and love.

When awareness (Shiva) guides energy (Shakti), the fire burns clean and bright.
When energy moves without awareness, it leads to pride or burnout.
Thus, the Tantric secret of Manipura is balance — to act powerfully yet remain humble, to shine brightly yet remain still within.

This is the **inner marriage of stillness and strength**, the sacred union that births enlightened action.

The Deeper Tantric Revelation

The hidden teaching of Manipura is this:
Transformation itself is sacred.

The fire of life — whether it takes the form of passion, ambition, or challenge — is not to be feared or extinguished but revered as the purifier of the soul.
To meet life's intensity with awareness is to awaken the solar fire of the spirit.

In the deepest Tantric understanding, awakening is not withdrawal from power, passion, or purpose —
it is the **illumination of them.**
When you act from the still point within the flame, your every breath becomes a ray of divine will —
steady, luminous, and free.

KUNDALINI AND THE ALCHEMY OF POWER
Emotion as the Fire of Awakening

Emotion is the fire of the soul — the heat through which consciousness learns to transform.
It is how the infinite breathes through the finite, how life itself evolves from feeling into knowing.
When Kundalini rises into the **Solar Plexus Chakra**

(**Manipura**), she enters the forge of transformation —
where raw emotion becomes radiant will, and passion refines
into purpose.

Here, the waters of the Sacral meet the flames of the Solar.
What was once fluid now begins to shimmer with heat and
light.
The emotional tides of Svadhisthana are purified in Manipura's
fire, revealing a deeper truth:
Emotion is not meant to be controlled or denied — it is meant
to be **transmuted**.

Emotion as Energy Transformed

In the Solar Plexus, emotion becomes the raw material of
strength.
The currents that once surged through the Sacral now rise
upward, burning brighter and cleaner.
Each feeling becomes fuel for awakening, each reaction an
invitation to mastery.

The Tantric sages taught:

"That which burns you also illumines you — if you meet it with
awareness."

When Kundalini ignites within Manipura, she consumes the
heaviness of old emotions — anger, fear, shame, doubt — and
releases their hidden gold.
This is not destruction but purification: the sacred fire refining
emotion into essence.
It is through this process that awareness gains brilliance, and
will becomes divine.

The Fire of Transformation

Where water washes, fire clarifies.
The emotional debris that the Sacral stirred to the surface now
meets the solar flame.
This inner fire does not reject feeling — it distills it.

Anger becomes courage.
Fear becomes focus.
Desire becomes determination.
Grief becomes compassion in action.

This is the alchemy of Manipura — the **conversion of emotion
into illumination**.
Each emotion, when embraced consciously, is burned clean of
attachment, leaving only wisdom in its wake.
This is how Kundalini teaches that nothing in us is wasted —
everything can become light.

The Dance of the Inner Sun

When the fire of the Solar Plexus awakens, it moves through the
body as light in motion.
You may feel waves of heat rising through the abdomen, a pulse
of energy expanding outward, or a quiet radiance emanating
from the core.
This is **Shakti as flame** — not wild, but aware; not consuming,
but creative.

You begin to move from the center, act from presence, and
radiate from strength.
Breath deepens, posture lifts, and the spine feels alive with
golden current.
This is the dance of the inner sun — the awakening of luminous
power through consciousness.

In this state, emotion no longer rules you; it **fuels** you.
Each feeling becomes a spark of insight, guiding your next
inspired action.

The Gold Within the Flame

Every emotion carries hidden light.
Within every shadow lies brilliance waiting to emerge.
When you meet your emotions in the fire of awareness, their
secret alchemy unfolds:

• Fear becomes faith.
• Anger becomes vitality.
• Shame becomes dignity.
• Doubt becomes discernment.
• Desire becomes divine will.

This is the golden purification of Manipura — where what once
bound you now empowers you.
The fire burns not to punish, but to liberate; not to erase, but to
reveal the radiance already within.

The Hidden Tantric Truth

Kundalini does not awaken by escaping emotion — she
awakens by **illuminating** it.
Each flame of feeling is an invitation to know the divine within
form.

When anger transforms into courage, or pain into purpose, you
witness the divine alchemy of fire.
When will aligns with awareness, you become a vessel of
sacred power — radiant, steady, alive.

Tantra teaches that enlightenment is not cold detachment, but
conscious combustion — the fire of presence consuming
illusion and revealing truth.

To burn is to become light.
To feel deeply and act consciously is to allow Shakti to rise —
no longer as water seeking its path, but as fire realizing its
brilliance.

Through this alchemy, you become both flame and light —
the luminous expression of divine power awakened within.

SECRET USES OF THE SOLAR PLEXUS: SOLAR MYSTERIES, FIRE TRANCE, AND THE ALCHEMY OF WILL

Beyond its link to confidence and power, the **Solar Plexus
Chakra (Manipura)** holds ancient teachings on transformation
through light, rhythm, and intention.
In many esoteric traditions, this radiant center was not merely a
symbol of strength, but a **sun within the human temple** — the
inner star through which spirit becomes luminous in matter.

Here, fire is not destruction but revelation. Manipura conceals
the mysteries of illumination, teaching how awareness, emotion,
and will fuse to create the gold of spiritual mastery.

Solar Mysteries: The Sun Within

In Tantric and alchemical cosmology, Manipura is ruled by the
sun — the eternal flame of consciousness that rises each day to
banish shadow.
Its rhythm mirrors the cycles of dawn, noon, and dusk — the
sacred pattern of awakening, action, and rest.

Ancient adepts practiced **solar meditation** at sunrise to absorb
the prana of the new day, visualizing the inner sun igniting
within the navel. This was not mere visualization — it was
communion with cosmic intelligence.

To work with Manipura is to learn the **art of illumination** — knowing when to shine outward in action, when to conserve power inward, and when to rest in still light.
This solar rhythm restores balance between doing and being, teaching that true strength radiates, not forces.

When aligned with the sun's cycle, the fire of will becomes luminous rather than consuming — a steady brilliance that warms, heals, and inspires.

Fire Trance and the State of Radiant Presence

Where the Sacral's lunar trance moves through rhythm and flow, the Solar trance moves through stillness and flame — the **radiant awareness of presence.**

In ancient temples, initiates would gaze into fire, chant bija mantras, or perform rhythmic breath (Agni Pranayama) until the boundary between self and flame dissolved.
In this state, the practitioner became the fire — steady, clear, and self-luminous.

Modern seekers experience this as the **flow state of focus and brilliance** — when purpose and action merge into one seamless movement.
The artist, the healer, and the mystic all touch this inner sun: a creative trance where awareness burns through distraction, and energy moves with pure intention.

Here, the fire of Manipura does not destroy — it clarifies. The ego melts away, leaving only the radiance of conscious creation.

The Alchemy of Will: Turning Fire into Light

Just as the alchemist turns lead into gold, the initiate of Manipura turns instinct into insight and emotion into power.

Every impulse, once purified by awareness, becomes the fuel of transformation.

Anger becomes direction.
Fear becomes faith.
Doubt becomes discernment.
Ambition becomes purpose.

This is **solar alchemy** — the art of refining personal will into divine will.
Through breath, focus, and intention, the flames of emotion are directed upward, energizing the heart with compassion and the mind with clarity.

Nothing is wasted in this process. The same heat that once fueled reaction now powers creation, and the self begins to shine as a vessel of conscious light.

Fire Bonding: Communion with the Flame

Just as the Sacral's ritual was water bonding, the Solar's sacred act is **fire bonding** — the communion with the eternal flame.
In ancient rites, initiates sat before sacred fires or the rising sun, offering breath, herbs, or mantra into the flames as a symbol of surrender and renewal.

The practice continues today whenever you light a candle with intention, gaze into fire for meditation, or bask in sunlight with gratitude.
Fire bonding reconnects you to the element of transformation, teaching the rhythm of release: what to burn away, what to keep, and how to rise renewed from your own ashes.

Spiritually, it reminds us that the same fire that warms the body also illuminates the soul.

Primal Power and the Flame of Creation

Where the Root expresses primal survival and the Sacral expresses primal creation, the Solar Plexus expresses **primal transformation** — the power to evolve, act, and manifest.

This is the domain of **Tejas Shakti**, the fiery radiance of consciousness.
It is the energy that fuels not only the digestive fire of the body but also the fire of intellect, purpose, and personal evolution.

When channeled consciously, Tejas becomes the light of divine will — capable of illuminating others without burning out the self.
To awaken this current is to claim your birthright as a conscious creator — one who shapes reality not through force, but through presence.

The Hidden Wisdom

The Solar Plexus reveals that true power is luminous, not loud.
Its secret is not domination, but radiance — the kind of light that burns away illusion and reveals truth.

Just as the Root grounds and the Sacral flows, the Solar **transforms**.
It turns emotion into insight, impulse into integrity, and energy into purpose.

To honor Manipura is to remember that the sun within you is eternal — a steady flame fed by awareness.
When you live from this radiant center, you no longer strive to control life; you **illuminate** it.

You do not conquer darkness — you dissolve it by shining.

WESTERN MYSTICISM: THE FIRE OF ILLUMINATION AND THE TEMPLE OF DIVINE WILL

In Western mystical and esoteric traditions, **fire** has long symbolized purification, transformation, illumination, and divine will.
Just as the Root corresponds to earth — the stone of foundation — and the Sacral to water — the current of emotion — the **Solar Plexus** corresponds to **fire**, the living flame that animates and enlightens the temple.

These teachings remind us that spirit does not reside only in silence, but also in radiance — in the act of shining, refining, and transforming.
Manipura is the altar of that sacred flame — the lamp of the soul through which divine purpose burns into form.

The Fire of Genesis

In the beginning of creation, after the waters were stirred, came **light**:

"And God said, 'Let there be light.'"

This moment — the birth of illumination — is the awakening of Manipura in the cosmic body.
It represents the ignition of awareness, the moment consciousness begins to see itself.

Western mystics viewed this divine light not only as external creation but as **inner revelation** — the awakening of the Christic or solar flame within the human heart and mind.
In energy language, it is the moment Kundalini reaches the Solar Plexus, transforming emotion into illumination.

This "light of understanding" was called by medieval mystics the **Lux Intellectus** — the light of the intellect, which does not

reason but perceives truth directly.
Thus, Manipura is the seat of **illumined knowing** — not
knowledge as accumulation, but as radiant comprehension.

The Temple of Divine Will

If the Root builds the temple's foundation and the Sacral fills it
with living waters, the Solar Plexus **ignites the altar flame** at
its center.
This is the **Temple of Divine Will** — where devotion becomes
action, and energy becomes creation.

In the Christian mystical tradition, this fire was seen as the
flame of the Holy Spirit — the burning heart that empowers
disciples to act with courage, clarity, and faith.
Medieval mystics spoke of it as "the interior sun," the divine
spark that lights the soul from within.

In Kabbalistic tradition, this center corresponds with **Tiferet**,
the sefirah of beauty, balance, and radiant will — the solar heart
of the Tree of Life.
Tiferet unites the higher spheres of divine wisdom with the
lower realms of manifestation, just as Manipura transforms
emotion into enlightened action.
It is solar, harmonizing, and luminous — the point where **will
aligns with love**.

To awaken Manipura is to awaken this divine will — the
courage to act not from egoic desire but from conscious
purpose.

Alchemy and the Element of Fire

In the alchemical tradition, fire represents **coagula** — the power
that fixes, transforms, and manifests.
Where water dissolves, fire crystallizes. It brings clarity,

definition, and form to that which has been softened by emotion and reflection.

The alchemist must first dissolve the old self in water (solve), then refine and recombine it in fire (coagula).
This is the alchemy of Manipura — where feeling meets form, and energy becomes directed will.

The alchemical flame, often depicted as the **solar furnace or athanor**, symbolizes this internal process of purification.
The impurities of ignorance, fear, and self-doubt are burned away, revealing the **gold of consciousness** — the Philosopher's Stone within.

In this fire, personality becomes presence, and will becomes wisdom.

Mysteries of the Sun and the Christic Light

Western mystics, from the Hermetic philosophers to the Rosicrucians, revered the **Sun** as both a celestial and spiritual symbol — the visible body of the invisible God.
In this solar wisdom, Christ is the inner sun — the Logos or divine intelligence that radiates through creation.

The Hermetic axiom "As above, so below" speaks directly to Manipura's purpose: the light that shines in the heavens must also shine within man.
When the inner sun is awakened, one becomes a microcosm of divine radiance — a living reflection of the cosmic fire.

This is echoed in the Christian mystic's prayer, "Christ in me, the hope of glory," and in the Hermetic ideal of the *Illuminated Man* — the adept whose inner flame mirrors the divine Sun.

Just as Isis, Mary, and Sophia carried the lunar mysteries, Christ, Apollo, and Helios carried the **solar mysteries** — the

radiant consciousness that guides and sustains creation.
Together, they reveal the cosmic polarity of light and reflection,
fire and water, consciousness and feeling — the same dynamic
Tantra expresses through **Shiva and Shakti.**

The Shared Wisdom

Across Western mysticism, the solar message mirrors that of the
East:
Fire is sacred because it transforms.

It is the agent of divine will — not a force of destruction but of
illumination.
Through fire, the soul learns not only to see but to act, to create,
and to embody light.

Whether through the alchemist's furnace, the Rosicrucian's
inner sun, or the mystic's Pentecostal flame, Western traditions
whisper the same revelation that Tantra declares through
Manipura:

The fire within you is the light of divine intelligence.
When your will aligns with that flame, God acts through you.

To live from this solar center is to live as both vessel and flame
— a radiant instrument of conscious creation, a sun within the
human temple, burning not to consume, but to enlighten.

Chapter 8 – Balancing & Healing Practices

Reiki Positions and Energy Protocols for the Solar Plexus Chakra

The **Solar Plexus Chakra (Manipura)** governs power, confidence, vitality, and the ability to act from one's true will. In Reiki and other energy modalities, it is often treated after the Sacral — once emotional flow is restored — to help energy rise upward and transform into strength and purpose.
Balancing this chakra restores clarity, motivation, and the courage to stand in one's authentic light.

Hand Positions for the Solar Plexus Chakra

Reiki placements for the Solar Plexus are located between the navel and sternum — the area of the stomach, diaphragm, and solar plexus nerve complex. This region stores both personal and ancestral emotions related to control, confidence, and self-worth.
Always approach with calm, focused presence, as this chakra holds deep patterns of identity and empowerment.

• **Upper Abdomen (Solar Plexus):** Hands placed just above the navel ignite inner strength and confidence, awakening the will to act in harmony with purpose.
• **Diaphragm and Rib Cage:** Positioning hands over the diaphragm supports emotional release, assisting in the transformation of suppressed anger, fear, or anxiety into calm

strength.
• **Back of Solar Plexus:** Placing hands on the upper lumbar or lower thoracic spine balances front and back energy flow, integrating willpower with inner peace.
• **Front and Back Together:** One hand on the upper abdomen and one behind the spine stabilizes energy, harmonizing assertiveness (front) with personal integrity (back).

ENERGY PROTOCOLS

1. Igniting the Inner Sun

Invite Reiki to flow as a warm, golden light within the solar plexus.
Visualize it gently illuminating the abdomen — softening tension, releasing self-doubt, and rekindling self-belief.
This is the light of personal power awakening from within.

2. Clearing the Fire

Manipura can accumulate energetic "smoke" from suppressed emotion, stress, or overcontrol.
Move your hands in slow, circular motions over the solar plexus to clear stagnant fire energy, allowing the inner flame to burn steady and clean.

3. Balancing Will and Surrender

Alternate placements between the solar plexus and heart.
This bridges power with compassion, teaching that true strength flows from love, not dominance.
As energy moves upward, visualize it as a column of radiant gold linking the navel to the heart.

4. Radiating Confidence

See the chakra spinning as a bright yellow sun, emanating warmth through the entire torso.

This radiance purifies fatigue, fear, and insecurity, restoring vitality and purpose.
Let the light expand until it fills the aura, strengthening boundaries and personal magnetism.

5. Sealing the Flame

Conclude by placing your hands gently over the solar plexus, affirming:
"The fire within me burns steady and true."
This seals the energy field with stability, courage, and peace.

SYMBOLIC SUPPORT

Advanced Reiki practitioners may use symbols to deepen the activation and purification of Manipura:

• **Cho Ku Rei (Power Symbol):** Strengthens personal energy, authority, and confidence; clears energetic toxins and fear.
• **Sei He Ki (Harmony Symbol):** Balances emotional charge within the digestive fire; releases anger, frustration, and resistance to change.
• **Dai Ko Myo (Master Symbol):** Awakens divine will — aligning personal purpose with universal intelligence. It transforms ego-driven ambition into radiant, spiritual service.

THE PRACTITIONER'S ROLE

Working with the Solar Plexus requires neutrality, empowerment, and humility.
Because this center governs will and identity, practitioners must embody **calm confidence** rather than control.
Through presence and intention, the practitioner helps the client remember their innate sovereignty — not giving power, but awakening it.

Reiki for Manipura is not about inflating ego; it is about restoring balance between action and peace.
The healer becomes the mirror in which the client sees their own light reflected clearly once again.

Healing Reminder

Reiki at the Solar Plexus teaches one of the great spiritual paradoxes:
Power and peace are not opposites — they are one when guided by consciousness.

As Manipura's flame is purified, life becomes purposeful and radiant.
The inner sun rises, bringing strength without struggle and direction without force.

Through this radiance, the soul remembers:
"I am strong. I am clear. I act with light."

Bridging the Root Chakra to the Heart Chakra Through the Solar Plexus

The chakras are not separate energy centers but a continuous current — a river of consciousness flowing upward and downward through the human experience.
Between the grounded base of the Root and the expansive openness of the Heart lies the transformative realm of the Solar Plexus — the **alchemical fire** that refines instinct into awareness and emotion into purpose.

This is the journey from survival to self-realization, from reaction to response, and from dependence to empowerment.

The Path from Root to Heart

As energy ascends through these lower and middle chakras, it evolves in vibration — from density to radiance, from matter to meaning:

- **Root (Muladhara):** Establishes grounding, stability, and safety — the firm foundation that anchors physical existence.
- **Sacral (Svadhisthana):** Awakens flow, emotion, and creative movement — transforming security into connection and experience.
- **Solar Plexus (Manipura):** Ignites confidence, will, and personal power — shaping emotional energy into purposeful direction.
- **Heart (Anahata):** Opens compassion and unity — expanding individual will into service, empathy, and divine love.

Through this continuum, Manipura acts as the **refining fire** that tempers emotion into clarity and transforms the raw waters of the Sacral into radiant expression.

The Role of the Solar Plexus in the Bridge

The Solar Plexus is the **crucible of transformation** — where the dense energy of the lower chakras is purified before rising to the heart.
It is here that instinct becomes will, and will becomes intention.

Without the warmth of Manipura's fire, emotion (Sacral) cannot rise to love (Heart); it remains unrefined, reactive, or uncertain. And without the grounding of the Root beneath it, the Solar Plexus burns too quickly — confidence becomes control rather than compassion.

When balanced, Manipura harmonizes these forces, creating a steady flame that warms rather than consumes.
It teaches emotional maturity — the ability to act with awareness, to hold power with grace, and to channel energy into creation rather than reaction.

The Energetic Ascent: From Instinct to Illumination

Each chakra along this path expresses a stage of consciousness:

- **Root:** "I am safe."
- **Sacral:** "I feel."
- **Solar Plexus:** "I act."
- **Heart:** "I love."

Together, these statements trace the evolution of the human spirit — from basic existence to radiant compassion.
When energy flows freely through them, the inner journey becomes effortless: stability fuels emotion, emotion fuels will, and will opens into love.

Blocked energy at the Solar Plexus, however, can stall this ascent.
Fear, shame, or doubt extinguish the flame, leaving one feeling powerless or emotionally disconnected.
But when the fire of Manipura is clear and strong, it transforms fear into courage and hesitation into trust.

It is the **sacred forge** through which the soul learns to act from love rather than react from fear.

Living the Bridge

To bridge Root and Heart through the Solar Plexus is to live as a being of both power and tenderness.
It means standing firmly in who you are while remaining open to connection.

It is the practice of transforming energy through awareness —
letting life's challenges become fuel for growth rather than
weight for suffering.

When the Root is steady, the Sacral flowing, and the Solar
Plexus luminous, energy rises into the Heart with ease.
Love becomes not an ideal, but a lived reality — expressed
through confidence, compassion, and clear purpose.

In this state, your actions align with your soul.
You embody strength without domination, passion without
chaos, and love without condition.

This is the golden bridge between earth and heaven within you
— the **path of transformation through the Solar Fire**, where
the light of being and the warmth of love finally meet.

Bridging Root to Heart Across Cultures

Across ancient traditions, the journey from the base of the spine
to the center of the chest has been honored as a sacred passage
— the transformation from matter to spirit, from instinct to
compassion.
In yogic philosophy, this ascent flows through **four key
chakras** — the **Root (Muladhara)**, **Sacral (Svadhisthana)**,
Solar Plexus (Manipura), and **Heart (Anahata)** — forming
the *energetic bridge between survival and love*.

While the Root grounds us in the earth and the Heart opens us
to divine connection, the Sacral and Solar Plexus serve as the
currents of transformation between them — emotion and will,
flow and fire, feeling and empowerment.

Across cultures, this passage has been portrayed as the meeting
of elements — earth, water, fire, and air — a continuum of

awakening where instinct becomes emotion, emotion becomes strength, and strength becomes love.

Eastern Traditions: The River and the Flame

In the Tantric and yogic traditions of India, the lower chakras represent ascending stages of consciousness — the refinement of life force (prana) from density to luminosity:

- **Muladhara (Root)** — *Bhumi Tattva* (Earth): stability, structure, belonging.
- **Svadhisthana (Sacral)** — *Apah Tattva* (Water): emotion, creativity, adaptability.
- **Manipura (Solar Plexus)** — *Agni Tattva* (Fire): power, transformation, and will.
- **Anahata (Heart)** — *Vayu Tattva* (Air): compassion, love, and expansion.

Together, they form a sacred progression — **Earth → Water → Fire → Air** — the alchemy of grounding, flowing, burning, and breathing.
The Sacral serves as the *river of life*, awakening emotion and pleasure; the Solar Plexus becomes the *inner sun*, transforming emotion into empowered action.
As Kundalini Shakti rises through these centers, she learns to **feel through water, act through fire, and love through air** — carrying the soul from survival to transcendence.

Indigenous and Shamanic Wisdom: The Heart of Earth, Water, and Fire

In many Indigenous cosmologies, creation begins with the union of Earth and Water — the womb of the Great Mother — and evolves through the element of Fire, the animating spirit of transformation.
The Root connects us to the land and ancestry (Earth).
The Sacral connects us to emotion, fertility, and creative flow

164 | DR. CONSTANCE SANTEGO

(Water).
The Solar Plexus embodies the sacred flame of will and vitality (Fire).
And the Heart unites them in harmony (Air/Spirit).

Shamanic journeys often move through these same stages: descent into the underworld of feeling (Sacral), purification by the fire of personal power (Solar Plexus), and emergence into the upper world of heart and vision.
This path teaches that love must be embodied — that true compassion is born only after emotion has been felt and personal power purified.

Taoist Philosophy: From Jing to Qi to Shen

In Taoist internal alchemy, the body is viewed as a sacred laboratory of transformation.
Energy condenses and refines through three primary centers:

- The **Lower Dantian** (Root and Sacral): the cauldron of *jing* — essence, grounded vitality, and sexual energy.
- The **Middle Dantian** (Solar Plexus and Heart): the crucible where *jing* transforms into *qi* (vital energy) and then into *shen* (spirit).

When the grounded essence of Earth blends with the fluid adaptability of Water, Fire naturally ignites — giving rise to vitality and purpose.
As this energy ascends to the Heart, it becomes compassion and higher consciousness.
Taoists call this the **Water-and-Fire Union**, or the **Way of the Gentle Flame** — mirroring the chakra system's teaching that **feeling (Water)** must be guided by **awareness (Fire)** to open the Heart.

Western Mysticism and Alchemy: The Sacred Marriage of the Elements

Western alchemists described the soul's transformation as the union of four elemental forces:

- **Salt (Earth)** — the body, matter, and grounding (Root).
- **Mercury (Water)** — the emotions, adaptability, and flow (Sacral).
- **Sulphur (Fire)** — will, passion, and transformation (Solar Plexus).
- **Air/Spirit** — love, wisdom, and unity (Heart).

The alchemist's task was to balance these within the alembic of the soul — to marry the fixed with the volatile, the cool waters of emotion with the steady flame of will.
Only through this sacred union could the "Philosopher's Stone" — the enlightened heart — be formed.

This Western alchemy mirrors the inner journey of the chakras: Earth stabilizes, Water feels, Fire empowers, and Air liberates. When these elements unite, the soul becomes whole — the temple of the human heart filled with living light.

Psychological Perspectives: From Survival to Self-Realization

Modern psychology echoes this same archetypal ascent:

- **Root Chakra (Muladhara):** The developmental foundation of safety, trust, and belonging — our attachment to life itself.
- **Sacral Chakra (Svadhisthana):** Emotional and relational development — learning to feel, play, and connect.

- **Solar Plexus Chakra (Manipura):** Personal identity, willpower, and self-esteem — the formation of confidence and purpose.
- **Heart Chakra (Anahata):** Emotional integration and compassion — transcending ego to embrace empathy and love.

If early experiences damage safety, repress emotion, or undermine confidence, love struggles to rise.

Healing, therefore, retraces this path — **restoring security (Root), freeing emotion (Sacral), empowering will (Solar Plexus), and awakening compassion (Heart).**

Psychology and energy medicine converge on the same truth: emotional and personal empowerment are the bridges that carry us into love.

The Universal Bridge

Across all traditions, the wisdom remains constant:

The journey from the Root to the Heart cannot skip the waters or the flame in between.

You must **feel before you can act**, **act before you can open**, and **open before you can love**.

The Root grounds you in the world.

The Sacral teaches you to flow with life.

The Solar Plexus teaches you to act with integrity and purpose.

The Heart reveals that love is the divine movement through all of them.

Together, they form the **sacred bridge of embodiment** — the path where instinct becomes awareness, emotion becomes power, and power becomes love.

Meditation & Visualization Exercises for the Solar Plexus Chakra

The Solar Plexus Chakra is the temple of fire — the seat of personal power, confidence, and transformation.
Meditation here is not about passivity but illumination. These practices awaken the inner sun, cleanse fear and doubt, and strengthen your sense of identity, direction, and radiant will.
As the fire of Manipura burns steady and bright, it transforms emotion into clarity and action into purpose.

1. THE GOLDEN SUN VISUALIZATION

Purpose: To ignite and balance the Solar Plexus through light and warmth.

1. Sit comfortably with your spine tall and shoulders relaxed.
2. Bring your awareness to the space just above your navel — the center of your personal sun.
3. Visualize a radiant golden orb glowing within this area, pulsing gently with each breath.
4. With every inhale, the sun expands — warming your entire abdomen. With every exhale, it radiates light throughout your body.
5. Whisper inwardly:
   "I am strong. I am radiant. My inner light guides me."
6. Continue until you feel warmth spreading through your torso, dissolving tension and filling you with luminous peace.

2. THE FIRE BREATH MEDITATION (AGNI PRANAYAMA)

Purpose: To energize the body and purify the mind through rhythmic breath.

1. Sit with a straight spine. Place one hand lightly over the Solar Plexus.
2. Inhale deeply through the nose, exhale forcefully through the nose — short, quick bursts powered by your abdomen (like gentle bellows).
3. Continue for 20–30 seconds, then return to normal breathing.
4. Feel the warmth build in your core — the fire of Manipura awakening.
5. Visualize this inner flame burning away fear, doubt, and fatigue.
6. End with the affirmation:
   "My energy is powerful and pure. I burn with purpose and clarity."

(Note: Beginners should practice gently and rest if lightheaded.)

3. THE SOLAR FLAME MEDITATION

Purpose: To transform emotional heaviness into radiant self-assurance.

1. Sit quietly and imagine a small flame flickering in your Solar Plexus.
2. Each time you inhale, feed the flame with your breath. Each time you exhale, let it grow stronger, steadier, and more golden.
3. Visualize this flame consuming self-doubt, fear, or judgment — transmuting them into light and strength.

4. Whisper:
   "All that I am becomes light. All that I fear becomes fuel."
5. Sit in stillness, feeling your body glowing with calm, unwavering power.

4. THE WARRIOR'S STANCE BREATH

Purpose: To ground confidence and awaken empowered presence.

1. Stand tall with feet hip-width apart.
2. Place your hands over your Solar Plexus and take deep, steady breaths.
3. With each inhale, feel energy rising from your feet into your core.
4. With each exhale, feel yourself standing stronger, taller, more certain.
5. Imagine a golden circle of light expanding around your body — your field of protection and confidence.
6. Repeat silently:
   "I stand in my power. I am centered in strength. I act with courage and grace."
7. Feel your breath stabilize and your energy align — clear, strong, and balanced.

5. THE INNER SUN RISING

Purpose: To connect the Root, Sacral, and Heart chakras through the Solar Plexus — harmonizing grounding, emotion, will, and love.

1. Begin by visualizing energy rising from the **Root Chakra** (base of spine) as a deep red glow.
2. As it flows upward into the **Sacral Chakra**, the energy turns orange — warm and fluid.

3. When it reaches the **Solar Plexus**, it ignites into a brilliant golden light — radiant and alive.
4. Allow this golden light to continue upward, entering the **Heart Chakra**, where it softens into emerald green, expanding with compassion.
5. Whisper:
   "From earth I rise. Through fire I shine. In love I radiate."
6. Rest in this balanced current — grounded, passionate, confident, and kind.

6. THE BIJA MANTRA MEDITATION – RAM

Purpose: To activate Manipura through sound vibration.

1. Sit comfortably with a tall spine and close your eyes.
2. Focus awareness at your Solar Plexus.
3. Inhale deeply, and as you exhale, chant **RAM** (pronounced "rahm"), letting the "ah" vibrate in your abdomen and the "m" hum softly in your chest.
4. Feel the vibration clearing heaviness, awakening courage, and kindling vitality.
5. Continue for several minutes, then sit in silence, feeling the afterglow of strength and light.
6. Close with the affirmation:
   "I am the fire of transformation. I act with confidence, purpose, and love."

Each of these meditations awakens the solar power within — the strength that acts without aggression, the confidence that shines without ego, and the light that warms the heart without burning it.

When practiced consistently, the fire of Manipura becomes steady — illuminating the path between instinct and love, body and spirit, self and soul.

Crystals for the Solar Plexus Chakra

Crystals connected to the Solar Plexus Chakra carry the radiant, empowering vibration of fire and sunlight.
Their energy strengthens confidence, motivation, and inner strength while burning away fear, doubt, and self-criticism.
These stones help you claim your personal power, take decisive action, and shine with authentic vitality.
By working with Solar Plexus crystals, you awaken your inner sun — feeling capable, purposeful, and confident in your place in the world.

Citrine

- **Qualities:** Abundance, empowerment, joy.
- Known as the "stone of success," citrine channels the energy of the sun — bright, warm, and life-giving. It clears the mind of negativity, boosts motivation, and attracts prosperity. Citrine ignites optimism and supports manifestation through inspired action.
- **Use:** Keep near your Solar Plexus during meditation, wear as jewelry to strengthen confidence, or place in your workspace to enhance focus, creativity, and abundance.

Tiger's Eye

- **Qualities:** Courage, grounding, discernment.
- Tiger's Eye bridges Earth and Fire energies, bringing balance between confidence and humility. It promotes clarity in decision-making and helps you act from strength rather than impulse.
- **Use:** Carry in your pocket when you need to make bold choices or hold during affirmations of courage. It's an excellent crystal for grounding personal power in integrity and calm confidence.

Yellow Jasper

- **Qualities:** Endurance, stability, protection.
- Yellow Jasper provides steady, nurturing energy for those working on long-term goals. It strengthens willpower without aggression and helps maintain optimism through challenges.
- **Use:** Meditate with Yellow Jasper over the Solar Plexus to build perseverance and resilience. It is also beneficial during times of stress or self-doubt, restoring patience and inner balance.

Pyrite

- **Qualities:** Manifestation, strength, leadership.
- Often called "Fool's Gold," Pyrite is anything but foolish — it embodies masculine energy, vitality, and determination. It stimulates the intellect, enhances confidence, and protects the aura from negativity.
- **Use:** Place Pyrite on your desk to attract success and creative problem-solving or meditate with it to fortify your energetic boundaries and assertive power.

Golden Topaz (Imperial Topaz)

- **Qualities:** Motivation, clarity, divine will.
- Golden Topaz aligns the Solar Plexus with higher purpose, transforming personal ambition into spiritual service. It encourages clarity, optimism, and aligned action — helping you follow through on your goals with grace and determination.
- **Use:** Wear near the Solar Plexus or Heart to bridge will and compassion, or hold during visualization practices focused on manifesting your true path.

Amber

- **Qualities:** Vitality, purification, ancient wisdom.
- Amber, a fossilized resin, holds the energy of sunlight preserved through time. It purifies the Solar Plexus, clearing energetic stagnation while infusing the body with warmth and life force. It is both grounding and uplifting — connecting personal power to the wisdom of nature.
- **Use:** Wear as a pendant to keep your energy bright and protected, or place on the abdomen to restore strength after illness or emotional depletion.

Solar Plexus Crystal Affirmation

"I am radiant, confident, and strong.
I stand in my truth and act with purpose.
My inner fire burns steady and bright."

HOW TO WORK WITH SOLAR PLEXUS CRYSTALS

- **Placement:** Lay stones on or just above the navel during meditation or energy healing to activate confidence, willpower, and inner strength. You may also place them in a triangular formation around the abdomen to symbolize balance, direction, and focus.
- **Sun Charging:** Place your Solar Plexus crystals in morning sunlight for a few hours to energize them with warmth, clarity, and life force. (Avoid prolonged exposure for light-sensitive stones like Citrine or Amber.)
- **Empowerment Spaces:** Keep these crystals in areas where you make decisions or take action — your workspace, studio, or altar — to encourage confidence, motivation, and follow-through.

- **Affirmation:** While holding a crystal, repeat:
  "I stand in my power. I act with purpose. My inner fire transforms and guides me."

Crystals for the Solar Plexus Chakra are more than symbols of strength — they are radiant allies for transformation. Each one carries the energy of the sun, reminding you that true power is not control but illumination. Through their light, you awaken courage, direction, and the steady flame of confidence that burns within.

CHARGING CRYSTALS WITH THE ELEMENT OF FIRE

Because the Solar Plexus Chakra is governed by the element of fire, charging your crystals through heat, light, and intention restores vitality, confidence, and willpower.
Fire is the purifier and transformer — it burns away stagnation, activates inner strength, and reawakens your radiant life force. Charging your stones with this element aligns them to Manipura's essence: illumination, clarity, and empowered action.

1. Sunlight Charging (Physical or Symbolic)

Sunlight carries both strength and life-giving warmth — the essence of Solar Plexus energy.

Direct Method (for sun-safe stones such as Citrine, Tiger's Eye, or Pyrite):

- Place your crystal in direct morning sunlight for one to three hours.
- As it absorbs the light, visualize golden rays infusing the stone with courage and purpose.
- Speak with an intention such as:
  "I charge this crystal with the light of the sun. May it

burn away doubt and awaken radiant confidence within me."
- Avoid intense afternoon heat for light-sensitive stones (like Amber or Topaz).

Symbolic Method (for delicate stones):

- Place your crystal near a candle flame or window where sunlight enters indirectly.
- Let it absorb the warmth and brilliance symbolically, without direct contact.
- You can wave the crystal gently through the air above the flame, imagining it drinking in fire's energy.

2. Candle Flame Charging

Candlelight represents sacred transformation — gentle fire that illuminates without consuming.

- Light a yellow or gold candle and hold your crystal safely in front of it.
- With each breath, imagine the flame's warmth entering the stone, cleansing shadows and awakening confidence.
- Whisper:
  "Flame of truth, light of will — ignite the strength within this crystal and within me."

3. Fire Breath Charging

To charge crystals energetically through your own solar power:

1. Sit comfortably and hold the crystal over your Solar Plexus.
2. Inhale deeply through the nose; exhale through the mouth in a long, steady breath, as though breathing warmth into the stone.

3. Visualize golden light radiating from your abdomen — your inner sun — flowing into the crystal.
4. See it glowing brighter with each breath, filled with energy, courage, and vitality.
5. End by placing your hand over the crystal and affirming: *"Through the fire of my spirit, this stone is charged with strength and purpose."*

4. Sound as Fire

Sound, like flame, moves in waves that cleanse and transform energy.

- Use a singing bowl tuned to the note **E** (the Solar Plexus frequency), a chime, or even rhythmic drumming.
- As the sound resonates, visualize it stoking the crystal's inner flame — awakening its power and brilliance.
- Each vibration kindles courage and restores clarity.

5. Sacred Fire Ritual

For deep personal activation:

- Arrange your Solar Plexus crystals (Citrine, Tiger's Eye, or Pyrite) in a circle around a burning candle.
- Add a few drops of essential oils such as **lemon, ginger, or frankincense** to enhance purification and focus.
- Sit before the flame, breathe steadily, and feel its warmth expand through your abdomen.
- Visualize both you and your stones absorbing the sun-fire of divine empowerment.

Charging Affirmation

"With the power of fire, I awaken and renew.
Courage burns bright, willpower is clear.
My crystal shines with the light of divine purpose."

ESSENTIAL OILS FOR THE SOLAR PLEXUS CHAKRA

The Solar Plexus Chakra (**Manipura**) responds deeply to warm, spicy, and citrus aromas that stimulate vitality, confidence, and personal power.
These energizing oils awaken the fire within — clearing stagnation, transforming doubt into determination, and reigniting motivation and courage.
Essential oils for the Solar Plexus support digestion on both physical and emotional levels, helping you "process" life's experiences with strength, clarity, and purpose.
They empower self-expression, focus, and the courage to act from your authentic will.

Lemon

- **Qualities:** Clarity, focus, and mental brightness.
- The fresh, radiant scent of lemon clears mental fog and negativity, replacing hesitation with optimism. It energizes the Solar Plexus, stimulating decisiveness and motivation while supporting the body's natural cleansing processes.
- **Use:** Diffuse to refresh the atmosphere during work or study, or apply (diluted) to the abdomen to promote clarity and confidence before important decisions.

Ginger

- **Qualities:** Motivation, courage, and empowerment.
- Ginger's spicy warmth stokes the inner fire, dissolving fear and inertia. It inspires boldness and self-assurance, reminding you to act with conviction and follow through on your goals.
- **Use:** Add a few drops to a massage blend for the abdomen or soles of the feet to activate energy flow; diffuse when initiating new projects or seeking courage to lead.

Peppermint

- **Qualities:** Mental clarity, vitality, and focus.
- Peppermint refreshes the mind and awakens the senses. Its cool fire clears mental clutter, stimulates digestion, and restores alertness — harmonizing intellect with will.
- **Use:** Diffuse or inhale before physical activity or public speaking to invigorate confidence; apply (diluted) to the abdomen for digestive or energetic rejuvenation.

Bergamot

- **Qualities:** Self-worth, joy, and emotional balance.
- Bergamot uplifts the spirit and dissolves self-criticism. It bridges confidence and compassion, balancing the Solar Plexus with the Heart. Its sunny aroma helps release the need for external validation, restoring authentic self-esteem.
- **Use:** Diffuse in the morning to start the day with optimism, or anoint the Solar Plexus area (diluted) while repeating affirmations of worth and joy.

Frankincense

- **Qualities:** Centering, spiritual alignment, and higher will.
- Frankincense connects personal will (Solar Plexus) with divine will (Crown), harmonizing action with purpose. It brings calm strength, courage, and spiritual clarity.
- **Use:** Inhale deeply during meditation to align intention with higher purpose, or add to a carrier oil and massage the abdomen and heart for balanced empowerment.

Black Pepper

- **Qualities:** Inner fire, resilience, and transformation.
- Black Pepper embodies the alchemy of fire — it burns away fear and awakens courage. Its bold, grounding heat strengthens resolve and determination, especially during times of doubt or fatigue.
- **Use:** Apply (well diluted) to the Solar Plexus area or diffuse when reclaiming power after emotional depletion.

How to Use Solar Plexus Chakra Oils

- **Diffusion:** Add a few drops to a diffuser to energize your space with clarity, motivation, and warmth.
- **Massage:** Blend with a carrier oil and massage into the abdomen or mid-back to awaken vitality and stimulate digestion — physically and emotionally.
- **Sunlight Ritual:** Apply diluted oils such as lemon or bergamot and sit briefly in morning sunlight, visualizing your Solar Plexus glowing with golden light.
- **Meditation:** Inhale directly or cup your hands over the Solar Plexus while breathing deeply and affirming empowerment and inner strength.

Affirmation to Pair with Aromatherapy

"With each breath, I awaken my inner fire.
Confidence rises within me, courage guides my path,
and I act with strength, purpose, and radiant joy."

Energetic Insight

Essential oils for the Solar Plexus Chakra are not merely scents — they are living flames of transformation.
Each aroma carries the spark of life that ignites confidence and clarity. Through the power of scent, they remind the spirit that

true power is gentle, focused, and luminous — not dominance, but radiant presence.

They awaken the sun within, teaching that empowerment is not found in control but in conscious, purposeful action.

BLENDING FOR EMPOWERMENT: ESSENTIAL OIL COMBINATIONS FOR THE SOLAR PLEXUS CHAKRA

Blending essential oils for the Solar Plexus Chakra is the art of alchemical fire — merging aroma, intention, and vitality into one radiant expression.

Each blend becomes a spark of transformation, awakening motivation where there was doubt, and courage where there was hesitation.

Because Manipura is governed by **fire**, blends for this chakra should feel **warm, bright, and invigorating** — awakening willpower, digestion, and the inner flame of self-belief.

When creating your blend, focus on **intention** — your reason for blending becomes the purpose that fuels its power.

Combine up to three oils in a carrier such as **jojoba, fractionated coconut, or sunflower oil.** Shake gently and charge your blend with mindful breath before using.

1. Confidence & Courage

Purpose: To strengthen self-esteem, confidence, and motivation.

Blend:
• 2 drops Lemon
• 2 drops Ginger
• 1 drop Frankincense

Use: Apply (diluted) over the Solar Plexus before important meetings or creative pursuits. Diffuse to strengthen presence and courage.

Affirmation: *"I am confident, capable, and radiant with purpose."*

2. Empowered Action

Purpose: To overcome procrastination and activate willpower.
Blend:
• 2 drops Black Pepper
• 2 drops Peppermint
• 1 drop Bergamot
Use: Diffuse in your workspace or apply (diluted) to the abdomen or wrists when preparing to take decisive action.
Affirmation: *"I act with clarity, courage, and direction. My actions create my destiny."*

3. Inner Strength

Purpose: To restore vitality and resilience after burnout or fatigue.
Blend:
• 2 drops Rosemary
• 2 drops Lemon
• 1 drop Ginger
Use: Inhale deeply before meditation or morning exercise, or apply (diluted) over the Solar Plexus and heart.
Affirmation: *"My inner fire burns steady and strong. I am renewed with life and power."*

4. Clarity & Focus

Purpose: To clear mental fog and align action with intention.
Blend:
• 2 drops Peppermint
• 1 drop Frankincense
• 1 drop Grapefruit
Use: Diffuse during study, creative planning, or decision-making. Inhale directly to stimulate clear thinking and balanced energy.

Affirmation: *"My mind is clear, my will is focused, and my energy flows with precision."*

5. Sacred Sun Ritual Blend

Purpose: To honor the solar flame within — the sacred light of transformation and will.
Blend:
• 1 drop Lemon
• 1 drop Frankincense
• 1 drop Black Pepper (or Cinnamon Leaf for ritual intensity)
Use: Anoint your Solar Plexus before meditation, or add to a candle ritual at sunrise. As you breathe in, visualize golden fire awakening in your core — strong, steady, and radiant.
Affirmation: *"I am the light of the sun. My power shines with divine clarity and purpose."*

Charging Your Blends with the Element of Fire

Because the Solar Plexus Chakra is ruled by **fire**, charge your oil blends with light and heat to amplify their empowering vibration:

1. **Sunlight Charging:**
   Place your blend in a glass container under morning sunlight for one to three hours. Visualize golden rays infusing it with confidence and vitality.
2. **Candle Flame Activation:**
   Hold your blend near (but not above) a flame while repeating the affirmation:
   "Fire of life, awaken strength within this blend and within me."
3. **Breath of Power Ritual:**
   Cup the blend in your hands over your Solar Plexus. Inhale deeply, exhale warmth into the bottle, and imagine golden light filling it.
   Feel your inner fire transferring to the oils.

4. **Sound Infusion:**
   Chant the bija mantra **"RAM"** seven times over your blend to align it with Manipura's frequency.
   Let your voice vibrate through the container, igniting it with intention and strength.

Energetic Insight

Solar Plexus blends are not just aromatic creations — they are **elixirs of empowerment**.
Each scent carries the spark of divine will, reminding you that your purpose is not found outside you but within the radiant fire of your own being.
Through these blends, you awaken courage, focus, and luminous self-trust — the true light of Manipura.

CRYSTAL + AROMA ACTIVATION FOR INNER FIRE

The Solar Plexus Chakra is awakened not by force, but by presence.
It opens when will, breath, scent, and energy align — when body and spirit remember that power is not domination, but radiance.
This ritual unites two powerful allies — crystals and essential oils — to rekindle the inner flame of confidence, clarity, and purpose.

Preparation

Set aside 10–15 minutes in a quiet, bright space.
Natural sunlight or a single candle flame is ideal.
Sit comfortably with your spine tall, allowing your belly to soften and breathe.

Have these items ready:
• **One Solar Plexus Crystal:** Citrine, Tiger's Eye, Pyrite, or Yellow Calcite
• **Your Empowerment Blend:** Any essential oil combination from the previous section (or simply Lemon and Ginger diluted in a carrier oil)
• **A candle, gentle drumming, or uplifting instrumental music (optional)**

1. Centering Breath

Take three deep breaths into your Solar Plexus — the space between your ribs and navel.
Inhale through the nose, feeling your abdomen expand like a rising sun.
Exhale through the mouth, releasing any heaviness or self-doubt.
With each breath, sense a golden warmth awakening within you.

Whisper:
"I ignite. I trust. I shine."

2. Anointing the Energy Center

Warm a few drops of your oil blend between your palms.
Bring your hands to your Solar Plexus — the home of Manipura, your inner sun.

As you inhale, draw in the invigorating scent; as you exhale, imagine golden light glowing beneath your palms.
Feel it spread through your chest and spine like sunlight filling every cell.

If you wish, lightly anoint these points:
• Solar Plexus (seat of will and power)

• Throat (expression of truth)
• Heart center (to align power with love)

Affirm softly:
"I act from my center. My power is radiant, confident, and kind."

3. Crystal Infusion

Hold your chosen crystal in your right hand — your giving hand.
Close your eyes and visualize drawing energy up from the earth: a steady current of golden light flowing into the crystal.

Move the crystal in slow, clockwise circles over your Solar Plexus.
With each movement, imagine your inner flame glowing brighter — steady, contained, and powerful.

Repeat the mantra:
"RAM"

Let the vibration resonate in your abdomen, warming you from within — a hum of strength and clarity.

4. The Fire Meditation

Place the crystal gently on your Solar Plexus (or hold it there if sitting upright).
Visualize a radiant sun within your abdomen — golden, luminous, and alive.

With each inhale, the light expands outward, filling your entire being.
With each exhale, it burns away fear, hesitation, and self-doubt.

See yourself surrounded by a field of golden light — brilliant, centered, and strong.
Allow your breath to move like heat waves — calm yet powerful — radiating confidence through your body.

5. Integration

When the energy feels complete, bring one hand to your heart and one to your Solar Plexus.
Feel the bridge between love and power glowing in harmony.
You are both compassionate and strong — gentle and bold.

Whisper:
"My heart guides my power. My power serves my heart. I am radiant and free."

Take several grounding breaths and open your eyes slowly.
Sit in the afterglow of your own brilliance — peaceful, warm, and aware.

Aftercare

• Cleanse your crystal in sunlight or by holding it near candle flame briefly (avoid overheating).
• Store your oil blend in a warm, dry space charged with positive intention.
• Repeat this ritual weekly, or during the waxing moon or morning hours, to strengthen motivation, purpose, and confidence.

When practiced consistently, this ritual reminds you that **your power is sacred** — not to control, but to illuminate.
Through scent, crystal, and consciousness, you awaken the radiant fire of Manipura: **the light of your will, the warmth of your purpose, and the golden joy of being fully alive.**

FIRE RITUAL FOR INNER EMPOWERMENT

A Solar Plexus Chakra Sun & Candle Ceremony

Fire is the sacred element of **Manipura** — the spark of vitality, transformation, and will.
When we align with fire consciously, we awaken the sun within — the light of clarity, confidence, and radiant purpose.
This ritual can be performed with candlelight, sunlight, or even a symbolic flame in meditation.
Its purpose is to **ignite personal power, purify stagnation, and rekindle the strength of your inner sun.**

Preparation: Setting the Energy of Illumination

Choose a time when you will not be disturbed — ideally **at sunrise or midday**, when solar energy is strongest.
This ritual is especially potent during the **waxing moon** or in moments of transition when motivation or confidence feels dim.

Gather:
• One **candle** (gold, yellow, or white)
• 1–2 drops of **Lemon**, **Ginger**, or **Frankincense** essential oil
• A small dish of **sea salt** or **sand** (to anchor the fire element in balance)
• One **Solar Plexus crystal** (Citrine, Tiger's Eye, or Pyrite)
• Optional: A gold or yellow cloth, drum or upbeat instrumental music

Take a moment to center yourself and light your candle, saying softly:
"I awaken the fire within. I rise in strength and clarity."

Step 1: Blessing the Flame

Hold your hands a few inches from the flame or sunlight.
Take three deep breaths, inhaling through your nose, exhaling

through your mouth.
Visualize drawing in radiant golden light through your crown,
guiding it down into your Solar Plexus.
Then, exhale this light through your hands toward the flame,
linking your inner fire with the sacred outer fire.

Whisper:
**"As above, so within — as this flame burns, so too does my
power rise."**

Step 2: Anointing with Fire

Place a drop or two of your essential oil blend on your palms.
Rub your hands together briskly until you feel heat.
Then, place your hands over your Solar Plexus — the space
between your ribs and navel.
Feel the warmth radiating beneath your palms.

If you wish, lightly anoint these areas:
• Solar Plexus (your power center)
• Heart (to balance will with compassion)
• Throat (to express truth with courage)

Affirm softly:
"My power is pure. My will is aligned with divine purpose."

Step 3: Crystal Activation

Hold your chosen crystal (Citrine, Pyrite, or Tiger's Eye) in
your right hand — the channel of action and empowerment.
Close your eyes and envision golden light spiraling from your
Solar Plexus into the crystal, charging it with strength,
confidence, and focus.
Move it slowly in clockwise circles over your abdomen while
repeating the mantra:

"RAM."

Let the vibration resonate deep in your core — warm, steady, and strong.
See the golden light expand, illuminating your whole body like a sunrise.

Step 4: The Flame Meditation

Sit comfortably before your candle or with eyes closed if outdoors in sunlight.
Gaze softly into the flame, or visualize one burning within your Solar Plexus — bright, unwavering, eternal.

With every inhale, imagine this light expanding outward, filling your aura with gold.
With every exhale, release self-doubt, fear, or hesitation into the fire to be transformed.
Stay here for several minutes, breathing the rhythm of illumination.

Whisper:
"I am the light of my own becoming. My fire purifies, empowers, and renews me."

Step 5: Integration

When you feel complete, place one hand on your heart and one on your Solar Plexus.
Feel the warmth moving between them — the harmony of love and power, compassion and purpose.

Say aloud:
"My heart guides my power. My power serves my heart."

Take a final deep breath and extinguish the candle (or bow to the sun) in gratitude.
Visualize the flame remaining alive within you — glowing quietly at your center.

Aftercare

• Cleanse your crystal in sunlight or by placing it near your candle's flame (safely, without heat contact).
• Store your oil blend or ritual items on a sunlit altar or gold cloth to maintain the frequency of illumination.
• Repeat this ritual weekly, or whenever confidence wavers or purpose needs renewal.

When practiced with awareness, this Fire Ritual awakens the **radiant power of Manipura** — the will that transforms intention into action and light into life.
You emerge not only renewed, but **illuminated** — a living embodiment of the sun within.

SOMATIC PRACTICES FOR THE SOLAR PLEXUS CHAKRA

Reclaiming Power Through Movement and Breath

While meditation quiets the mind, somatic practice awakens the will.
The Solar Plexus Chakra — **Manipura**, the seat of power, confidence, and transformation — thrives on movement that builds warmth, stability, and inner strength.
Unlike the Sacral, which flows, Manipura ignites — it is the fire that fuels direction and purpose.

Healing this chakra means learning to trust your strength, to stand tall in your center, and to embody empowerment through the language of posture, breath, and motion.
When fear, shame, or self-doubt have dimmed the inner flame, somatic awareness rekindles it. It teaches you to move from your core — the radiant sun within — and to let power flow through every action with integrity and grace.

The following practices are designed to help you connect with the fire of Manipura — awakening clarity, willpower, and the confidence to shine.

1. Core Flame Breath: Igniting the Inner Fire

The core flame breath awakens Manipura by linking breath with abdominal strength and heat.
It activates digestion, circulation, and energy flow, empowering the solar center.

Practice:

1. Sit upright with your spine tall and shoulders relaxed.
2. Place one hand over your Solar Plexus (between the ribs and navel).
3. Inhale deeply through your nose, feeling the belly expand forward.
4. Exhale sharply through the mouth, drawing the navel inward toward the spine.
5. Continue rhythmically, inhaling slow and deep, exhaling with intention.
6. As warmth builds, visualize golden light glowing brighter in your core.

Mantra:
"With each breath, I awaken my inner fire."

2. Power Stance: Embodying Confidence

Posture is the physical expression of belief. When you align your body in strength, your energy follows.
This standing exercise grounds your will and awakens presence.

Practice:

1. Stand with feet hip-width apart, knees slightly bent.

2. Roll your shoulders back and down, chest open, chin level.
3. Engage your abdomen gently — not tense, but firm.
4. Breathe deeply into your Solar Plexus, imagining golden light radiating outward.
5. Feel the ground beneath you and the fire within you connect — earth and sun meeting in your body.
6. Hold for 2–3 minutes, breathing confidence into every cell.

Mantra:
"I stand in my power. My energy radiates strength and purpose."

3. Abdominal Sun Rotations: Cultivating Warmth and Flow

This gentle movement activates digestion, stimulates the diaphragm, and releases tension around the midsection — the physical home of Manipura.

Practice:

1. Sit cross-legged or stand comfortably.
2. Place your hands over your Solar Plexus.
3. Begin to make slow, circular motions with your upper body — clockwise, then counterclockwise — as if stirring light within your belly.
4. Inhale as you lean forward, exhale as you round back.
5. Move with awareness and ease, letting the motion build warmth and rhythm.

Mantra:
"I move from my center. My light flows in all directions."

4. The Warrior Flow: Moving from Power and Grace

In yoga, **Virabhadrasana (Warrior poses)** embody the Solar Plexus essence — courage in motion, rooted strength, and purposeful expansion.

Practice:

1. Step one foot back, front knee bent, arms extended wide.
2. Inhale — feel your chest lift and Solar Plexus open toward the horizon.
3. Exhale — sink gently into your stance, feeling the strength of your legs and the fire in your core.
4. Breathe through the posture for several rounds, visualizing sunlight pouring through your abdomen and radiating through your fingertips.
5. Switch sides and repeat.

Mantra:
"I move with strength and intention. My power flows with grace."

5. The Heat of Transformation: Breath & Stillness

Fire purifies through presence. This practice helps you absorb your own radiance and embody inner stability.

Practice:

1. Sit comfortably with your palms resting on your Solar Plexus.
2. Inhale deeply, visualizing a sphere of golden light expanding outward.
3. Hold the breath for a moment, feeling warmth build.
4. Exhale slowly, allowing the warmth to spread through your entire body.

5. Rest in stillness, basking in the glow of your awakened core.

Mantra:
"I am steady. I am radiant. I am transformed."

Energetic Insight

When the body moves with awareness from the Solar Plexus, willpower becomes wisdom.
These practices teach that strength is not tension, but alignment — a harmony between power and presence.

Through each breath, twist, and stance, you reclaim ownership of your energy, your choices, and your life.
As the fire of Manipura burns clear and steady, you embody your true essence: **radiant, confident, and unstoppable.**

YOGA AND BREATHWORK FOR THE SOLAR PLEXUS CHAKRA

Igniting Strength, Clarity, and Personal Power

The Solar Plexus Chakra (**Manipura**) governs energy, willpower, and transformation — all of which awaken through heat and focused movement.
Yoga and breathwork for this chakra restore vitality, confidence, and courage by engaging the core — the physical and energetic center where fire burns and life force gathers.

While Sacral Chakra practices flow like water, Solar Plexus practices ignite like flame.
Through purposeful postures, rhythmic breath, and inner focus, you learn to kindle energy without aggression — to burn away fear, stagnation, and doubt, revealing the radiant power of your true self.

When practiced consciously, Solar Plexus Yoga becomes a sacred fire ceremony within the body: each breath a spark, each movement a flame, each moment an offering of empowerment.

The Element of Fire in Yoga

Manipura corresponds to the element of **fire** — symbolizing transformation, illumination, and will.
Fire is both creator and purifier; it turns raw matter into energy, darkness into light, inertia into motion.
In Solar Yoga, you awaken this inner fire not to consume, but to illuminate — balancing strength with compassion, effort with ease.

As the heat builds, so does clarity.
The body becomes a forge where self-doubt melts into confidence, and intention becomes action.

Intention for Practice

**"I am the fire of transformation.
I act with strength, clarity, and purpose."**

Solar Plexus Yoga Principles

1. **Engage the Core** – Strengthen and stabilize the abdomen and diaphragm to awaken Manipura's energy.
2. **Build Heat with Awareness** – Use breath and movement to generate warmth, vitality, and focus.
3. **Align Power and Presence** – Let every posture radiate confidence and open the space between will and wisdom.
4. **Balance Fire with Stillness** – Rest in quiet luminosity after activation — the glow of contained strength.

Recommended Poses for Manipura Activation

1. **Navasana (Boat Pose)** – Builds core strength and confidence.
    o   Sit with legs lifted and spine tall. Breathe deeply into the belly, visualizing golden fire glowing at your center.
    o   *Mantra:* "I rise with strength and stability."
2. **Utkatasana (Chair Pose)** – Awakens endurance and personal power.
    o   Engage thighs, draw the navel toward the spine, and hold the pose as you breathe through inner resistance.
    o   *Mantra:* "I trust the fire within to sustain me."
3. **Virabhadrasana II (Warrior II)** – Embodies courage, focus, and determination.
    o   Gaze steadily over your front fingertips, chest lifted, belly engaged.
    o   *Mantra:* "I act with courage and grace."
4. **Plank or Chaturanga** – Builds strength, stability, and core alignment.
    o   Keep the fire steady — breath even, energy grounded.
    o   *Mantra:* "I am disciplined, focused, and alive."
5. **Dhanurasana (Bow Pose)** – Opens the Solar Plexus and stimulates digestive fire.
    o   As you lift, feel the abdomen press into the earth, awakening Manipura.
    o   *Mantra:* "I open my heart through the strength of my will."
6. **Ardha Matsyendrasana (Seated Twist)** – A detoxifying pose for energetic purification.
    o   Twists stimulate the digestive organs, clearing stagnation and rebalancing the fire element.
    o   *Mantra:* "I release the old and transform through clarity."

Breathwork (Pranayama) for the Inner Flame

1. **Kapalabhati (Skull Shining Breath)**
   o Short, sharp exhales through the nose ignite energy and cleanse Manipura.
   o Focus on the Solar Plexus as a radiant point of light growing brighter with each exhale.
   o *Mantra:* "My breath is the spark that awakens my light."
2. **Bhastrika (Bellows Breath)**
   o Powerful inhalations and exhalations stoke the digestive fire and awaken willpower.
   o Perform 10–20 rounds, then rest, feeling the inner warmth radiate outward.
   o *Mantra:* "I am filled with vitality and purpose."
3. **Agni Sara (Fire Cleansing Breath)**
   o Exhale completely, then pump the abdomen inward and outward several times before inhaling again.
   o This stimulates the navel center and awakens the energy of transformation.
   o *Mantra:* "I honor the fire that purifies and renews me."
4. **Solar Balancing Breath (Right-Nostril Breathing / Surya Bhedana)**
   o Close the left nostril, inhale through the right (the solar channel), exhale through the left.
   o This activates the Pingala Nadi — the channel of dynamic, masculine energy — balancing vitality and focus.
   o *Mantra:* "I breathe in clarity, I exhale confidence."

Energetic Insight

When practiced with awareness, Solar Plexus Yoga awakens your inner sun — the fire of transformation that burns away fear and illuminates truth.
It reminds you that power is not domination but direction — not control, but creation.

Through the breath of fire, the strength of the core, and the stillness that follows effort, you rediscover the radiant light of Manipura — **the power to act, the courage to lead, and the confidence to shine.**

YOGA POSES FOR THE SOLAR PLEXUS CHAKRA

Awakening Confidence, Strength, and Inner Power

Each of the following postures activates the core, strengthens the spine, and stimulates digestion — regions governed by **Manipura**, the chakra of willpower and transformation.
These movements build internal heat, awaken focus, and connect you with your personal fire — your power to act, decide, and create with clarity.

1. Boat Pose (Navasana) – Igniting the Inner Fire

Sit on the floor with knees bent and feet lifted off the mat.
Extend the arms forward, keeping the chest open and spine long.
Breathe deeply into the abdomen, feeling energy gather in your center.

Focus: Core activation, balance, and inner strength.
Affirmation: *"I am centered, strong, and radiant."*

2. Warrior II (Virabhadrasana II) – Embodying Courage and Focus

Step your feet wide apart and bend your front knee.
Extend your arms parallel to the ground, gaze softly over your front hand.
Feel your power rooted in the legs, guided by clarity in the core.

Focus: Grounded action, confidence, and determination.
Affirmation: *"I act with courage and purpose."*

3. Bow Pose (Dhanurasana) – Expanding the Solar Flame

Lie on your stomach, bend your knees, and reach back to hold your ankles.
On an inhale, lift the chest and thighs, pressing your belly into the earth.
Breathe into the stretch across your abdomen, awakening Manipura's heat.

Focus: Opening the front body and stimulating digestive fire.
Affirmation: *"I am open, powerful, and full of light."*

4. Plank Pose (Phalakasana) – Strengthening the Core of Will

Come into a high plank position, shoulders over wrists, body in one line.
Engage your abdomen, keeping the breath steady and eyes focused forward.
Feel strength radiate from your Solar Plexus through every limb.

Focus: Endurance, willpower, and stability.
Affirmation: *"My power is steady and unwavering."*

5. Revolved Chair Pose (Parivrtta Utkatasana) – Purifying Through Fire

Begin in Chair Pose with knees bent and palms together at the heart.
On an exhale, twist from the waist, placing one elbow outside the opposite knee.
Press the palms together and gaze upward, breathing through the heat of transformation.

Focus: Detoxification, digestion, and energetic cleansing.
Affirmation: *"I release what no longer serves me and rise renewed."*

6. Camel Pose (Ustrasana) – Radiating Confidence and Light

Kneel with knees hip-width apart and place your hands on your lower back or heels.
Lift your heart toward the sky, allowing the front body to open fully.
Feel your Solar Plexus expand — bright, courageous, and free.

Focus: Confidence, empowerment, and vulnerability in strength.
Affirmation: *"I shine my light without fear."*

7. Corpse Pose with Solar Awareness (Savasana with Manipura Focus)

Lie on your back with one hand over your abdomen and one over your heart.
Visualize golden light glowing within your belly — steady, calm, and radiant.
Each breath fans this inner flame, spreading warmth throughout your body.

Focus: Integration, peace, and embodied strength.
Affirmation: *"My power rests in balance. I am light and strength in harmony."*

Energetic Insight

Solar Plexus Yoga transforms effort into empowerment.
It teaches that true strength arises not from force, but from **alignment** — from the centered flame that burns clean and bright.
When Manipura is active and balanced, you feel energized, decisive, and confident — not to dominate the world, but to **shine within it**.

HEALING THROUGH FIRE RITUALS AND SOLAR CYCLES

Honoring the Element of Transformation and the Rhythms of Inner Power

The Solar Plexus Chakra (**Manipura**) is ruled by the **element of fire** and guided by the **solar cycles** of the sun.
Where the moon symbolizes flow and reflection, the sun represents purpose and radiance — the light of conscious action.

Just as dawn follows night and seasons turn with the sun's strength, your energy, confidence, and will also rise and fall in natural cycles.
To heal and balance the Solar Plexus Chakra is to **align with the rhythm of your own power** — to stoke the inner flame when it wanes and to rest in quiet luminosity when it burns bright.

Fire as a Sacred Healer

Fire transforms.
It consumes the old, illuminates truth, and forges strength
through change.
Across cultures, sacred fire has symbolized purification and
divine will — from the eternal temple flames of ancient Vedic
ritual to the Celtic Beltane fires and the ceremonial bonfires of
Indigenous traditions.

Where water cleanses through flow, **fire cleanses through
illumination.**
It burns away stagnation, fear, and self-doubt, leaving only
clarity and purpose in its wake.
In Manipura's teaching, fire does not destroy — it **refines**,
revealing the gold of the soul hidden beneath layers of
hesitation.

Intention for Practice

**"Like fire, I transform.
I release the old and rise renewed in light."**

Solar Ritual for Empowerment and Renewal

This ritual helps rekindle your inner flame, release
disempowering emotions, and restore confidence and direction.

You'll Need:

- A **candle** (yellow or gold) to represent your Solar Fire
- A **bowl of water** (to balance the fire element)
- 3 drops of **essential oils** such as lemon, ginger, or
  frankincense
- A **small piece of citrine, tiger's eye, or pyrite**
  (optional, for empowerment)

Steps:

1. Prepare the Space

Sit in a quiet, well-ventilated area.
Light the candle and place the bowl of water beside it to
symbolize harmony between heat and calm.
Take a deep breath and say aloud:

**"With this flame, I awaken my light.
With this breath, I reclaim my power."**

Add the oils to the bowl or diffuse them nearby.
Let the scent of warmth and spice awaken vitality.

2. Activate the Solar Flame

Bring your hands to your Solar Plexus — the space between
your ribs and navel.
Inhale deeply, feeling your abdomen rise.
Exhale slowly, imagining the flame before you merging with
the flame within.
See golden light radiating through your torso — bright, strong,
unwavering.

If you wish, hold your crystal over the flame (a safe distance)
and whisper:
"I charge this stone with courage and clarity."

3. Release Through Breath

As you breathe, visualize any heaviness — fear, guilt, or
indecision — melting into the fire.
With each exhale, whisper what you are ready to release:

"I release self-doubt."
"I release hesitation."
"I release what dims my light."

Feel the fire transmute each offering into radiant energy.

4. Seal with Empowerment

Place both hands on your Solar Plexus.
Close your eyes and imagine a golden sun expanding within
you — strong, calm, and luminous.
Whisper:

"I am light. I am power. I am aligned with my purpose."

When ready, extinguish the candle safely.
Touch the surface of the water and say:

"Fire purifies, water soothes, and I am balanced in both."

Pour the water into the earth or sink, offering gratitude for
transformation.

Purpose

This ritual is a reminder that empowerment is not about force —
it is about illumination.
Each time you light the candle, you awaken a truth: **the sun
never questions its right to shine.**
When you honor your inner fire, you step fully into your
radiance — warm, steady, and alive with purpose.

AFFIRMATIONS, MUDRAS, AND DAILY BALANCING PRACTICES FOR THE SOLAR PLEXUS CHAKRA

Awakening Strength, Clarity, and Inner Radiance

The Solar Plexus Chakra (**Manipura**) is the seat of your personal power — the inner sun where confidence, will, and transformation ignite.
To balance it is to awaken your fire without burning out — to act from clarity rather than control, and to move through life with purpose and radiant self-trust.

Daily affirmations, sacred hand mudras, and intentional rituals nurture Manipura's fire, transforming self-doubt into strength and inertia into decisive action.
Through these practices, you align with your **inner light** — steady, courageous, and alive.

Affirmations For Confidence And Empowered Action

Words are fuel for the Solar Plexus. When spoken with conviction, they awaken the nervous system and strengthen your energetic center.
Speak these affirmations aloud each morning while placing your hand over your abdomen — feeling warmth rise beneath your palm like the first rays of dawn.

MORNING ACTIVATION AFFIRMATIONS

- "I stand in my power with confidence and grace."
- "My inner fire burns with clarity and purpose."
- "I take action aligned with my highest truth."
- "I trust myself to make clear and empowered choices."
- "The light within me shines brighter every day."

EVENING INTEGRATION AFFIRMATIONS

- "I release the day's challenges with gratitude and peace."
- "My strength renews as I rest in my own light."
- "I am proud of who I am becoming."
- "I am balanced — strong, calm, and whole."
- "I honor the fire within me as sacred."

Mantra for Meditation

RAM — (pronounced "rahm")
This is the **bija mantra** of Manipura, the sound of fire and transformation.

Chant softly, feeling the vibration resonate in the diaphragm and abdomen.
Each repetition stokes the subtle flame of courage and clarity within your Solar Plexus.

Focus: Visualize a golden sun glowing brighter with every "RAM," radiating warmth through your entire being.

MUDRAS FOR BALANCING THE SOLAR PLEXUS CHAKRA

In yogic and tantric traditions, **mudras** are sacred seals that direct prana (life force) through the body.
For Manipura, they strengthen determination, clear energetic stagnation, and balance the digestive fire — both physical and spiritual.

1. Rudra Mudra — The Gesture of Inner Power

This mudra channels the energy of **Rudra**, the fiery aspect of Shiva, symbolizing strength and transformation.

It awakens courage, motivation, and willpower, making it ideal before meditation, public speaking, or creative projects.

How to Practice:

1. Sit comfortably with your spine straight.
2. Touch the tips of your **thumb**, **index finger**, and **ring finger** together.
3. Keep the other fingers extended.
4. Rest your hands on your thighs, palms facing upward.
5. Breathe deeply for 5–10 minutes, focusing on the warmth in your abdomen.

Affirmation:
"I am powerful and centered in my purpose."

2. Surya Mudra — The Seal of Solar Energy

Named after **Surya**, the Sun God, this mudra increases vitality and digestive fire, clears lethargy, and strengthens confidence. It helps transform apathy into dynamic energy and is especially beneficial when you feel drained or indecisive.

How to Practice:

1. Fold the **ring finger** down toward the palm and press it gently with the **thumb**.
2. Keep the other fingers extended.
3. Rest your hands on your thighs, palms upward.
4. Practice for 5–15 minutes while breathing evenly.

Affirmation:
"The fire within me shines bright and pure."

3. Matangi Mudra — The Gesture of Inner Harmony

This mudra balances power with peace. It harmonizes the energies of assertion and compassion, helping you act decisively while staying calm and centered.
It also strengthens digestion, posture, and energetic alignment through the solar plexus.

How to Practice:

1. Interlace your fingers at chest level.
2. Extend both **middle fingers** upward and press them together.
3. Hold the hands lightly against the Solar Plexus.
4. Breathe deeply into the abdomen for several minutes, visualizing golden light radiating outward.

Affirmation:
"My power serves peace. My strength creates harmony."

Daily Balancing Practices

1. **Morning Sun Connection:**
   Stand facing the rising sun.
   Inhale, drawing in golden light through your Solar Plexus; exhale, radiating it outward.
   Whisper: *"I welcome this day with power and purpose."*
2. **Core Activation Breath:**
   Place your hands over your abdomen and take three deep breaths, expanding and contracting the belly.
   Feel your center awaken — warm, alive, focused.
3. **Daily Reflection:**
   At day's end, place your hand on your Solar Plexus and ask:
   "Did I act from power or from fear today?"
   Listen gently, without judgment. Awareness brings alignment.

Energetic Insight

Balancing Manipura is not about dominance — it is about **directed energy**.
When your Solar Plexus Chakra is aligned, your fire burns steady, not wild.
You act from confidence, not control. You shine, not to overpower, but to illuminate.

Each breath, word, and gesture becomes an act of mastery — a reminder that **you are the light you seek.**

Food Therapy for the Solar Plexus Chakra

Nourishing Power, Vitality, and Inner Fire

The Solar Plexus Chakra (**Manipura**) governs **metabolism, digestion, and personal empowerment.**
It is the body's radiant sun — transforming food into energy, thought into action, and intention into manifestation.
To nourish Manipura is to feed your **inner fire** — with food, with breath, and with mindful awareness.

When balanced, you eat with confidence and clarity, intuitively knowing what fuels your strength.
When imbalanced, digestion may falter, cravings may reflect emotional instability, or control may replace trust — leading to fatigue, frustration, or burnout.
The goal is to restore **harmonious fire** — steady, bright, and life-giving — by eating foods that warm, strengthen, and empower your body and mind.

Energetic Principles

- **Element:** Fire
- **Sense:** Sight
- **Color:** Yellow, Gold
- **Location:** Upper abdomen (stomach, liver, pancreas)
- **Themes:** Confidence, willpower, digestion, transformation, vitality

FOODS THAT HEAL AND BALANCE THE SOLAR PLEXUS CHAKRA

Yellow and Golden Foods: Fuel for the Inner Sun

Yellow-colored foods vibrate at the same frequency as the Solar Plexus, stimulating warmth, confidence, and clarity.
They also nourish the digestive organs and support energy metabolism — the physical reflection of willpower.

Examples:
• Bananas, pineapples, lemons, yellow peppers
• Corn, yellow squash, golden beets
• Ginger, turmeric root, saffron

How to Use:
Enjoy these foods in lightly cooked, warm dishes to kindle digestive fire without overstimulation.
Drink lemon water in the morning to awaken your metabolism and clarity of mind.

Digestive and Metabolic Support Foods

Manipura governs **Agni** — the digestive flame. To keep this fire balanced, eat foods that support smooth digestion and steady energy.

Examples:
• Brown rice, quinoa, millet, oats
• Lentils, chickpeas, mung beans
• Lightly steamed vegetables — especially carrots, cauliflower, and zucchini
• Warm herbal teas (ginger, fennel, peppermint)

Ritual Practice:
Before eating, pause and take three conscious breaths.
Whisper:
"This meal becomes my strength. I receive it with gratitude and purpose."

Spices to Awaken the Solar Fire

Mildly heating spices activate the Solar Plexus and strengthen willpower and clarity.
They support digestion, circulation, and courage —
transforming lethargy into light.

Examples:
• Ginger, turmeric, black pepper
• Cumin, coriander, fennel, mustard seed
• Cardamom and cinnamon for gentle balance

How to Use:
Sauté spices briefly in oil before cooking to release their fire element.
A warm cup of ginger tea after meals keeps Manipura bright and steady.

Proteins and Power Foods

The Solar Plexus thrives on nourishment that sustains energy and supports determination.
Balanced proteins and wholesome grains stabilize blood sugar and ground action into endurance.

Examples:
• Lentils, beans, tempeh, tofu
• Eggs, fish, or chicken (if aligned with your diet)
• Nuts and seeds — especially sunflower, pumpkin, and sesame
• Ghee or olive oil to lubricate and sustain the digestive flame

Tip:
Avoid skipping meals — consistent nourishment keeps your energy centered and your decisions clear.

SUN-INFUSED FRUITS AND ENERGY-RICH VEGETABLES

Fruits that ripen under strong sunlight carry Manipura's frequency of joy and radiance.
They refresh without cooling the inner fire.

Examples:
• Pineapple, mango, papaya, apricot
• Yellow apples, peaches, golden melons
• Lightly roasted root vegetables — carrots, sweet potatoes, parsnips

How to Use:
Enjoy fruit in the morning when solar energy is rising.
Squeeze fresh lemon or ginger into your water to awaken alertness and focus.

FOODS TO BALANCE EXCESS SOLAR ENERGY

When Manipura is **overactive**, one may feel overheated, irritable, or overly driven.
To cool and calm the inner fire, focus on hydration and moderation.

Soothing and Cooling Choices:
• Cucumber, lettuce, celery

• Aloe vera juice or coconut water
• Cooling herbs such as mint or coriander
• Mild dairy or oat milk to soothe acidity

Avoid:
Excess caffeine, alcohol, or overly spicy foods that
overstimulate the fire element and lead to burnout.

RITUAL OF MINDFUL EATING

Manipura thrives on **awareness and intention.**
Turn each meal into a meditation by engaging the senses fully:
Notice the colors, aromas, and warmth of your food.
Chew slowly, with gratitude.
Imagine your inner sun transforming nourishment into radiant
energy.

Affirmation:
"Each bite fuels my strength.
Each breath fans my inner flame.
I am light, power, and vitality embodied."

ENERGETIC INSIGHT

Eating for the Solar Plexus is an act of **self-respect.**
It is not about control or discipline, but alignment — honoring
what strengthens you, while releasing what dims your light.
Through food, you learn the sacred art of balance: how to burn
brightly without burning out,
how to transform nourishment into power, and
how to live with radiant confidence in every action.

HEALING RITUAL: THE EMPOWERED EATING PRACTICE

Feeding the Inner Fire with Presence and Gratitude

1. **Choose one meal each day** to eat in silence — free from screens, noise, or conversation.
2. Before eating, **pause to observe** your food. Notice the warmth of color, the vitality of texture, the fragrance of spices kissed by sunlight.
3. Inhale deeply and whisper:
   "May this food become light within me."
   Offer gratitude to the **sun**, **fire**, and **earth** that brought this nourishment into being.
4. Take slow, deliberate bites. Savor each flavor as a spark of solar energy entering your body.
   Feel warmth gather in your abdomen — your **Solar Plexus**, glowing golden and alive.
5. With every swallow, imagine this light expanding — strengthening your will, sharpening your clarity, and radiating through your whole being.

This ritual restores **presence, vitality, and empowerment** to the act of eating.
Each meal becomes a sacred exchange between your inner fire and the nourishment of life itself.

Affirmation For Food As Light

"Every bite fuels my purpose.
Every breath fans my inner flame.
I honor the fire within me that transforms nourishment into power."

HERBAL AND TEA REMEDIES FOR THE SOLAR PLEXUS CHAKRA

Supporting Digestion, Confidence, and Calm Strength

The Solar Plexus Chakra (**Manipura**) is the fire within — the center of digestion, transformation, and willpower.
Just as the sun transforms darkness into light, Manipura transforms food, thought, and emotion into usable energy.

Herbs and teas that stimulate digestion, balance heat, and calm tension all serve this chakra. They help regulate the body's inner flame — ensuring that your energy burns steady, not erratic.

When your Solar Plexus is balanced, you experience vitality without aggression, confidence without arrogance, and calm strength that radiates from your core.

Energetic Principles of Herbal Healing

- **Element:** Fire
- **Body Systems:** Digestive, metabolic, muscular
- **Color Frequency:** Yellow–gold
- **Core Actions:** Stimulate, purify, empower, balance
- **Spiritual Lesson:** Transformation through mindful action

KEY HERBS FOR THE SOLAR PLEXUS CHAKRA
Ginger (Zingiber officinale)

Qualities: Warming, stimulating, empowering.
Ginger awakens digestion, strengthens willpower, and restores motivation. It brings gentle heat to the belly, reigniting your inner fire when you feel sluggish or uncertain.
Use:

Sip ginger tea before meals to activate Agni (digestive fire). Inhale its spicy aroma to lift confidence and clear indecision.

Affirmation:
"The fire within me burns steady and bright."

Lemon Balm (Melissa officinalis)

Qualities: Calming, harmonizing, uplifting.
Lemon balm soothes an overactive Solar Plexus — the kind that burns too hot with anxiety or overcontrol. It softens tension while maintaining clarity and focus.
Use:
Brew as a gentle afternoon tea to calm nerves and renew optimism.
Excellent for those with perfectionist tendencies or mental fatigue.

Affirmation:
"I act with peace, not pressure."

Chamomile (Matricaria recutita)

Qualities: Soothing, digestive, balancing.
Chamomile harmonizes the gut–mind connection, calming both stomach and spirit. It eases emotional knots stored in the abdomen and promotes relaxation after meals or stress.
Use:
Drink warm chamomile tea in the evening to release tension and aid digestion.
Can be blended with fennel or lemon balm for deeper calm.

Affirmation:
"I digest life with ease and grace."

Peppermint (Mentha × piperita)

Qualities: Cooling, clarifying, uplifting.
Peppermint balances an overheated Solar Plexus while
enhancing focus and energy flow. It clears mental fog and
supports the nervous system's link to the digestive tract.
Use:
Drink before or after meals to relieve bloating or heaviness.
Inhale the aroma to reawaken clarity and mental precision.

Affirmation:
"My mind and body work together in harmony."

Turmeric (Curcuma longa)

Qualities: Purifying, energizing, empowering.
Turmeric embodies the golden light of Manipura —
strengthening digestion, cleansing the liver, and brightening
mood. It clears energetic stagnation and infuses courage into the
blood.
Use:
Add to warm milk, teas, or cooking as a tonic for inner strength
and balance.
For ritual work, mix with honey to anoint the Solar Plexus
before meditation.

Affirmation:
"Golden light flows through every cell of my being."

Fennel (Foeniculum vulgare)

Qualities: Gentle warmth, digestive ease, emotional stability.
Fennel relaxes the gut while nurturing vitality. It is ideal for
those who hold emotion or tension in the stomach area.
Use:
Chew seeds after meals or brew tea for sweet, soothing energy
that restores comfort and confidence.

Affirmation:
"I trust the process of transformation."

SOLAR TEA BLENDS

1. Radiant Fire Digestive Blend

Purpose: To stoke inner fire while supporting smooth digestion.
Blend: Ginger, fennel, chamomile, and lemon peel.
Use: Drink mid-day to awaken metabolism and mental focus.
Affirmation:
"My energy flows clear and strong like sunlight."

2. Calm Confidence Blend

Purpose: To balance strength with serenity.
Blend: Lemon balm, chamomile, and peppermint.
Use: Sip during stressful times or before public speaking to settle the stomach and calm nerves.
Affirmation:
"I act with courage and peace."

3. Golden Vitality Elixir

Purpose: To energize the Solar Plexus with warmth and joy.
Blend: Turmeric, ginger, cinnamon, and a hint of honey.
Use: Drink in the morning to awaken your body and spirit.
Affirmation:
"I shine with the light of purpose and vitality."

RITUAL USE OF HERBAL INFUSIONS

1. **Morning Sun Ritual:**
    Hold your warm tea at your Solar Plexus.
    Close your eyes, inhale the rising steam, and whisper:
    "This light nourishes my purpose."

2. **Evening Release Ritual:**
   As you sip your tea, place a hand on your belly and
   exhale softly.
   Let go of any tension, self-judgment, or emotional
   residue from the day.
   Feel your inner fire settling — warm, balanced, and
   calm.

Energetic Insight

Herbs that feed Manipura are like teachers of balance — some
ignite, others soothe.
Together they teach that power is not in force, but in flow;
not in dominance, but in radiant steadiness.

When you honor the wisdom of your fire —
you digest life, not just food.
You become the **sun within**,
burning bright, clear, and alive.

COOLING AND SOOTHING HERBS FOR OVERACTIVE SOLAR ENERGY

When the Solar Plexus burns too hot, it can manifest as
irritability, anger, overcontrol, or digestive discomfort.
The inner fire that once empowered can become consuming,
leading to restlessness, tension, or burnout.
To restore balance, the body calls for **cooling, grounding, and
harmonizing herbs** — plants that temper intensity while
preserving vitality.

These herbs teach the wisdom of the steady flame: strong
enough to illuminate, soft enough to sustain.

Balancing Herbs for Manipura:

- **Lemon Balm** – Calms nervous energy and anxiety; balances ambition with peace.
- **Chamomile** – Soothes inflammation, anger, and digestive tension; brings gentle clarity to the mind.
- **Peppermint** – Cools excess fire in the gut; clears mental clutter and renews focus.
- **Fennel** – Eases bloating and emotional heat held in the stomach; restores inner harmony.
- **Rose Petal** – Opens the heart to compassion, cooling fiery emotions with softness and grace.

SOLAR PLEXUS HARMONY TEA BLEND

Supports clarity, digestion, and calm empowerment.

Ingredients:

- 1 tsp dried lemon balm
- 1 tsp chamomile flowers
- ½ tsp fennel seeds
- ½ tsp peppermint leaves
- Optional: A slice of fresh ginger or a drop of honey for balance

Instructions:

1. Steep the herbs in hot water for 5–7 minutes.
2. As the tea steeps, breathe in the rising steam — golden, aromatic, calming.
3. Sip slowly, letting the warmth settle into your belly. Feel the fire within you glow steady — not blazing, not dim, but radiant and calm.

Affirmation:
"My inner fire burns steady and true.

I act from clarity, not impulse.
I am peace in motion."

HERBAL BATH FOR INNER STRENGTH AND CALM

A ritual bath to cool the body, relax the mind, and harmonize Manipura's energy.
This practice helps release tension, overthinking, or emotional heat that gathers in the solar region.

Ingredients:

- 1 cup Epsom or sea salt
- 1 tbsp dried chamomile
- 1 tbsp rose petals
- 1 tsp fennel seeds or peppermint leaves
- 3 drops sandalwood or lemon essential oil

Instructions:

1. Add the herbs and salt to warm bathwater, swirling clockwise to infuse.
2. Step into the bath mindfully, feeling the water soothe your abdomen and chest.
3. Close your eyes and visualize golden light descending into your Solar Plexus — the light of the sun cooling into calm radiance.
4. With each exhale, release irritation or tension; with each inhale, invite serenity and strength.

Intention:
Let the heat of excess emotion dissolve into stillness.
Emerge clear, centered, and empowered.

Affirmation For Herbal Healing

"Like the sun, I shine without burning.
Like the earth, I ground my strength in peace.
Like herbs, I remember that true power is steady, clear, and kind."

Nature Practices for the Solar Plexus Chakra

Reconnecting to the Fire of Life

Where the Root Chakra anchors us in earth and the Sacral attunes us to water, the **Solar Plexus Chakra (Manipura)** awakens the element of **Fire** — the radiant power of transformation and vitality.
To heal and balance this chakra is to rekindle your **inner sun** — to remember that light is your nature and that warmth, clarity, and willpower are sacred expressions of your soul.

In nature, fire is seen in the glow of sunrise, the pulse of heat in your body, and the golden shimmer of sunlight on your skin. Manipura invites you to reconnect to this living light — to move from passivity into purpose, from self-doubt into illumination.

1. Sunlight Meditation: Absorbing Solar Energy

The Solar Plexus is ruled by the **Sun**, the ultimate symbol of life force and confidence.
Spending time in natural sunlight (especially morning or late afternoon light) strengthens and purifies this energy center.

Practice:

- Stand or sit comfortably facing the sun.
- Place your hands over your upper abdomen, just below the rib cage.
- With every inhale, imagine golden light entering through your Solar Plexus.
- With every exhale, see it radiating outward like a gentle sunbeam.
- Whisper:
  "I am filled with the light of purpose. My power shines with clarity and grace."

Tip:
Avoid midday intensity; soft light harmonizes without overstimulating.
You may also perform this meditation in filtered sunlight indoors or visualize the sun's warmth if outdoors is not possible.

2. Fire Ritual for Transformation

The Solar Plexus governs transformation — the alchemy of turning energy into action.
A simple fire ritual helps release self-doubt, anger, or fear, transmuting them into empowerment.

Practice:

- Write on a small piece of paper what you wish to release — limiting beliefs, procrastination, or old guilt.
- Light a candle or small safe fire.
- Hold the paper to your heart, then to your Solar Plexus.
- Say softly:
  "I release this into the fire of truth. May it transform into strength and clarity."

- Burn the paper and visualize its smoke rising like liberated energy.

Symbolism:
Fire consumes and renews. What you release becomes light.

3. Walking Meditation in Sunlight

This moving meditation aligns body and spirit with the rhythm of life.
Each step fans the inner flame of motivation and confidence.

Practice:

- Walk under natural light, ideally during sunrise or sunset.
- Feel the warmth on your skin, the steadiness of your breath.
- With each step, silently affirm:
  "I walk with purpose. Each step ignites my strength."
- Let your shoulders relax, your chest open, and your breath deepen into the solar center.

This practice awakens **presence in motion**, merging mindfulness with empowerment.

4. Candle Gazing (Trataka) for Focus and Willpower

Fire refines energy — it sharpens attention and burns away distraction.
Candle gazing strengthens Manipura and awakens the subtle fire of awareness.

Practice:

- Sit in a darkened room with a candle at eye level.

- Gaze softly at the flame without blinking for several seconds, then close your eyes.
- Visualize the flame glowing at your Solar Plexus, steady and bright.
- Repeat for 5–10 minutes.

Mantra:
"My inner flame burns clear and constant."

This technique enhances concentration, determination, and intuitive clarity.

5. Mountain Connection: Grounding Fire in Form

Fire needs earth to contain it. Too much drive without grounding leads to burnout.
The mountains teach how to hold fire with stability — calm strength instead of volatility.

Practice:

- Stand tall on solid ground — mountain, hill, or firm earth.
- Inhale deeply into your belly, feeling your spine lengthen upward.
- Exhale down into your feet, anchoring your fire in the earth.
- Whisper:
  "I am grounded power. My strength supports, not consumes."

This balances ambition with patience, passion with stability.

6. The Dance of Light

Movement releases stagnant energy and awakens confidence. Dance in sunlight or by candlelight — not to perform, but to **express warmth and radiance.**

Practice:

- Put on music that feels empowering.
- Let your hips, spine, and arms move freely, as if tracing golden rays around you.
- Imagine your Solar Plexus expanding, glowing, and illuminating the space.
- End by bringing your hands to your belly, smiling softly, and whispering:
  "I am light. I am life. I am love in motion."

Affirmation for Nature Connection

"The fire within me reflects the sun above.
I burn with purpose, not anger.
I shine with steady light, transforming all I touch into gold."

Chapter 9 – Advanced Practitioner Applications

Energetic Fire, Emotional Transmutation, and Empowered Resonance

For advanced practitioners, the **Solar Plexus Chakra (Manipura)** presents one of the most potent opportunities for energetic transformation.
Where the Root establishes grounding and the Sacral teaches flow, the Solar Plexus refines both into **purposeful power** — the capacity to act with clarity, confidence, and discernment.

Mastery at this level requires fluency in **fire energy**: sensing its intensity, regulating its heat, and transmuting its burn into illumination.
To work with Manipura is to become a **keeper of sacred fire** — one who knows when to stoke, when to temper, and when to let the light simply shine.

ENERGETIC DYNAMICS OF THE SOLAR FIELD

The energy of Manipura moves like a **radiant flame** — spiraling upward in waves of warmth, expansion, and brilliance.
While the Sacral flows in curves and ripples, the Solar radiates in pulses and rays, extending from the diaphragm outward into the world.

In a client's field, this may be perceived as:

- Warmth or heat emanating from the abdomen.
- A pulsing rhythm, often synchronized with the heartbeat.
- Expansive golden light that radiates through the upper body.

When balanced, the energy feels **steady, bright, and confident** — neither dull nor consuming.
When blocked, it may appear dim or dense, accompanied by feelings of doubt, lethargy, or lack of motivation.
When overactive, it may blaze too fiercely — manifesting as irritability, dominance, anxiety, or exhaustion.

Advanced practice involves **modulating the fire** — learning to sense its temperature and bring it back into equilibrium.
You are not extinguishing the flame; you are refining its brilliance.

ENERGETIC ASSESSMENT: READING THE FIRE

Practitioners assess the Solar field by attuning to the **quality of heat and motion** around the upper abdomen.
Through Reiki scanning, intuitive sensing, or breath resonance, you can perceive subtle differences in Manipura's frequency.

Common energetic presentations include:

- **Dim Flame:** fatigue, lack of willpower, indecision, low confidence.
- **Scattered Sparks:** overextension, burnout, restlessness, mental overload.
- **Smoldering Ashes:** suppressed anger, resentment, digestive sluggishness.
- **Raging Fire:** aggression, overcontrol, perfectionism, nervous tension.

Each pattern reveals not only physical imbalance but also **the client's relationship with power** — how they claim, contain, or resist it.

From Fire to Light

In advanced energy work, emotions within Manipura are not simply released; they are **transmuted** — transformed into refined energy through conscious awareness and breath.
This process mirrors alchemy: turning the dense matter of fear or anger into the golden light of empowerment.

Protocol:

1. **Anchor the Root:** Begin by grounding the client's base energy to prevent overstimulation.
    Visualize strong red roots descending into the earth.
2. **Ignite the Solar Flame:** Move your hands to the upper abdomen.
    Visualize a golden-yellow spiral rotating clockwise, brightening with each breath.
3. **Invite Awareness:** Encourage the client to breathe into their solar center.
    Ask: *"What emotion lives here?"* — frustration, fear, uncertainty, pride.
    Do not seek to remove it; simply witness it.
4. **Channel Reiki or Light Energy:**
    As you channel, imagine the emotion glowing brighter until its sharpness softens into warmth.
    Energy may shift from dense to radiant, from agitation to calm clarity.
5. **Seal and Integrate:**
    Visualize the entire Solar region filled with golden sunlight — calm, radiant, and expansive.
    Whisper or affirm:

"All that was tension becomes strength.
All that was fear becomes light."

TANTRIC RESONANCE AND POLARITY INTEGRATION

The Solar Plexus governs the **balance of will and surrender, assertion and receptivity.**
It is the alchemical midpoint where personal power merges with divine will.

Within advanced practice, healers may harmonize two primary polarities:

- **Yang (Solar/Masculine Energy):** Focused, decisive, radiant, projective.
- **Yin (Lunar/Feminine Energy):** Receptive, cooling, reflective, intuitive.

When Yang dominates, power becomes control.
When Yin dominates, confidence wanes.
When balanced, **action and awareness move in unison —**
power guided by wisdom, energy governed by heart.

Integration Practice:
Place one hand over the Solar Plexus (will) and one over the Heart (compassion).
Breathe deeply, feeling energy flow between them — a golden current linking strength and love.
Repeat silently:
"Power guided by love is pure.
Love strengthened by power is divine."

RESONANCE PRACTICE: THE FIRE WITHIN

For advanced self-practitioners, use this energetic alignment technique to refine Manipura's brilliance.

Steps:

1. Sit upright, spine aligned, and close your eyes.
2. Inhale through the nose, drawing breath into your Solar Plexus.
3. Exhale through the mouth, visualizing golden fire spreading evenly through your body.
4. With each breath, refine the flame — from red to orange to gold to white.
5. Feel clarity, focus, and gentle warmth radiating outward from your core.

End by resting your hands over the Solar Plexus and affirming:
"I act from centered strength. My will serves the highest light."

ADVANCED INSIGHT: THE ALCHEMY OF POWER

To master Manipura is to master **transformation itself**.
This chakra refines all forms of input — food, emotion, experience — into usable life force.
Its intelligence lies in discernment: knowing what to burn, what to release, and what to illuminate.

At this level, energy healing becomes **energetic leadership**.
You no longer merely balance energy — you **embody clarity** so profoundly that your presence becomes the catalyst for transformation in others.

When your Solar Plexus radiates with harmony:

- Confidence replaces control.
- Purpose replaces striving.

- Radiance replaces resistance.

You become the calm flame —
the healer who shines, not burns.
The teacher who empowers, not dominates.
The light that illuminates, never blinds.

HANDS-ON PROTOCOLS FOR THE SOLAR PLEXUS CHAKRA & STABILIZING CLIENTS

Restoring Power, Inner Calm, and Energetic Integrity

Working hands-on with the **Solar Plexus Chakra (Manipura)**
calls for precision, presence, and deep energetic awareness.
This is the center of personal power — where confidence, will,
and identity are forged.
Here, energy transforms from emotion into action, and from
feeling into purpose.
Practitioners entering this field engage with the **fire of
transformation** — a potent force that must be tended with
respect and clarity.

When approached skillfully, the hands become instruments of
refinement — regulating excess fire, reigniting depleted power,
and restoring harmony to the luminous flame that governs
vitality and purpose.

Client Preparation and Energetic Containment

Before working directly with the Solar Plexus, establish a
grounded and stable container.
Manipura's energy can rise quickly — activating emotion, heat,
or assertive impulses.
Grounding ensures that fire becomes **focused light** rather than
scattered flame.

Begin each session by:

1. **Grounding the Space**
   - o Invite the client to take three slow, centered breaths.
   - o Affirm aloud: "You are safe, supported, and empowered in this space."
   - o Allow stillness to settle before beginning.
2. **Connecting to the Root and Sacral Centers**
   - o Begin by placing hands at the feet or base of the spine.
   - o Channel grounding energy upward through the lower chakras, preparing the field for Solar activation.
   - o This anchors Manipura's fire in stability and flow.
3. **Invoking Permission**
   - o Explain that you will be working around the upper abdomen, ribs, and mid-back — regions associated with the solar center and digestion.
   - o Confirm comfort and consent.
   - o Maintain warmth and professionalism; hovering techniques are equally effective.

This preparatory stage allows the client's system to trust the process — essential when addressing issues of control, power, and self-worth.

Hand Placements for the Solar Plexus Chakra

The Solar Plexus Chakra is located between the navel and the base of the sternum.
It radiates through the diaphragm, stomach, liver, and adrenal region — the body's energetic furnace.

Primary Positions:

1. **Front Placement (Personal Power and Confidence)**
   - Place one hand gently between the navel and sternum.
   - The second hand may rest over the heart to connect will with compassion.
   - This position harmonizes confidence with empathy, transforming power into purpose.
   - Focus on steady, rhythmic breathing to cool and stabilize the internal flame.
2. **Back Placement (Energetic Integration and Strength)**
   - Place your hands over the mid-back at the level of the diaphragm.
   - This area often stores tension from stress, fear, or suppressed anger.
   - As warmth builds beneath your palms, visualize golden light radiating outward like sunlight breaking through clouds.
3. **Side Anchors (Balancing Action and Receptivity)**
   - Rest one hand on each side of the rib cage.
   - This balances the dual aspects of Manipura — assertive will and receptive wisdom.
   - Move energy in gentle waves, sensing where heat concentrates or cools.
4. **Hovering Position (For Sensitive Clients)**
   - Hold hands 2–3 inches above the abdomen.
   - Visualize a golden orb of light expanding between your palms and the client's body.
   - See it glowing steadily — warm but not burning — symbolizing balanced power.

Energy Movement Sequence: "Flame of Clarity" Technique

This advanced sequence awakens Manipura's fire while maintaining control and calm focus.

Steps:

1. **Stabilize the Root:**
   Begin at the base of the spine or feet to ensure grounding.
   Visualize red energy anchoring deeply into the earth.
2. **Activate the Solar Flame:**
   Move to the upper abdomen and trace small clockwise spirals with your palms.
   Imagine drawing forth golden fire that flickers gently — bright, clear, contained.
3. **Breathe with the Client:**
   Synchronize your breath:
     - Inhale as the flame rises.
     - Exhale to spread warmth through the body.
       Encourage slow diaphragmatic breathing to calm nervous tension.
4. **Transmute Emotion into Empowerment:**
   If anger, anxiety, or heat arises, place one hand over the Solar Plexus and the other on the Heart.
   This channels fire upward into love, transforming intensity into illumination.
5. **Cool the Flame:**
   Visualize soft yellow light turning to gold-white — the temperature of inner peace.
   End by placing hands on the knees or feet to return excess energy to the earth.

Signs of Activation and Release

During Solar Plexus work, clients may experience sensations such as:

- A gentle or rising heat through the abdomen or chest.
- Spontaneous deep breathing or sighs of relief.
- Tingling or warmth radiating through the spine or arms.

- Emotional expression — laughter, empowerment, tears, or clarity.
- A renewed sense of motivation or mental sharpness.

Practitioner Note:
Maintain neutrality and compassion.
Power, like fire, refines when witnessed without judgment.
Your calm presence allows transformation to occur safely.

Stabilizing Clients After Solar Activation

Following Manipura activation, clients may feel exhilarated or emotionally charged.
Grounding and cooling techniques are essential to integrate the new frequency.

Stabilization Steps:

1. **Return to the Root:**
   - Place hands at the feet or base of spine.
   - Channel cool, grounding energy until the body feels calm and stable.
2. **Cooling the Fire:**
   - Move one hand to the Heart and one to the Solar Plexus.
   - Visualize the light shifting from bright yellow to soft gold.
   - Guide slow, steady breathing: *inhale strength, exhale calm.*
3. **Energetic Sealing:**
   - Sweep your hands from crown to feet, smoothing the aura.
   - Affirm softly:
     "Your power is balanced.
     Your light shines with peace and purpose."
4. **Hydration and Nourishment:**

- o Encourage clients to drink water, herbal tea (such as chamomile or peppermint), or eat grounding foods after the session.
- o Suggest gentle movement, such as stretching or walking, to harmonize energy flow.

Advanced Reiki Integration

For Reiki Masters and energy practitioners, Solar Plexus work benefits from deliberate symbol integration:

- **Cho Ku Rei (Power Symbol):**
  Strengthens the internal fire and restores balanced confidence.
- **Sei He Ki (Harmony Symbol):**
  Cools excess emotion, transforming reaction into calm discernment.
- **Dai Ko Myo (Master Symbol):**
  Invokes spiritual illumination — converting willpower into divine purpose.

Visualize these symbols as golden glyphs revolving within the Solar Plexus — refining, harmonizing, and radiating outward in perfect equilibrium.

Practitioner Awareness

Manipura reflects the healer's own relationship with **power, ego, and control.**
If your client's energy feels overwhelming or your own center tightens, pause and breathe.
Draw awareness back to your Root.
Remember: **you guide the fire by embodying calm flame.**

Your mastery lies not in dominance but in radiance —
in allowing strength to express through serenity.

When the healer's fire burns steady,
the client's flame remembers how to shine.

Energetic Ethics and Boundaries for Practitioners Working with the Solar Plexus Chakra

Holding Safe Space for Power, Confidence, and Transformation

The **Solar Plexus Chakra — Manipura** — governs willpower, personal authority, and energetic transformation.
Because it regulates identity and power dynamics, it is one of the most crucial centers for practitioners to approach with humility, ethics, and discernment.

Here, energy is refined from raw emotion into empowered direction. Clients come into contact with their deepest fears of inadequacy, control, or failure — as well as their hidden reservoirs of courage and strength.
To work with Manipura is to stand beside another's **inner fire**, ensuring it burns bright without consuming.

Working in this chakra demands energetic clarity and ethical strength.
The practitioner must embody both compassion and neutrality — serving as a **mirror of centered power**, not a source of dominance or persuasion.
Healing here is not about empowering someone for them, but guiding them to **reclaim their own authority** in a balanced and sacred way.

The Foundation of Energetic Integrity

Before addressing another's Solar Plexus, practitioners must examine their own relationship with **power, ego, and control.** This is not merely a technical practice but an energetic initiation — every interaction with Manipura reveals one's inner alignment with humility and purpose.

Ask yourself before each session:

- Am I acting from confidence or from the need to prove myself?
- Do I feel clear, centered, and free from judgment or pride?
- Can I guide transformation without trying to control its outcome?

If the answer to any of these is uncertain, pause.
Ground yourself. Breathe into your center.
Your inner equilibrium defines the ethical integrity of the healing space.

"The healer's steadiness becomes the flame by which others learn to burn without fear."

Creating Safety Through Consent and Communication

Because the Solar Plexus governs self-esteem and personal autonomy, the **tone of interaction** between practitioner and client is paramount.
Every instruction, gesture, or silence carries energetic influence.
Consent here is not only physical — it is **energetic permission** for empowerment.

Best Practices:

1. **Empower Through Dialogue:**
   - Clearly explain what the session involves — especially if you will work around the upper abdomen, diaphragm, or back.
   - Reinforce that the client retains full agency throughout the process.
   - Use language of empowerment, not authority: *"You are in charge of your healing process."*
2. **Gain Informed Consent:**
   - Invite verbal or written acknowledgment before each new technique.
   - Encourage clients to voice preferences or limits without hesitation.
   - Respect any request to pause or redirect energy at once.
3. **Observe Energetic Boundaries:**
   - Pay attention to posture, tone, or subtle cues that may signal emotional resistance or discomfort.
   - Meet these with patience and understanding, not persuasion.
   - When in doubt, choose stillness and breath over action.

Maintaining Energetic Boundaries

Manipura governs **personal power and boundaries** — both physical and energetic.
Because its element is fire, uncontained energy can lead to burnout, dominance, or conflict.
Boundaries here act as sacred vessels — structures that hold fire without suppression.

To maintain ethical energetic boundaries:

- Anchor firmly in your **Root Chakra** before every session.
- Visualize a golden field of light around your Solar Plexus — radiant yet contained, strong yet gentle.
- Set the internal command: *"Power flows through me, not from me."*
- After each session, clear residual energy through breathwork, nature, or intentional grounding practices.

Boundaries are the geometry of light. They protect integrity without dimming compassion.

Recognizing Power Dynamics in Healing Work

Working with Manipura means entering a space where **authority, validation, and confidence** can easily become entangled.
Both client and practitioner bring unconscious patterns around power — control, submission, leadership, or dependency.
Ethical awareness prevents misuse of influence and ensures empowerment remains the goal.

Practitioner Guidance:

- Stay rooted in humility. Healing is facilitation, not dominance.
- Avoid promises of transformation or authority over another's process.
- When offering intuitive insights, present them as invitations for reflection, not directives.
- If the client projects admiration or dependency, gently redirect them to their own inner power:
  "The wisdom you feel from me is a reflection of what already lives within you."

Energetic Entanglement and Projection

Manipura amplifies energy exchange — it is the chakra through which we send and receive will.
Without self-awareness, subtle cords of control, judgment, or expectation can form between healer and client.

Signs of entanglement may include:

- Feeling drained, restless, or emotionally charged after sessions.
- A desire to "fix" or "save" the client.
- The client seeking approval, direction, or validation beyond the session.

Response:

- Pause and breathe into your own center.
- Affirm silently: *"I honor your power and release all cords not of pure light."*
- Visualize golden fire purifying the connection between you and the client.
- If persistent, seek supervision, peer dialogue, or refer the client to another professional.

Energetic ethics demand that compassion be balanced with **detachment born of respect.**

Working with Emotional or Will-Based Release

During Solar Plexus activation, clients may experience strong emotional reactions — bursts of anger, tears, or laughter.
These expressions are not failures of control; they are the **fire of transformation,** releasing old imprints of shame or suppression.

Practitioner Approach:

- Stay calm, grounded, and nonreactive.
- Allow expression without judgment; energy burns clean when witnessed in safety.
- If intensity rises, place your hands on the client's hips or feet to draw the energy downward and stabilize.
- Encourage slow, steady breathing to regulate the nervous system.

Never suppress or magnify the release — simply **contain the fire** until it softens to warmth.

Transference, Ego, and the Temptation of Power

Because Manipura governs personal authority, both practitioner and client may experience **ego activation** — subtle tests of humility and integrity.
This may manifest as feelings of superiority, pride in "results," or the desire to control outcomes.

Awareness Practice:

- Observe your motivation before and during each session.
- Ask: *"Am I empowering or impressing?"*
- Maintain transparency and honesty in communication.
- If you sense energetic or emotional transference, return focus to the Root and Heart chakras for grounding and compassion.

Power in its purest form is service. True mastery shines quietly.

Post-Session Integration and Aftercare

Solar Plexus work can awaken deep realizations about purpose, confidence, or self-worth.

Clients may leave feeling lighter, inspired, or occasionally overstimulated.
Gentle integration ensures their new empowerment stabilizes into balanced strength.

Offer these aftercare suggestions:

- Drink water to cool and ground the fire element.
- Eat warm, nourishing meals to anchor energy in the body.
- Journal on the question: *"Where do I give away or misuse my power?"*
- Rest, breathe, or spend time in natural sunlight to harmonize the solar field.

Closing Affirmation:
"You are centered in your power.
Your light is steady and wise.
You act with strength and compassion."

The Sacred Duty of the Practitioner

To work with the Solar Plexus Chakra is to **walk beside the inner fire of humanity** — the power to choose, to create, and to transform.
Your role is not to command this flame but to protect its purity — to keep it burning with purpose, never pride.

True mastery is the art of **presence without dominance** — of igniting strength in others without needing to claim the source.
When ethics and awareness unite, the healing space becomes luminous —
a forge where both practitioner and client are refined in the same fire of awakening.

"The healer's light does not overpower — it illuminates.
When one flame burns steady, it teaches all others how to
shine."

THE ROLE OF MANIPURA IN REMOTE HEALING

Channeling Power, Intention, and Energetic Direction Across Distance

While the Sacral Chakra carries the emotional current of
connection, the **Solar Plexus Chakra (Manipura)** governs the
transmission of focused energy and intention — the fire that
gives direction, clarity, and vitality to distant healing.
In remote or distant work, Manipura becomes the radiant sun at
the center of the practitioner's field — the energetic engine that
propels healing light across space and time.

Where the Sacral feels, the Solar Plexus **directs**.
Where emotion flows, intention ignites.
It is through Manipura that the practitioner learns to send
energy with precision and strength — not through effort, but
through alignment with inner will.

Energy Beyond Physical Contact

In distant healing, the absence of physical proximity places
greater emphasis on the **power of focus and intention.**
The Solar Plexus is the seat of **energetic projection**,
transforming inner conviction into radiant output.

Manipura governs our ability to act from clarity — to send,
direct, and stabilize energy without distortion.
When the practitioner attunes to a client remotely, this chakra
becomes the transmitter — radiating energy outward in
coherent waves of light and will.

Through the **Solar Plexus**, the healer projects confidence, direction, and healing fire.
Through the **Heart**, this power is tempered with compassion.
Together, they form the energetic balance that makes distance work both **effective and ethical**.

How Manipura Functions in Remote Sessions

The Solar Plexus acts like a **spiritual command center**, regulating the quality, strength, and precision of the energy transmitted during a session.
When the practitioner's Manipura is balanced, energy flows as focused rays of golden light — clear, empowered, and unwavering.

Practitioners may experience:

- A steady warmth or gentle heat radiating from the upper abdomen.
- Pulsations or expansion in the solar area as energy begins to move outward.
- A sense of heightened clarity or focus, as though light is emanating from within.
- Subtle awareness of the client's vitality level — not as emotion, but as energetic brightness or density.

These perceptions are not mental constructs or imagination; they are the energetic "language" of will.
The healer does not control this flow — they **align with it**, becoming the conduit through which divine will and universal life force move.

"In distant healing, intention becomes light — traveling not through space, but through resonance."

Establishing Connection Through Intention and Focus

To work effectively with Manipura in remote healing, practitioners must cultivate **focused presence** — the fire of attention without the heat of control.
This balance ensures that energy is both powerful and pure.

Preparation Practice:

1. **Ground Through the Root:**
    Visualize deep red roots anchoring into the earth.
    This grounds your fire, ensuring stability and safety.
2. **Activate the Inner Sun:**
    Bring awareness to your Solar Plexus, two inches above the navel.
    Visualize a radiant golden sun expanding gently within, glowing brighter with each breath.
3. **Set the Intention:**
    Silently affirm:
    "Energy flows through me, guided by divine intelligence.
    I direct healing light with clarity, compassion, and purpose."
4. **Link to the Client:**
    Visualize the client surrounded by golden light.
    From your solar center, send a gentle ray — not a beam of control, but a bridge of illumination — connecting your inner light to theirs.
5. **Sustain the Flow:**
    Maintain awareness of your breath and heart.
    Allow energy to radiate naturally — not forced, but continuous, like sunlight shining through open space.

Maintaining Energetic Clarity and Detachment

Because Manipura channels **willpower and projection**, practitioners must take care not to impose personal will or outcome on the client's process.

In remote work, this fine distinction — between intention and control — defines the ethics of true healing.

To maintain purity of transmission:

- Visualize your energy as **golden light**, not fiery heat.
- Repeat silently: *"I send light, not opinion. I guide, not command."*
- Stay connected to your **Heart Chakra**, ensuring that every transmission arises from compassion, not ego.
- After the session, consciously **release all energetic cords** and return to stillness.

This maintains your integrity as a clear transmitter of divine energy rather than a personal force.

Balancing Power and Sensitivity in Distance Work

The Solar Plexus gives strength to the current of healing, but it must always be balanced by the cooling waters of emotion and empathy from the lower centers.

Too much fire leads to exhaustion or energetic burnout; too little, and the current lacks focus.

Practitioners can balance Manipura during remote sessions by:

- Pairing each directed breath (fire) with conscious release (water).
- Alternating between visualization of **gold light** (strength) and **silver light** (calm).
- Concluding with grounding in the Root or Heart to harmonize power and peace.

Through this rhythmic exchange, the healer sustains both **vitality and serenity**, allowing healing to move efficiently across distance.

The Ethics of Empowered Intention

The Solar Plexus Chakra demands impeccable energetic ethics.
Its fire can heal, but when unchecked, it can dominate or
overwhelm.
True practitioners understand that **light must illuminate, not
control.**

Always remember:

- Intention must serve, not dictate.
- Energy should empower, not impress.
- Manipura's purpose is not to command others' energy
  but to awaken their own inner flame.

When this is honored, distance healing becomes **a communion
of light** — a shared act of will aligned with higher purpose.

Closing Reflection

The Solar Plexus in remote healing is the **sun that never sets**
— radiant, constant, unwavering.
It teaches that distance is not an obstacle but an illusion; the
light of intention transcends all boundaries.

When your inner fire burns steady and your heart remains open,
your presence becomes luminous across time and space.
You are no longer merely sending energy —
you are **being** energy.

**"The healer's light travels not through distance, but
through resonance —
where one steady flame kindles another across the unseen."**

SOLAR PLEXUS TECHNIQUES FOR REMOTE HEALING

While each practitioner refines their own unique approach, certain techniques align especially well with **Manipura's radiant, focused nature.**
Where the Sacral Chakra heals through flow, the Solar Plexus heals through **illumination and precision** — cutting through confusion, dissolving fear, and restoring confidence and vitality across distance.

1. Visualization of Golden Light Projection

Visualize a **sun of golden light** glowing within your Solar Plexus.
From this inner sun, a **beam of radiant energy** extends toward the client — not as force, but as illumination.
This golden current carries **strength, clarity, and empowerment**, dispersing fear or self-doubt in its path.

As it connects, repeat silently:

"I send the light of confidence and peace.
The flame of power burns steady within us both."

The beam expands into a sphere, enveloping both practitioner and client in a shared field of balanced, luminous energy.

2. Intention Transmission through Breath and Will

Manipura governs **will and directed focus.**
To transmit healing across distance, synchronize breath with intention:

1. Inhale to draw energy from the earth and Source into your center.

2. Exhale through the Solar Plexus, sending focused intention outward — like sunlight radiating from your core.
3. Sense the client receiving not your energy, but the **frequency of empowerment and restoration.**

You may notice gentle warmth or pressure in the upper abdomen as energy aligns.
Let the current remain steady and compassionate, avoiding any sense of pushing or forcing.
It is light, not dominance, that heals.

3. Fire-to-Light Transmutation

If the client's field feels heavy, confused, or emotionally charged, work with **fire as the alchemical element of transformation.**

Visualize golden flames surrounding both your Solar Plexus and the client's energetic core.
These flames are cool, intelligent, and purifying — burning away fear, inertia, or shame while leaving clarity in their wake.
Whisper inwardly:

"What was fear becomes light.
What was burden becomes purpose."

This method clears energetic residue and rekindles the will to act, evolve, and trust one's own power.

4. The Mirror of Empowerment

Because Manipura transmits **confidence and self-trust**, one of the most powerful distant-healing techniques is **energetic mirroring.**
Visualize yourself and the client standing in identical light — both radiating equally, both sovereign in strength.

This reminds the soul that no healer gives power; they simply **reflect it back** until it is remembered.

Intend mutual activation, not dependence:

"Your light shines as brightly as mine.
Together, we remember the fire within."

Balancing The Practitioner's Energy After Sessions

Working through the Solar Plexus amplifies willpower and energetic projection.

Without conscious closure, practitioners may feel overstimulated, restless, or mentally fatigued after distance work.

To restore equilibrium, you must **cool the fire** and **return to center.**

After the session:

1. Visualize the golden ray retracting softly, returning all energy to its Source in gratitude.
2. Place both hands over your Solar Plexus and take three deep, cooling breaths.
3. Affirm:

   "All light returns purified to the Source.
   My energy is calm, clear, and complete."

4. Visualize cool blue or white light enveloping your abdomen, bringing balance to the inner flame.
5. Finally, ground through your feet — imagine roots drawing nourishing earth energy upward, tempering fire with stability.

This restores clarity, prevents energy depletion, and ensures that the Solar current remains **radiant but contained.**

THE GIFT OF SOLAR CONNECTION IN REMOTE HEALING

In distant work, the Solar Plexus Chakra teaches one of the greatest truths of energy mastery:
that empowerment transcends presence.
Confidence, purpose, and vitality are frequencies that can be transmitted across any distance through focused will and integrity.

Through Manipura, the practitioner learns:

- To project energy with intention, not control.
- To transmit strength through clarity, not force.
- To embody the principle of true leadership — power in service of illumination.

In the realm of remote healing, the Solar Plexus reveals that all distance is illusion.
When the inner sun shines without attachment, its light travels effortlessly — restoring others not by what it sends, but by
what it awakens.

"When the healer's light burns steady,
distance dissolves — and all beings remember the fire within."

Clearing Ancestral Fear and Karmic Imprints

Releasing Patterns of Control, Shame, and Powerlessness to Restore Inner Strength and Purpose

Just as the Root Chakra carries the memory of physical survival and the Sacral holds the memory of emotion, the **Solar Plexus Chakra (Manipura)** stores the energetic patterns of **personal**

power, courage, and self-worth inherited from our ancestors.
It is the fire that defines how we act, assert, and believe in our
right to exist — and it is often dimmed by generations of fear,
suppression, or misuse of will.

Where Muladhara holds the fear of not surviving, and
Svadhisthana holds the fear of feeling, **Manipura holds the
fear of being seen, heard, or powerful.**
These ancestral and karmic imprints influence how we express
leadership, confidence, and purpose — shaping our capacity to
trust our inner fire.

Inherited Patterns of Power and Fear

Every lineage carries energetic memories about strength,
success, and self-expression.
Families who have endured persecution, poverty, repression, or
domination often pass down unspoken beliefs such as:

- "It's dangerous to stand out or succeed."
- "Better to stay small than to be judged."
- "Power corrupts — humility means silence."
- "Speaking truth brings conflict or rejection."

These patterns may manifest as chronic self-doubt, fear of
failure, or guilt about ambition.
They are not personal flaws but **ancestral codes of survival** —
the fire once suppressed to keep generations safe.
When left unhealed, they continue to dim the individual's
radiance, preventing the full embodiment of soul purpose.

"The fire you fear was once the fire that protected your
ancestors.
Now it asks to be reclaimed — purified, not extinguished."

Karmic Patterns of Power and Will

Karma in the Solar Plexus is not punishment; it is **unfinished mastery of will.**
Across lifetimes, souls experience both sides of the spectrum — domination and submission, misuse of power and fear of it.
Manipura is where these lessons converge for integration.

Recurring patterns such as:

- Giving away authority to others.
- Attracting controlling or dismissive relationships.
- Struggling with procrastination or lack of motivation.
- Feeling unseen despite effort and talent.
- Alternating between overdrive and burnout.

These are not failures but **initiations** — opportunities to transmute fear into strength, and control into conscious leadership.
Through this fire, the ego is refined, not destroyed — becoming a vessel of divine will rather than personal force.

Recognizing Signs of Ancestral and Karmic Imprints in Manipura

When ancestral fear or karmic lessons are stored in the Solar Plexus, they often express as:

- Chronic insecurity or imposter syndrome.
- Fear of conflict, visibility, or responsibility.
- Digestive issues, adrenal fatigue, or tension in the solar region.
- People-pleasing or overcompensation through work and achievement.
- Difficulty making decisions or trusting intuition.
- Sudden bursts of anger, frustration, or guilt around power dynamics.

These symptoms reflect the **body's memory of suppression** — the times when courage was punished, will was broken, or voice was silenced.

Healing these imprints allows the inner flame to rise again, steady and sovereign.

PRACTICES FOR CLEARING ANCESTRAL FEAR AND POWER KARMA

1. Fire Ritual of Release

Since Manipura is governed by the element of fire, this ritual transforms ancestral fear into light.

- Write down beliefs or patterns you wish to release — e.g., "I fear success," "I must shrink to be safe."
- Place the paper in a safe fireproof bowl or outdoor fire.
- As it burns, visualize golden flames consuming the energy behind the words, rising upward as light.
- Whisper:

  "I release what is not mine to carry.
  I reclaim the courage of my lineage in purity and strength."

Allow the smoke to symbolize freedom — the return of all suppressed will to divine truth.

2. Reiki or Energy Clearing

During energy work, focus on the upper abdomen and diaphragm.

Visualize **bright golden light** expanding outward, dissolving cords of fear or ancestral authority that suppress confidence.

Channel Reiki or light codes to harmonize the solar field, balancing humility with empowerment.

Affirm:

"Power flows through me, not from me.
I lead with integrity and light."

3. Breath of Empowerment (Agni Prana)

Breath awakens Manipura's inner flame and clears karmic
residue through oxygen and focus.

- Sit upright and place your hands over your navel.
- Inhale deeply into the Solar Plexus; exhale forcefully
  through the nose or mouth.
- Repeat rhythmically for 1–3 minutes, feeling energy
  ignite at your core.
- Visualize stagnant energy lifting as smoke from the fire.

End by breathing gently, letting the flame burn warm and calm
— a symbol of balanced will.

4. Lineage Visualization and Forgiveness Meditation

Close your eyes and imagine your ancestors standing behind
you, hands on your shoulders.
They represent both your heritage and your inherited fears.

Silently affirm:

"I honor your survival.
I release your fear.
I now choose to live in strength, integrity, and love."

Feel the golden light of your Solar Plexus radiate backward
through time — healing those who came before you, freeing
both them and yourself.

5. Creative Reclamation of Will

Transform old family patterns by taking action that your lineage avoided — speak truth, share art, set boundaries, or step into leadership.
Each act of courageous self-expression rewrites your ancestral code.

Creation is fire given form.
Every empowered choice becomes an offering to the ancestors — proof that fear has become wisdom.

THE FIRE RESTORED

When ancestral fear and karmic shame are cleared, the Solar Plexus shines as it was meant to — **a steady sun of courage and clarity.**

Confidence no longer feels like arrogance.
Action arises naturally from alignment.
You no longer carry the fear of being seen, judged, or punished for your light.

You remember that strength is sacred when guided by love.
You become a living flame of integrity — transforming the inherited shadow of fear into luminous self-mastery.

"The ancestors once hid their fire to survive.
You are the one who keeps it burning —
not in defiance, but in grace."

RELEASING POWER CORDS AND RESTORING
PERSONAL SOVEREIGNTY

Returning to Wholeness Through Conscious Empowerment and Inner Fire

The **Solar Plexus Chakra (Manipura)** is the seat of personal power — the energetic forge of will, confidence, and purposeful action.
Through this center, we connect to others in the dynamic exchange of influence, responsibility, and authority. Every interaction — with family, mentors, leaders, lovers, or institutions — leaves an energetic impression.

Where the **Sacral Chakra bonds through emotion**, Manipura bonds through **power and purpose**.
Healthy connections inspire mutual strength. But when power cords become distorted by fear, control, obligation, or domination, they begin to drain vitality and dim the inner fire.
Healing here is not about isolation, but alignment — learning to share energy through integrity rather than dependency or submission.

Understanding Power Cords

Energetic cords form whenever there is a **transfer of will or influence** between souls.
Some cords uplift — shared visions, mutual respect, healthy mentorships.
Others bind — when one's fire is used to fuel another's fear or authority.

In Manipura, these cords may appear as **threads of golden light** connecting the upper abdomen to others.
When balanced, the exchange is empowering — energy circulates freely between equals.
When distorted, the current becomes one-sided: giving without replenishment, leading to fatigue, resentment, or loss of direction.

Common examples of draining power cords:

- Feeling responsible for others' happiness or success.
- Giving away authority to teachers, leaders, or systems.
- Staying small to avoid conflict or judgment.
- Needing validation before making choices.
- Being pulled into others' crises or emotional storms.

These cords anchor themselves in the Solar Plexus because it governs **will, identity, and personal direction.**
Releasing them restores energetic sovereignty — the ability to act from inner truth rather than inherited obligation.

Recognizing Signs of Power Entanglement

When Manipura is enmeshed with others' energy, you may experience:

- Sudden fatigue after conversations or sessions.
- Indecision, confusion, or a sense of being "pulled" in multiple directions.
- Digestive discomfort or tightness in the upper abdomen.
- Chronic self-doubt or over-dependence on others' opinions.
- A recurring pattern of giving more than you receive.

These are not failures — they are invitations to **reclaim the fire of discernment** and restore balance between serving and self-honoring.

Energetic Anatomy of Empowered Detachment

True detachment is not withdrawal; it is **alignment without entanglement.**
It is the art of standing fully in your own light while allowing others to stand in theirs.

In the Solar Plexus, detachment means no longer surrendering your will to fear, guilt, or manipulation.

Energetic sovereignty does not come from walls but from **clarity** — knowing where your energy ends and another's begins.
In this space, love remains, but control dissolves. Power is shared, not stolen.

When cords dissolve:

- Clarity replaces confusion.
- Strength replaces obligation.
- Purpose burns bright again.

Through awareness and compassion, what once felt like domination or depletion becomes an act of liberation — for both souls.

RELEASING POWER CORDS PRACTICE

(To be performed with neutrality and compassion, never anger or resistance.)

1. Prepare the Space

Sit comfortably.
Place your hands on your Solar Plexus — the area above the navel, below the sternum.
Take several deep breaths, inhaling confidence, exhaling tension.
Visualize a warm golden sun glowing in your abdomen — radiant, steady, and strong.

2. Identify the Connection

Bring to mind a person, system, or situation that feels energetically draining or controlling.
Without judgment, sense where this connection lives in your body — perhaps a golden cord extending from your Solar Plexus outward.

3. Call in Light and Awareness

Visualize a column of golden fire descending from Source above, meeting your inner sun.
Whisper silently:

"Only wisdom and strength remain.
All else returns to divine neutrality."

4. Dissolve the Cord with Fire

Rather than cutting or tearing, imagine the cord transforming in light — dissolving like mist in the sun's warmth.
Feel energy returning to its rightful source, cleansed of fear or control.
As the bond releases, both you and the other are freed — luminous, sovereign, complete.

5. Seal and Empower

Visualize your Solar Plexus glowing brighter, spinning freely in perfect balance.
Whisper:
"My will is my own.
My energy is clear.
I lead with integrity and light."

Sit in this radiance until you feel calm and centered.
You may notice warmth spreading through your torso — the
sign of Manipura's restored flow.

The Return of Personal Sovereignty

As power cords dissolve, the energy once scattered in worry or
obligation returns to your center.
You feel decisive, grounded, capable — no longer seeking
permission to shine.
The Solar Plexus becomes what it was always meant to be: a
sun of self-trust, radiating strength from within rather than
reflecting borrowed light.

You begin to act not from reaction, but from vision.
You no longer give power away — you **share it consciously.**
Your fire warms without burning, guides without controlling.

This is the true essence of Solar healing:
To stand in your own authority while honoring the autonomy of
all beings.
To lead from luminosity, not dominance.
To shine because it is your nature, not your defense.

"When I reclaim my fire, I illuminate the world.
When I release control, I become power in motion.
When I stand in my light, others remember their own."

CROSS-REFERENCING WITH TCM MERIDIANS: STOMACH AND SPLEEN

The Fire of Transformation and the Alchemy of Power

The **Solar Plexus Chakra (Manipura)** corresponds
energetically with the **Fire and Earth dynamics** within
Traditional Chinese Medicine (TCM), especially as expressed
through the **Stomach and Spleen meridians.**

Both systems describe this region of the body as the **center of transformation** — where energy is digested, refined, and directed into life force.

Where the Sacral governs flow and movement, the Solar Plexus governs **metabolism and mastery** — the ability to transform input (food, emotion, experience) into vitality, confidence, and purpose.

In both TCM and yogic systems, this center determines how well we "digest life."

When balanced, we feel capable, clear, and powerful.

When imbalanced, energy stagnates — manifesting as worry, fatigue, or difficulty asserting boundaries.

STOMACH MERIDIAN – ASSIMILATION AND PERSONAL POWER

In TCM, the **Stomach** is called the *"Sea of Nourishment."* It receives, processes, and distributes energy from food — both physical and emotional — providing the foundation for qi (vital energy).

Likewise, Manipura governs the **metabolic fire (Agni)** that digests life experience.

When this fire is balanced, we assimilate lessons, emotions, and nourishment with ease, transforming them into confidence and wisdom.

When weak, we feel drained, indecisive, or overly dependent on external validation.

When Stomach Qi Is Balanced:

- You feel centered and self-assured.
- Digestion (literal and metaphorical) is strong.
- You maintain healthy motivation and enthusiasm for life.

When Imbalanced:

- Digestive discomfort, nausea, or bloating.
- Overthinking or "rumination" that depletes mental energy.
- Feeling "stuck" or powerless to move forward.

Balancing Techniques

- Practice **solar breathing**: inhale into the upper abdomen, exhale through the mouth to release worry.
- Apply gentle Reiki or heat to the stomach region to stimulate digestive and emotional metabolism.
- Eat warm, cooked foods and avoid excessive cold or raw items that weaken inner fire.

Affirmation:

"I digest life with clarity and strength.
My inner fire transforms experience into purpose."

SPLEEN MERIDIAN – INTEGRATION AND STABILITY

The **Spleen** in TCM transforms and transports the essence extracted by the Stomach, distributing nourishment throughout the body and spirit.
Energetically, it represents **trust in one's own capacity** — the ability to rely on inner strength rather than external reassurance.
Just as the Solar Plexus integrates experience into identity, the Spleen integrates nourishment into qi and confidence.

When the Spleen's energy (Spleen Qi) is strong, you feel capable of sustaining effort without exhaustion.
When weakened, overthinking, worry, or self-doubt consume the fire meant for action.

Signs of Spleen Qi Deficiency:

- Fatigue, muscle weakness, or sugar cravings.
- Lack of focus or chronic worry.
- Feeling unsupported, unstable, or emotionally "ungrounded."

Balancing Techniques

- **Abdominal massage** or acupressure along the Spleen meridian (inside of the legs) to strengthen digestion and personal power.
- **Mindful eating** — chew slowly, breathe between bites, and eat with gratitude to anchor awareness in the body.
- Incorporate **yellow and golden foods** (corn, millet, ginger, turmeric, squash) to harmonize with Manipura's frequency.

Affirmation:

"I am nourished by trust and stability.
I draw strength from the center of my being."

THE FIRE ELEMENT: THE ESSENCE OF TRANSFORMATION

The Fire Element, expressed through the Solar Plexus and TCM's digestive meridians, is the **engine of evolution.**
It transforms nourishment into energy, thought into will, and emotion into action.
When this inner fire is balanced, you feel radiant, decisive, and courageous — neither aggressive nor submissive, but empowered through alignment.

When it weakens, fear and inertia dim the flame.
When it flares excessively, anger, control, or burnout may arise.

Balance is achieved through steady transformation — the sacred alchemy of turning life's raw material into luminous purpose.

Solar–Fire Integration Practice

1. Sit comfortably and bring your awareness to your upper abdomen.
2. Visualize a **golden flame** glowing within, steady and strong.
3. As you breathe, imagine the flame digesting any tension, doubt, or fear — transforming it into clear light.
4. With each exhale, feel this light expanding through your body, infusing every cell with confidence and vitality.

Affirmation:

"I am the fire of transformation.
I digest life with ease and radiate strength from within."

FLOW SYNCHRONIZATION: ALIGNING PRACTITIONER AND CLIENT IN THE FIELD OF EMPOWERMENT

Energetic Coherence, Confidence Transmission, and the Radiance of Shared Will

When working with the **Solar Plexus Chakra (Manipura)**, the practitioner's personal vibration of confidence, clarity, and inner stability profoundly affects the client.
This chakra governs **personal power, will, and energetic metabolism** — it entrains to the vibrational frequency of focus and strength.

If the practitioner stands firm in centered authority, the client's energy begins to mirror that steadiness, reigniting their own internal fire.
However, if the practitioner feels uncertain, anxious, or

energetically scattered, that instability can unintentionally ripple into the session — weakening the field of empowerment.

Synchronization at the Solar Plexus level is therefore an **alignment of intent and frequency**, not emotion — a steady, luminous resonance between practitioner and client that awakens courage, purpose, and energetic discipline.

Why Synchronization Matters

- **Energetic Coherence:**
  Manipura responds to consistency and focus. When practitioner and client share a stable frequency of purpose, the nervous system relaxes and the energy field becomes organized, allowing deep release and empowerment.
- **Confidence Transmission:**
  The Solar Plexus learns through resonance. A practitioner embodying self-trust naturally radiates that vibration, helping the client rediscover their own authority and self-belief.
- **Restoration of Will:**
  Synchronization prevents energetic domination or depletion. When both fields are harmonized, energy circulates freely — supporting empowerment without competition or control.

Practitioner Preparation

1. Center in Your Power Field

Before beginning, place one hand on your upper abdomen. Breathe slowly into this area until you feel warmth behind your navel.
Visualize a golden sun expanding with each breath.
Silently affirm:

"I am centered in my strength.
I radiate calm, balanced power."

2. Clarity Check-In

Ask yourself:

- Am I acting from calm authority or striving to control the outcome?
- Is my intention aligned with the client's highest good?
- Can I hold focus without attachment?
  Release any tension or ego-driven motivation through a few cleansing breaths.

3. Set the Intention

As you prepare for the session, state inwardly:

"May this space radiate confidence, clarity, and divine will.
May strength flow in harmony between practitioner and client."

Synchronization Techniques

1. Shared Solar Breathing

- Invite the client to place a hand over their Solar Plexus.
- Inhale together for 4 counts, feeling the abdomen expand; exhale for 4 counts, releasing tension.
- Imagine the breath feeding a shared flame of calm empowerment between you.
- Continue until both breathing patterns align naturally.

2. Resonance Mirroring

- Sense the rhythm of the client's energy field — perhaps fast, diffuse, or sluggish.

- Subtly attune your own breath and focus to their pace, then gradually slow and stabilize your rhythm.
- This gently guides the client's energy into coherence, allowing Manipura to harmonize without resistance.

3. Energetic Linking

- Visualize a **golden ray of light** connecting your Solar Plexus to the client's.
- See both centers glowing like twin suns, pulsing in rhythm.
- Allow this ray to balance and strengthen, radiating mutual trust and grounded vitality.

4. Closing Synchronization

- Toward the end, imagine both golden suns shining brightly and evenly.
- With gratitude, allow the connecting ray to dissolve into pure light, leaving both fields radiant and independent.
- Invite the client to breathe deeply and sense the warmth in their abdomen — the rekindled fire of personal power.

Key Considerations

- **Boundaries with Strength:**
  Solar synchronization is about clarity, not control. Maintain awareness of your own energetic perimeter. You share light, not force.
- **Presence Over Performance:**
  Clients feel your conviction more than your technique. The steadiness of your inner sun creates safety and trust — the foundation of transformation.
- **Integration Practices:**
  After the session, encourage the client to ground their new energy:

- o Journaling insights on confidence and self-trust.
- o Gentle core exercises or mindful movement.
- o Sitting in sunlight or candlelight for continued connection to fire energy.

Practitioner's Affirmation Before Synchronization

"I am steady, radiant, and calm.
My presence empowers, not overpowers.
Through clarity and will, I invite balance and strength."

Practitioner Energy Hygiene After Solar Work

Working with the Solar Plexus engages the energetic centers of confidence, will, and transformation — both yours and the client's.
Because Manipura is the engine of motivation, it can easily absorb remnants of others' fear, frustration, or ambition.
Maintaining energy hygiene ensures your inner flame stays bright and pure rather than becoming overloaded or depleted.

After each session:

- Stand upright, feet grounded.
- Sweep your hands over your abdomen and solar region, brushing away residual energy.
- Visualize your inner fire clearing itself — a golden blaze burning away what is not yours.
- Drink water or herbal tea to cool and stabilize the body.
- Take a few moments in sunlight or candlelight, reaffirming:

  "All energy returns to its rightful place.
  My fire is steady, my purpose clear."

When practitioner and client resonate in Solar alignment, healing becomes an act of empowerment rather than release — a remembering of inner authority through shared luminosity.

"When my fire burns steady, others remember their light. When I stand in power, I awaken power in all I serve."

WHY ENERGY HYGIENE MATTERS

• **Energetic Boundaries:**
The **Solar Plexus Chakra** governs will and personal power. Without conscious clearing, practitioners may unconsciously absorb clients' anxiety, fear, or overexertion — dulling their inner fire or distorting their sense of purpose.

• **Fire Balance:**
Excess Solar energy can cause irritability, overconfidence, or burnout, while depletion manifests as fatigue, self-doubt, or indecision.
Maintaining balance ensures your power remains steady — strong yet compassionate.

• **Professional Longevity:**
Consistent energetic hygiene keeps the practitioner's field clear, preserving focus and vitality over years of service.
It prevents "compassion fatigue" and supports sustained confidence, clarity, and presence in each session.

POST-SESSION RESET PRACTICES
1. Fire Purification Ritual

After each session, wash your hands and forearms under warm running water.
Visualize **golden light** streaming through your palms, carrying away all residual energy that is not your own.
Say silently:

"I release all external energy.
I stand clear and empowered in my own light."

When possible, step into sunlight for a moment, allowing the warmth to replenish your Solar center.

2. Core Breath Reset

Sit or stand tall. Place one hand over your **Solar Plexus** and the other over your **heart**.
Inhale through the nose, drawing breath deep into your upper abdomen.
Exhale through the mouth, releasing tension, heat, or fatigue.
Repeat 3–5 times, imagining your internal fire stabilizing into a calm, steady flame.

3. Power Realignment Movement

Manipura governs action and movement.
After each session, engage in a brief physical reset:
roll your shoulders, twist gently at the waist, or perform light stretching.
Visualize your golden energy circulating evenly through your core — not confined or scattered, but radiant and contained.

4. Aromatic or Sound Renewal

Diffuse or apply essential oils that support clarity and courage, such as **lemon, rosemary, or frankincense.**
You may also tone the sound **"RAM"** — the bija mantra of the Solar Plexus — feeling its vibration center your will and cleanse your field.
Affirm:

"Only clarity, strength, and peace remain in my energy field."

5. Reconnection to the Earth and Heart

To prevent overstimulation, always finish by grounding.
Visualize roots of golden light extending from your feet deep
into the earth while your Solar fire gently merges with the
heart's compassion.
This integration ensures your power stays aligned with purpose,
not ego.

LONG-TERM MAINTENANCE

• **Rest and Reflection:**
Schedule regular periods of stillness to prevent overextension.
True power thrives on renewal, not constant output.

• **Nourishment and Warmth:**
Eat warm, cooked meals and avoid excessive stimulants.
Support the digestive fire (Agni) that fuels both body and spirit.

• **Physical Strengthening:**
Engage the core daily — yoga twists, mindful walking, or light
exercise help sustain energetic and muscular balance.

• **Solar Baths or Sun Meditation:**
Once a week, sit or soak in warm water infused with **ginger or
turmeric**, or simply rest in natural sunlight.
Visualize any stagnation dissolving as your body absorbs
radiant gold energy.

• **Energetic Journaling:**
Reflect on moments where you gave away power or felt
depleted.
Use these insights to refine boundaries and reinforce your center
of command.

PRACTITIONER'S CLOSING AFFIRMATION

"I honor my energy as sacred.
I stand clear, focused, and strong.
I release all that is not mine.
My power is balanced, my light steady, and my purpose aligned."

Chapter 10 – Transformation Through Manipura

Case Studies: Reclaiming Confidence, Purpose, and Inner Strength

The **Solar Plexus Chakra (Manipura)** governs personal power, confidence, and the ability to transform experience into wisdom.

Transformation at this level is rarely about emotion — it is about empowerment.

When Manipura heals, passivity gives way to purpose, doubt transforms into confidence, and fear into decisive, inspired action.

The following case studies illustrate how balancing the Solar Plexus Chakra can restore self-esteem, activate willpower, and rekindle the inner fire of transformation.

True healing at Manipura does not mean dominance or control — it is the quiet, radiant certainty that one's light can lead without burning out.

CASE STUDY 1 – FROM SELF-DOUBT TO INNER POWER

Client Presentation:
A 46-year-old woman presented with chronic indecision and low self-confidence following a major career change. She

described feeling "invisible" and overwhelmed by others' opinions. Physically, she experienced digestive discomfort and fatigue, particularly after stressful interactions.

Assessment:
Energetic evaluation revealed depletion in the Solar Plexus with weak outward flow. The Root and Sacral were balanced, but Manipura was dim — her internal fire suppressed by self-doubt and perfectionism.

Therapeutic Process:

- **Reiki & Solar Activation:** Hands-on energy work over the upper abdomen using the *Cho Ku Rei* symbol to strengthen will and confidence.
- **Core Breathwork:** Focused diaphragmatic breathing to ignite warmth behind the navel.
- **Affirmation Practice:** "I act with clarity and courage. I trust my inner guidance."
- **Digestive Healing:** Encouraged warm teas and slow, mindful eating to strengthen gut vitality and energetic digestion.

Outcome:
Within four sessions, her posture straightened, her voice grew stronger, and she began initiating changes in her business. Digestive issues improved, and she reported feeling "lit from within."

Transformation:
Fear dissolved into faith. The client rediscovered her inner authority — no longer seeking permission to shine.

CASE STUDY 2 – RELEASING CONTROL AND TRUSTING LIFE

Client Presentation:
A 38-year-old man sought help for chronic anxiety, insomnia, and the need to "control everything." He described burnout, muscle tightness, and a constant sense of urgency.

Assessment:
Manipura energy was hyperactive — the fire burned too hot. His field felt sharp and restless, extending forward as if constantly bracing for impact. The Heart Chakra was partially closed, limiting emotional balance.

Therapeutic Process:

- **Cooling Breathwork (Shitali Pranayama):** To calm internal heat and soothe the nervous system.
- **Guided Visualization:** A golden sun within the abdomen radiating light steadily, not fiercely.
- **Reiki Polarity Balancing:** Placing one hand on the Solar Plexus and the other on the Heart to harmonize will and compassion.
- **Journaling on Trust:** Encouraged reflection on the difference between control and alignment.

Outcome:
After one month, the client reported reduced anxiety and improved sleep. He learned to delegate tasks at work and spend time in nature without guilt.

Transformation:
The fire of Manipura shifted from force to flow — strength became presence, not pressure.

CASE STUDY 3 – RESTORING PURPOSE AFTER PERSONAL LOSS

Client Presentation:
A 52-year-old teacher experienced a deep sense of purposelessness after early retirement. She felt "lost without a role," describing her life as dull and directionless. Physically, she reported mid-back pain and digestive sluggishness.

Assessment:
Energy scanning revealed low frequency in the Solar Plexus and Heart Chakras. The flow of creative energy from the Sacral was intact, but it lacked focus and structure — inspiration without direction.

Therapeutic Process:

- **Empowerment Meditation:** Visualization of a radiant golden sun rising from the abdomen to the heart, symbolizing renewed purpose.
- **Mantra Work:** Chanting *RAM*, the bija mantra of Manipura, to awaken inner strength and motivation.
- **Service Integration:** Encouraged her to mentor younger teachers, reigniting a sense of contribution.
- **Physical Activation:** Gentle yoga twists and core strengthening to awaken willpower through movement.

Outcome:
Within six weeks, her energy field brightened, and she described feeling "alive with direction." The physical discomfort eased, and she began a new volunteer program supporting youth education.

Transformation:
The inner flame of purpose rekindled — her service became her strength.

KEY LESSONS FROM MANIPURA HEALING

1. **Empowerment Restores Clarity:**
   When power returns to its rightful place within, confusion dissolves. True confidence comes from alignment, not control.
2. **Fire Must Be Tended, Not Forced:**
   Manipura thrives in balance — too little and we lose direction, too much and we burn out. Healing is the art of steady flame.
3. **Purpose is the Pathway to Healing:**
   When the will serves a higher purpose, ego transforms into devotion. The Solar Plexus becomes a sun that warms, not scorches.
4. **Integration of Fire and Heart:**
   Empowerment without compassion becomes domination; compassion without strength becomes depletion. Balance both for true mastery.

PRACTITIONER'S REFLECTION

Transformation at the Solar Plexus is the art of *energetic leadership.*
The practitioner's role is not to give strength but to reflect it — to help the client remember their own radiance.

Each awakening at Manipura may express differently: courage, conviction, creativity, or calm determination.
Yet beneath all expressions lies the same truth:

When the inner fire burns steadily, the spirit leads with confidence,
and every action becomes an act of light.

Chapter 11 – Reflection & Integration

Daily Self-Care Rituals for Solar Empowerment

Healing the **Solar Plexus Chakra (Manipura)** is not a single moment of awakening — it is a disciplined dance with your own power.
Where the Sacral teaches flow, the Solar Plexus teaches focus.
Its strength lies in consistency: the ability to act without aggression, to lead without domination, and to shine without burning out.

Daily self-care at the level of Manipura means tending to the inner flame — keeping it bright, balanced, and steady.
These rituals cultivate confidence, direction, and the calm vitality that sustains purposeful living.

1. Morning Solar Activation

Begin each day by lighting your inner fire.

• **Movement:** Before engaging with technology, stand tall and roll your shoulders back. Perform gentle core twists or sun salutations to awaken your center.
• **Breath:** Inhale deeply into the upper abdomen, feeling warmth spread behind the navel. Exhale through the mouth, releasing self-doubt.
• **Intention:** Whisper,

"Today I stand in my power and act with clarity."

This morning ritual fuels self-belief and sets the tone for focused, radiant presence throughout the day.

2. Confidence Journal Check-In

The Solar Plexus thrives on self-awareness and accountability. Take a few minutes daily to reflect on your relationship with power and action.

Write:
• Where did I act with confidence today?
• Where did I give my power away?
• What one thing can I do now to realign with my purpose?

Over time, these reflections build emotional intelligence rooted in strength rather than reaction.

3. Fire Element Rituals

Because Manipura is ruled by the element of fire, working consciously with heat, light, and warmth helps stabilize and empower this chakra.

• **Morning Light:** Step into natural sunlight or gaze at a candle flame for one minute, breathing in its radiance.
• **Digestive Fire:** Eat warm, nourishing meals — soups, teas, grains, and gentle spices like ginger or turmeric.
• **Evening Flame Meditation:** At night, light a candle and focus on its glow within your core.
Visualize your inner fire burning steadily — not fierce, but unwavering.

"My light is constant. My purpose is clear."

4. Willpower Practice

The Solar Plexus governs self-discipline and motivation.
Each day, commit to one action that reinforces your integrity or
moves you toward a goal.

• Complete a small but meaningful task before noon.
• Follow through on one promise to yourself.
• Replace one negative thought with an empowering truth.

This practice strengthens the energetic muscle of will,
transforming intention into manifestation.

5. Empowerment Through Breath

Midday, pause and place a hand over your Solar Plexus.
Inhale for four counts, exhale for six.
With each breath, imagine any tension or insecurity melting
away.
Feel your body expand with calm assurance.

"I breathe in confidence. I exhale doubt."

This simple breathing ritual maintains inner balance amid
external demands.

6. Evening Reflection & Stillness

At day's end, sit quietly with your spine straight.
Visualize a golden sun within your abdomen, radiating warmth
throughout your body.
Ask yourself:
• Did I act from strength or fear today?
• What am I proud of?
• Where can I bring more calm leadership tomorrow?

Forgive any imbalance and end with gratitude.
Affirm:

"I am strong, centered, and at peace with my power."

7. Weekly Solar Renewal

Once per week, devote time to rekindling and refining your power.

Options include:
• Practicing yoga poses that activate the core (boat, plank, warrior).
• Spending quiet time in sunlight or around a campfire to commune with the fire element.
• Performing a confidence ritual — writing intentions, burning old fears, or visualizing success.
• Taking a day of rest from external pressure to reconnect with inner direction.

These moments restore equilibrium between will and surrender — ensuring that your power remains luminous, not consuming.

Integration Insight

Solar strength is not control — it is presence.
When this chakra is balanced, you lead with assurance, act with purpose, and move through life as a calm flame rather than a wildfire.

Through consistent daily rituals of clarity, courage, and reflection, you transform the Solar Plexus into a temple of empowerment — where action becomes meditation, confidence becomes compassion, and power becomes light.

"When my inner fire burns steady, I walk my path with grace. I lead not by force, but by radiance."

JOURNALING PROMPTS FOR THE SOLAR PLEXUS CHAKRA

Embodying Confidence, Purpose, and Personal Power

The **Solar Plexus Chakra (Manipura)** thrives on clarity, action, and self-trust.
Journaling is one of the most powerful practices for balancing this chakra because it transforms confusion into understanding and hesitation into direction.
Through writing, you reclaim your authority — aligning thought, emotion, and will into a single, radiant current of purpose.

These prompts are designed to help you strengthen boundaries, release fear, ignite motivation, and stand firmly in your own light.

1. Confidence and Self-Worth

• Where in my life do I feel strong and capable?
• What situations cause me to doubt myself — and why?
• How do I respond when my power is challenged?
• What would change if I believed, fully, that I am enough?

2. Purpose and Direction

• What goals or dreams feel most aligned with my authentic self?
• When have I acted from purpose rather than pressure?
• Where am I giving my energy to things that drain instead of fuel me?
• How can I lead my life, rather than wait for permission to act?

3. Boundaries and Personal Power

• What boundaries do I need to strengthen or communicate more clearly?
• Where do I overextend myself out of guilt or obligation?
• How do I feel when I say "no"?
• What would healthy, empowered boundaries look like in my daily life?

4. Inner Fire and Motivation

• What inspires me to take bold action?
• When do I feel most alive, passionate, and engaged?
• How do I react when I lose momentum — with frustration, apathy, or self-compassion?
• What practices help me rekindle motivation when I feel depleted?

5. Fear and Transformation

• What fears hold me back from pursuing what I truly want?
• How have past failures taught me strength or resilience?
• What part of myself am I ready to release so I can grow?
• How can I use fear as fuel for transformation rather than avoidance?

6. Leadership and Integrity

• What does leadership mean to me — control, service, or inspiration?
• How do I influence others through my words and energy?
• Where can I bring more authenticity and humility into my power?
• What legacy do I want to create through my daily actions?

7. Sacred Affirmations

After reflecting, close your journaling session with one or more of these Solar affirmations:

"I act with confidence and clarity."
"My power is calm, focused, and aligned with love."
"I transform challenges into strength."
"I honor my inner fire and use it to illuminate my path."
"I am the author of my destiny — guided by wisdom and courage."

Integration Note

Journaling for the Solar Plexus Chakra is not about control — it's about *alignment*.
Let your words ignite awareness, not pressure.
If anger or frustration arises, see it as energy ready to transform.
If pride or joy shines through, let it remind you of your brilliance.

Each sentence is a spark — a reminder that your light is both your compass and your power.
Through writing, you learn to command your energy with grace, and to live as a steady flame: radiant, confident, and free.

GUIDED EXERCISE: IGNITING THE FIRE OF MANIPURA

Awakening Confidence, Willpower, and the Inner Light of Transformation

The **Solar Plexus Chakra (Manipura)** is the seat of your personal power — the center where will, clarity, and confidence ignite.
Where the Sacral teaches flow, the Solar Plexus teaches direction.

It is the alchemical fire that transforms energy into purpose, turning intention into action and fear into courage.

This guided exercise awakens the golden flame within your abdomen, harmonizing strength with serenity — so your power becomes radiant, not forceful; steady, not consuming.

Preparation

Find a quiet space where you can sit upright or lie comfortably. Have a yellow or gold candle nearby, or simply visualize its light.
If you wish, play soft instrumental music to support focus.

Close your eyes.
Place one hand over your upper abdomen — between your navel and your sternum — and the other over your heart.

Take several deep, steady breaths.
Inhale through your nose, expanding the belly slightly.
Exhale slowly through your mouth, releasing any heaviness or self-doubt.

Allow your awareness to settle in the warmth of your center.
Feel the quiet strength that lives behind every breath.

Step 1: The Breath of Power

Breathe deeply into your upper abdomen — the seat of your inner sun.
With each inhale, imagine drawing in light.
With each exhale, imagine that light spreading through your torso.

Your breath becomes the bellows of transformation — steady, rhythmic, awakening your fire without strain.

Say softly to yourself:

"With every breath, I awaken my power.
My strength rises with calm purpose."

Continue for several breaths until you feel warmth building in your core.

Step 2: The Light of Purpose

Visualize a radiant golden-yellow light glowing behind your navel.
See it flicker, then grow brighter — like dawn breaking inside you.

With each inhale, the light strengthens.
With each exhale, it expands — filling your abdomen, your spine, your entire body with confidence and clarity.

If tension or doubt appears, imagine it melting into the golden fire, transmuted into wisdom and resolve.

Whisper:

"All fear dissolves in the fire of truth.
I trust my inner strength."

Step 3: The Fire in Motion

Gently begin to engage your body:
If seated, roll your shoulders back and lift your chest slightly.
If lying down, visualize your spine lengthening and straightening.

As you breathe, imagine the flame at your core spinning gently — not wild, but controlled, circular, and balanced.

Each rotation sends waves of energy through your body —
warming, energizing, empowering.
Feel vitality rising up the spine, illuminating every cell.

Repeat inwardly:

"I am energy in motion.
I am strong, clear, and alive."

Step 4: The Heart Connection

Now bring your focus to your heart while maintaining
awareness of the golden fire at your center.

See a radiant stream of light connecting your heart (green) and
Solar Plexus (yellow).
As they merge, the light becomes golden-green — compassion
infused with courage.

Feel this current linking love and strength, softening the edges
of power with empathy.

Whisper:

"My strength serves love.
My confidence is guided by compassion."

Step 5: Affirmation and Stillness

Let movement fade into stillness.
Your breath becomes calm, steady, luminous.
Feel warmth radiating through your torso — your body relaxed,
your spirit awake.

Affirm silently or aloud:

"I am centered in my power.
I act with purpose and integrity.
My light is steady, my will aligned with truth.
I shine from within."

Rest here for a few moments, basking in the glow of your own strength.
When you're ready, take one final deep breath and open your eyes.

If you wish, drink a warm herbal tea or place your hands briefly over a candle flame (from a safe distance) to anchor the element of fire within you.

Integration

This exercise can be practiced daily or anytime you feel uncertain, passive, or drained.
Each breath and visualization strengthens Manipura's current — training your mind and body to associate *action with peace, not pressure.*

Over time, this inner fire becomes self-sustaining — a steady radiance that fuels your purpose and confidence in all areas of life.

The more you honor your power,the more your Solar Plexus becomes a sun of consciousness — shining steadily between the warmth of your heart and the grounding of your roots.

Chapter 12 – Understanding the Journey So Far

How Love Descends into the Body to Become Creation

If you've been following the *Chakra 101 Series* from the beginning, you've already experienced something unusual — this journey doesn't begin at the Root, as most chakra systems do.

Instead, we began with the **Heart Chakra**, the bridge between the physical and spiritual realms. From there, we have been descending — carrying love downward through the body to anchor it into form.

This path is called **Involution before Evolution** — a journey where love first *descends into matter* before rising again as wisdom. It's the same movement of energy that happens in every healing process: Spirit flows into the body so that it can be felt, lived, and expressed.

THE FOUR BOOKS SO FAR

Book	Chakra	Element	Primary Lesson
1. Heart Chakra 101 – The Bridge	Air	Love & Compassion	The first initiation — opening to divine love and awareness.
2. Root Chakra 101 – Building Safety, Survival, Foundation	Earth	Grounding & Belonging	Learning to anchor love into the body and into the world.
3. Sacral Chakra 101 – Creativity, Pleasure, Emotions	Water	Flow & Feeling	Allowing love to move through emotion, creativity, and pleasure.
4. Solar Plexus Chakra 101 – Power, Confidence, Transformation	Fire	Will & Manifestation	Empowering love to act — transforming energy into purpose and creation.

Each step has brought love deeper into your being — from spirit into body, from feeling into form.

Where the Heart awakened love, the Root gave it roots, the Sacral gave it movement, and now the Solar Plexus gives it power.

WHY WE BEGAN AT THE HEART

In traditional chakra teachings, energy flows upward — from
Root to Crown.
But in integration work, the real healing often begins with **the
awakening of the Heart.**

When the Heart opens, compassion awakens, and that love
naturally seeks to ground itself.
It wants to be lived, not just understood.
That's why this path leads downward first — into embodiment,
emotion, and empowered action — before rising back upward
toward communication, intuition, and divine connection.

This sequence mirrors how many spiritual awakenings unfold:

First, love awakens.
Then safety is built.
Emotion begins to flow.
Purpose ignites.
And finally — truth is spoken, vision expands, and spirit unites
with form.

MANIFESTATION: THE DESCENT OF LOVE INTO FORM

Now, in this *Solar Plexus* stage, you have reached the moment
where **love becomes creation.**
You've already built the foundation and opened the emotional
current — now, it's time to learn how to direct that energy
consciously.

Manifestation is not about forcing the universe to obey your
will.
It is about aligning your will with your heart's truth — so that
what you create carries the vibration of love.

Through the **Root**, you learned how love feels when it is safe.
Through the **Sacral**, you learned how love moves as emotion and creativity.
Now, through the **Solar Plexus**, you will learn how love *acts* — through courage, confidence, and purposeful action.

This is the alchemy of embodiment:

Love descending through Earth, Water, and Fire until it becomes visible in your life.

True manifestation is not the mind commanding matter — it is the **Heart expressing itself through the body.**
When your lower chakras align beneath the Heart's guidance, willpower becomes service, desire becomes inspiration, and every action becomes an act of love in motion.

HOW THE TRINITY WORKS TOGETHER

Manifestation is a cycle, not a single act.
Each chakra builds on the one before it:

Chakra	Element	Manifestation Role	Key Lesson
Root	Earth	Ground the intention	"I am safe to receive."
Sacral	Water	Energize through emotion	"I feel and flow with my desire."
Solar Plexus	Fire	Act with confidence	"I create through inspired action."

Earth stabilizes, Water energizes, Fire mobilizes.

If any part of the trinity is missing, manifestation falters:

- Without **Earth**, there is no foundation — ideas drift.
- Without **Water**, there is no emotional magnetism — nothing moves.
- Without **Fire**, there is no transformation — dreams stay as thoughts.

When all three align beneath the Heart, manifestation becomes effortless.
Love descends into the body, finds ground, gathers momentum, and becomes creation.

The Trinity in Action: How Your Chakras Mirror the DREAM Method

If you've read my book *Manifestation – The DREAM Method in 5 Steps*, you already know that manifestation begins long before anything becomes visible. It starts in the unseen — in your thoughts, beliefs, emotions, and energy.

The lower three chakras — Root, Sacral, and Solar Plexus — are the living engine that moves this process through your body. They translate your *inner world* (thoughts and feelings) into your *outer world* (experiences and results).

Just as the DREAM Method moves from the **unconscious to conscious thought**, into **action**, and finally into **manifestation**, the chakras mirror that same evolution — but through energy rather than intellect.

Let's explore how this happens within you.

ROOT CHAKRA – THE REALM OF THE UNCONSCIOUS (EARTH)

Manifestation begins below awareness — in the deep soil of the subconscious.
Your Root Chakra stores early memories, family beliefs, and survival instincts.
These unseen patterns either support or limit what you believe is possible.

Before you can consciously manifest anything, you must feel *safe* to have it.
When you ground your dreams here — when the body feels secure — your vision gains roots.

"I am safe to receive what I desire."

SACRAL CHAKRA – THE REALM OF CONSCIOUS CREATION (WATER)

Once the idea feels safe, it rises into awareness.
You begin to *imagine* it, to *feel* it, to let emotion give it life.
This is the domain of the Sacral Chakra — where thought becomes energy in motion.

Your feelings act like water: they give shape and texture to your intentions.
If you try to manifest from thought alone, the current stays dry.
But when you add emotion, the water begins to flow — and life starts to respond.

"I allow my emotions to guide creation through joy, not fear."

SOLAR PLEXUS – THE REALM OF ACTION (FIRE)

Energy that is grounded and emotionalized must now be expressed.

This is where the Solar Plexus — the fire of will — steps forward.

Here, you choose, act, and take aligned steps toward your vision.
Manifestation becomes real only when love and feeling move into motion.
This is not forceful effort — it is confident participation in creation.

"I act with clarity, courage, and trust in my purpose."

HEART – THE REALM OF MANIFESTATION (AIR)

When your actions are aligned with love, creation returns to you in form.
The Heart receives what the lower chakras have prepared — grounding, feeling, and doing — and turns experience into wisdom.

This is where manifestation is realized not just as a result, but as a reflection of who you've become.

"I receive with gratitude the love I have brought into form."

THE CYCLE OF MANIFESTATION

You can think of the Trinity and the DREAM Method as two sides of one truth:

DREAM Step	Chakra Equivalent	Purpose
Unconscious Thought	Root (Earth)	Seed of creation — belief and safety
Conscious Thought	Sacral (Water)	Emotionalization — energy in motion
Action	Solar Plexus (Fire)	Transformation — will made visible
Manifestation	Heart (Air)	Realization — love experienced in form

Each step is essential.
Without grounding, emotion floats.
Without emotion, action feels empty.
Without action, love has nowhere to land.

When you embody all three — **Root stability**, **Sacral flow**, and **Solar fire** — you turn the unseen into the seen.
You don't just *think* your dreams into being — you *feel* them, *move* them, and *live* them.

THE FLOW IN SIMPLE TERMS

1. **Root – Unconscious Thought:**
   Beliefs and fears held in the subconscious set the energetic tone.
   → "Do I feel safe to have this?"
2. **Sacral – Conscious Thought:**
   Awareness and emotion give shape to the desire.
   → "Can I imagine and feel this as real?"
3. **Solar Plexus – Action:**
   Willpower and confidence bring the idea into motion.
   → "Am I willing to act on what I feel?"
4. **Heart – Manifestation:**
   The created reality returns to you as experience.
   → "Can I receive with love and gratitude?"

REFLECTION

Take a moment to ask yourself:

- Do my beliefs support what I'm asking for? (Root)
- Do my emotions align with my desires? (Sacral)
- Am I taking consistent, inspired action? (Solar Plexus)

If all three say yes, manifestation becomes effortless — because your energy, emotion, and will are moving in the same direction.
That is the true magic of the Trinity — when love, grounded in the body, becomes visible as life itself.

REFLECTION

Take a moment to pause and feel how far you've come.
You have journeyed through Earth, Water, and Fire — from
stillness to movement, from emotion to will.
You've learned that love isn't just something you feel; it's
something you *live*.

Let this next chapter teach you how to direct that love through
intention, courage, and manifestation —
so that everything you create in the world becomes an echo of
your heart made visible.

"With the body now anchored, emotionalized, and empowered,
we rise once more to the Heart — not as seekers,
but as creators returning home to love, ready to give it voice
through the Throat Chakra."

Preparing for What Comes Next

RETURNING TO THE HEART — EMPOWERED BY LOVE

When you first began this journey with *Heart Chakra 101 – The Bridge*, you were invited to awaken the pure vibration of love — to open, forgive, and reconnect with the sacred intelligence of your heart.
At that time, love may have felt like a quest: something to remember, to heal, or to reclaim from within.

Since then, you've descended into the body — you have **rooted** that love into safety, **flowed** it through emotion, and **ignited** it into purpose.

Now, you return to the Heart transformed.

This time, you are not a seeker reaching for love — you are a **creator expressing love through form.**

When the Heart reopens after the awakening of the body, its vibration changes.
Love becomes less about emotional need and more about compassionate service.
You no longer ask, *"Who will love me?"*
Instead, you naturally radiate, *"How can I bring love into this moment?"*

The Heart that once sought to heal now becomes the center of **alignment and manifestation** — the place where heaven and earth meet within you.
It integrates everything you have built below it:

- The **Root's** stability gives love structure.
- The **Sacral's** flow gives love feeling.

- The **Solar Plexus'** fire gives love purpose.

Together, they create the frequency of **embodied compassion** — love that is not just felt, but lived.

WHY THE FOUNDATIONS MATTER
The Risks Of Rising Too Soon

Every chakra builds upon the one below it.
Just as a tree cannot reach toward the sky without strong roots, your spiritual expression cannot sustain itself without a stable foundation in the body.

Moving to the Throat before mastering the lower centers may lead to energy that is brilliant but **ungrounded** — truth that speaks without wisdom, vision that lacks embodiment, or creativity that burns out before it becomes real.

Here's how that imbalance can appear:

If This Chakra Is Unstable	Expression in the Throat May Become...
Root (Earth) – fear, insecurity, or disconnection from the body	Words that sound spiritual but feel hollow — unanchored truth that others can't feel.
Sacral (Water) – emotional suppression or over-identification	Expression that swings between emotional flooding and emotional silence.
Solar Plexus (Fire) – misuse of power or fear of visibility	Words that manipulate, defend, or hide — the voice either dominates or withdraws.

If This Chakra Is Unstable	Expression in the Throat May Become...
Heart (Air) – conditional love or unresolved grief	Expression that seeks approval or performs love, rather than speaking from it.

When the lower chakras are balanced, energy flows upward **cleanly and powerfully.** Your truth then carries the resonance of embodiment — not just ideas, but lived experience.
Your voice becomes magnetic, healing, and real because it vibrates with the weight of authenticity.

Chapter 13 – Quick Reference Toolkit

Solar Plexus Chakra (Manipura)

The Seat Of Personal Power, Purpose, And Inner Radiance

CORE OVERVIEW

Location: Upper abdomen, between the navel and sternum
Element: Fire
Color: Yellow or gold
Bija Mantra: *RAM*
Governing Principle: Transformation through will and clarity
Primary Function: Personal power, confidence, motivation, and self-discipline
Associated Glands/Organs: Pancreas, liver, digestive system, diaphragm, adrenals
Sense: Sight (perception and inner vision)
Astrological Associations: Sun, Mars, Leo
Symbol: Ten-petaled lotus containing a downward-pointing triangle representing the transformative fire of action and will

KEY THEMES

- Personal Power & Self-Confidence
- Purpose, Willpower & Motivation
- Self-Discipline & Integrity
- Transformation through Action
- Healthy Ego & Leadership

• Balance Between Control and Surrender
• Trusting Inner Guidance

WHEN BALANCED

• Clear sense of purpose and direction
• Confidence without arrogance
• Healthy digestion (physically and emotionally)
• Warmth, vitality, and enthusiasm for life
• Ability to take action with calm authority
• Emotional resilience and independence
• Inner strength guided by love

WHEN IMBALANCED

Underactive Solar Plexus (Deficient):
• Low self-esteem or indecisiveness
• Fatigue, poor digestion, lack of motivation
• Fear of rejection or failure
• Difficulty asserting boundaries

Overactive Solar Plexus (Excessive):
• Dominance, aggression, or perfectionism
• Need for control, power struggles
• Anger, frustration, or impatience
• Burnout from overexertion

BALANCING TECHNIQUES

Physical Practices:
• Core-strengthening yoga (Boat, Warrior, Plank, Bow)
• Sun salutations and breath of fire (Kapalabhati)
• Brisk walks, hiking, or martial arts for focused strength

Energetic Practices:
• Visualization of a radiant yellow sun in your abdomen
• Chanting *RAM* to awaken confidence and willpower
• Fire meditations to transform fear into courage

Emotional/Spiritual Practices:
• Journaling about personal goals and boundaries
• Affirmations of empowerment and authenticity
• Working with forgiveness and self-respect

AROMATHERAPY & CRYSTALS

Essential Oils:
Lemon – clarity and positivity
Grapefruit – motivation and lightness
Ginger – courage and inner warmth
Peppermint – focus and mental clarity
Black Pepper – strength and endurance

Crystals:
Citrine – joy, abundance, and confidence
Tiger's Eye – strength and grounded will
Amber – purification and courage
Yellow Jasper – endurance and balance
Golden Calcite – empowerment and vitality

FOODS & NUTRITION

Supportive Foods:
• Complex carbohydrates (brown rice, oats, quinoa)
• Yellow fruits and vegetables (bananas, corn, pineapple, squash)
• Digestive spices (ginger, turmeric, cumin, cinnamon)
• Herbal teas for digestion and clarity (chamomile, lemongrass, peppermint)

Avoid Excess:
• Heavy, greasy foods that dull energy
• Caffeine or sugar dependency that causes burnout
• Overeating or emotional eating tied to control

AFFIRMATIONS

"I stand in my power with confidence and ease."
"My inner fire fuels my purpose."
"I transform challenges into growth."
"I act with integrity and strength."
"My will is aligned with divine wisdom."

MUDRA & MANTRA

Mudra: *Rudra Mudra (Gesture of the Sun God)*
– Touch the tips of the thumb, index, and ring fingers together.
– Rest your hands on your knees with palms up.
– This mudra activates energy, enhances digestion, and strengthens willpower.

Mantra: *RAM* (pronounced "Rahm")
– Chant slowly and steadily, feeling vibration in the upper abdomen.
– Visualize the sound awakening golden light within your core.

MEDITATION FOCUS

Visualize a glowing sun radiating from your Solar Plexus.
With each inhale, it expands — bright, warm, and steady.
With each exhale, it purifies fear, doubt, and hesitation.
Feel confidence, direction, and empowerment flowing through your being.

"I am the flame of transformation.
My light illuminates my path and empowers my purpose."

INTEGRATION INSIGHT

Manipura's mastery is not domination — it is *illumination.*
When this chakra is balanced, your power becomes peaceful,
your will becomes wise, and your actions flow effortlessly from
clarity.

You no longer push — you radiate.
You no longer control — you lead.
And in doing so, your inner sun becomes a beacon for others to
rise.

Conclusion: The Power of Presence and Purpose

The Solar Plexus Chakra, **Manipura**, is the radiant fire of transformation — the meeting point between the physical and spiritual will.
It is where individuality awakens, not in defiance of others, but in service to truth.
Through its light, we remember that confidence is not noise; it is the quiet certainty that arises when we align with purpose.

When the fire of Manipura burns too low, we feel doubt, hesitation, or dependency — as though our inner sun has dimmed.
When it burns too fiercely, we risk domination, pride, or burnout — consuming rather than creating.
But when this fire burns evenly — bright, steady, and warm — we live with clarity, courage, and compassion.
We act not to prove, but to express the truth of who we are.

Manipura teaches that power is not control — it is **conscious direction**.
It is the ability to channel energy, to move forward with integrity, and to transform challenge into growth.
This is the alchemy of the Solar Plexus: turning the lead of fear into the gold of confidence.

Through breath, awareness, and discipline, we master the art of balanced action — doing without forcing, shining without burning.
We learn that true leadership begins within — when self-trust

replaces self-doubt, and confidence flows from connection to Source rather than ego.

The balanced Solar Plexus allows the fire of will to rise upward — to fuel the heart with courage and illuminate the path of love. In this way, Manipura becomes the **bridge between passion and compassion, personal power and spiritual purpose**.

"I am the light within the flame.
My will serves wisdom.
My strength is guided by love."

As you integrate the teachings of Manipura, remember that empowerment is not something you acquire — it is something you remember.
The power you seek has always been within you, waiting to be claimed with grace, humility, and devotion.

Carry this light forward into your daily life — let it guide your choices, inspire your words, and strengthen your boundaries.
For the fire of Manipura is not just your personal strength — it is the spark of divine purpose that ignites transformation in the world around you.

SOLAR PLEXUS CHAKRA BENEDICTION: THE BLESSING OF FIRE

(Manipura – The Radiant Sun Within)

May the flame within your belly burn steady and true.
May it warm your courage and illuminate your path.
May it cleanse away all doubt, fear, and hesitation, transforming resistance into radiant strength.

May your will be guided by wisdom, your power tempered with compassion.

May you act not from the need to control, but from the joy of creation.

May your fire never consume, but always refine — burning away illusion until only truth remains.

Let this golden light within you rise, from the center of your being to the heart above, uniting passion with purpose, action with love.

When shadows approach,
may your inner sun remind you who you are — a spark of divine intelligence, a vessel of radiant purpose, a living flame of transformation.

And as you walk your path, may every breath feed this sacred fire, so that wherever you go, you become the light that awakens others.

"I am the fire that transforms.
I am the light that leads.
I am the strength of Spirit made manifest."

**Blessed be the Fire of Manipura —
The Sun Within that never fades.**

THE TRUE ASCENT

The chakra journey is not a ladder to climb — it is a **spiral of embodiment.**
Each time your energy rises, it carries greater awareness and refinement.
Each time it descends, that awareness takes root more deeply in your lived experience.
Like breath, the journey of energy is cyclical — inhale, exhale; expansion, return; heaven meeting earth within you.

The descent through the Root, Sacral, and Solar Plexus was a sacred preparation — teaching love how to live in your body.
Now, as you rise again, the same love begins to **remember its higher song.**

From this renewed Heart, energy lifts once more —
upward through your chest, throat, and into the realms of expression and communication.
It is drawn not by effort, but by resonance — a natural upward movement of energy ready to be shared.

Your next initiation awaits in the **Throat Chakra (Vishuddha)** —
the center of authentic expression, vibration, and creative truth.

The Throat is not simply the place of speech.
It is the **bridge between your inner world and outer reality**, where vibration transforms into sound and truth takes shape in form.
It is where the invisible becomes audible — your energy translated into word, art, music, movement, or message.

Here, you begin to express not only what you think, but who you *are.*

SPEAKING AS THE SOUL

In the Throat Chakra, every word becomes an act of creation.
Each vibration you send forth carries the frequency of your
inner alignment.

If your foundations are balanced — if love is grounded (Root),
emotionalized (Sacral), and empowered (Solar Plexus) — your
voice becomes clear, magnetic, and healing.
Your words naturally carry the energy of wisdom, not reaction;
connection, not persuasion.

When your voice flows from an embodied Heart, your truth
resonates deeply with others because it rings with integrity.
It does not need to convince — it *connects.*
It does not strive to be heard — it *harmonizes.*

This is the difference between speaking *from* love and speaking
as love.

To speak from love is to remember compassion in your words.
To speak as love is to let Spirit itself speak through you.

The Throat Chakra is where that divine exchange occurs.

BEFORE YOU RISE

Before you begin this next chapter of your evolution, pause here
— between the Solar Plexus and the Throat — and breathe.
Feel your energy pulsing upward from the fire of your Solar
Plexus, rising into the calm rhythm of your Heart.
Here, the flames of will soften into the breeze of love, preparing
your words to become light.

Remember what the Heart first taught you in Book One: that
love is not something to seek, but something to *be.*
That truth, once felt and embodied, now seeks to be expressed

through you — through your sound, your actions, your very presence.

You are not beginning a new story.
You are continuing the same current of divine love — now ready to **speak, sing, write, teach, and create** in its name.
Your voice becomes the messenger of everything you've integrated.

Let this affirmation be your guide as you ascend:

"I return to my Heart, not to be healed, but to express the love that I am.
Through my voice, love moves beyond my body and into the world."

When you are ready, step forward into **Throat Chakra 101 – Expression & Truth** — the next sacred bridge in your journey, where energy becomes language, and love learns to speak its name.

Bibliography

CLASSICAL & YOGIC SOURCES

- Feuerstein, Georg. *The Yoga Tradition: Its History, Literature, Philosophy, and Practice.* Hohm Press, 2001.
- Avalon, Arthur (Sir John Woodroffe). *The Serpent Power: The Secrets of Tantric and Shaktic Yoga.* Dover Publications, 1974.
- Swami Sivananda. *The Chakras.* Divine Life Society, 1994.
- Easwaran, Eknath (trans.). *The Upanishads.* Nilgiri Press, 2007.
- Vivekananda, Swami. *Raja Yoga.* Advaita Ashrama, 1896. *(Foundational for understanding prana, will, and concentration — key aspects of Manipura energy.)*

CHAKRA & ENERGY HEALING WORKS

- Judith, Anodea. *Wheels of Life: A User's Guide to the Chakra System.* Llewellyn Publications, 1987.
- Myss, Caroline. *Anatomy of the Spirit.* Harmony Books, 1996.
- Brennan, Barbara Ann. *Hands of Light: A Guide to Healing Through the Human Energy Field.* Bantam, 1988.
- Sills, Franklyn. *Foundations in Craniosacral Biodynamics: The Breath of Life and Fundamental Skills.* North Atlantic Books, 2012.
- Leadbeater, C. W. *The Chakras.* Quest Books, 1972. *(Influential in shaping early Western models of chakra color and function.)*

REIKI & SPIRITUAL HEALING

- Takata, Hawayo. *Reiki: Hawayo Takata's Story.* Reiki Alliance, 1998.
- Petter, Frank Arjava. *This Is Reiki: Transformation of Body, Mind and Soul from the Origins to the Practice.* Lotus Press, 2012.
- Rand, William Lee. *Reiki: The Healing Touch.* Vision Publications, 1991.
- Santego, Constance. *Reiki Wisdom Series.* Maximillian Enterprises, 2024–. *(Especially relevant to energy harmonization and practitioner ethics.)*

PSYCHOLOGY, PERSONAL POWER & SELF-TRANSFORMATION

- Assagioli, Roberto. *Psychosynthesis: A Manual of Principles and Techniques.* Hobbs, Dorman & Co., 1965. *(Explores will and integration of personality — core Solar Plexus themes.)*
- Jung, Carl G. *The Archetypes and the Collective Unconscious.* Princeton University Press, 1969.
- Csikszentmihalyi, Mihaly. *Flow: The Psychology of Optimal Experience.* Harper Perennial, 1990. *(Modern psychological parallel to balanced Manipura energy.)*
- Hillman, James. *The Soul's Code: In Search of Character and Calling.* Random House, 1996.
- Tolle, Eckhart. *A New Earth: Awakening to Your Life's Purpose.* Penguin, 2005.

CROSS-CULTURAL & MYSTICAL REFERENCES

- Halevi, Z'ev ben Shimon. *Kabbalah: Tradition of Hidden Knowledge.* Thames & Hudson, 1991.
- Hanh, Thich Nhat. *Peace Is Every Step.* Bantam, 1992.
- Ibn Arabi. *Journey to the Lord of Power.* Inner Traditions, 1981.

- Underhill, Evelyn. *Mysticism: A Study in the Nature and Development of Spiritual Consciousness.* Dover Publications, 2002.
- Campbell, Joseph. *The Hero with a Thousand Faces.* Princeton University Press, 1949. *(The archetypal journey of empowerment mirrors the Solar Plexus path of transformation.)*

MODERN SCIENCE & RESEARCH

- Pert, Candace B. *Molecules of Emotion: The Science Behind Mind-Body Medicine.* Scribner, 1997.
- Lipton, Bruce H. *The Biology of Belief.* Hay House, 2005.
- McCraty, Rollin, et al. *Science of the Heart: Exploring the Role of the Heart in Human Performance.* HeartMath Institute, 2015.
- Dispenza, Joe. *Becoming Supernatural: How Common People Are Doing the Uncommon.* Hay House, 2017.
- Kauffman, Stuart. *At Home in the Universe: The Search for Laws of Self-Organization and Complexity.* Oxford University Press, 1995. *(Explores transformation and self-organization — metaphors for Solar Plexus empowerment.)*

ADDITIONAL RESOURCES

- Eden, Donna. *Energy Medicine.* TarcherPerigee, 2008.
- Osho. *The Book of Secrets: 112 Meditations to Discover the Mystery Within.* St. Martin's Griffin, 1998.
- Chopra, Deepak. *Quantum Healing.* Bantam, 1989.
- Hay, Louise. *You Can Heal Your Life.* Hay House, 1984. *(Affirmations and the psychosomatic link to the digestive system and self-worth.)*

OPTIONAL ADDITIONS FOR ADVANCED READERS

- Wilber, Ken. *The Spectrum of Consciousness.* Quest Books, 1977.
- Paramahansa Yogananda. *The Divine Romance.* Self-Realization Fellowship, 1944.
- Sivananda Radha, Swami. *Kundalini Yoga for the West.* Timeless Books, 1978.

Message From The Author

By the time you've reached this fourth book in the *Chakra 101* series, you've journeyed through the sacred foundations of your being.

You have opened the **Heart** — the gateway of love and compassion.
You have rooted into the **Earth** — discovering safety and belonging.
You have flowed with the **Sacral waters** — awakening creativity and emotional truth.

Now you arrive at the **Solar Plexus**, the radiant **Fire of Transformation**, where all that you have gathered becomes power in motion.

Here, the soul learns a new rhythm — not just to feel, but to *act*; not just to dream, but to *manifest.*
The Solar Plexus Chakra teaches the mastery of will — how to direct energy with clarity, courage, and grace.

It reminds us that true power does not come from control or force, but from alignment — the harmony of purpose, passion, and presence.
This is where self-trust is born, where confidence is kindled, and where the light of your spirit begins to shine through action.

Where the Root gave you stability, the Sacral gave you flow, and the Heart gave you compassion —
the Solar Plexus now gives you *sovereignty.*

As you explore these teachings, may you learn to burn bright without burning out.

May your will become a reflection of your soul's truth.

And may you remember that empowerment is not becoming something more — it is realizing the light that has been within you all along.

With love, fire, and faith in your unfolding,
Dr. Constance Santego

About the Author

Dr. Constance Santego, Ph.D., DNM, is an award-winning author, teacher, and natural medicine doctor who has dedicated

more than 25 years to the study and practice of energy healing. A Grand Reiki Master and founder of multiple wellness and educational programs, she has trained thousands of students worldwide in Reiki, holistic therapies, and intuitive development.

Her passion is to bring ancient wisdom into practical, modern tools that anyone can use for healing and self-discovery. She has authored more than forty books, ranging from the *Reiki*

Wisdom series and *Secrets of a Healer* guides to spiritual fiction exploring the Nine Spiritual Gifts. Her teaching blends Eastern philosophies, Western natural medicine, and modern energy science — always with compassion at the center.

Dr. Santego's mission is to help people connect with their inner wisdom, awaken their intuitive gifts, and live with greater balance, joy, and love. When she is not writing or teaching, she enjoys life in British Columbia, surrounded by nature's beauty, which continues to inspire her work.

ALSO AVAILABLE

For additional information on

Constance Santego's

wide range of Motivational Products, Coaching Sessions,
Spiritual Retreats,
Live Events and Educational Programs

Go to

www.ConstanceSantego.ca

Follow on Instagram - Constance_Santego and
Facebook - constancesantegoo

Subscribe and receive Free Information and Meditations on her
YouTube Channel - Constance Santego

Secrets of a Healer, Magic of Reiki

ISBN: 978-1-7772220-0-0

Secrets of a Healer, The Reiki Master's Manual

ISBN: 978-1-990062-34-6

www.ingramcontent.com/pod-product-compliance
Lightning Source LLC
Chambersburg PA
CBHW071707120626
46550CB00001B/141